Alfred John Church

Stories of the Old World

Alfred John Church

Stories of the Old World

ISBN/EAN: 9783744725118

Printed in Europe, USA, Canada, Australia, Japan

Cover: Foto ©ninafisch / pixelio.de

More available books at **www.hansebooks.com**

Classics for Children.

STORIES OF THE OLD WORLD.

BY THE
REV. ALFRED J. CHURCH, M.A.,
AUTHOR OF "STORIES FROM HOMER," "STORIES FROM VIRGIL," "STORIES FROM LIVY," ETC.

BOSTON:
PUBLISHED BY GINN & COMPANY.
1885.

CONTENTS.

THE STORY OF THE ARGO.

CHAPTER I.	7
CHAPTER II.	19
CHAPTER III.	30

THE STORY OF THEBES.

CHAPTER I.	47
CHAPTER II.	57

THE STORY OF TROY.

CHAPTER I.	69
CHAPTER II.	86
CHAPTER III.	109
CHAPTER IV.	128
CHAPTER V.	147
CHAPTER VI.	156
CHAPTER VII.	171

THE ADVENTURES OF ULYSSES.

CHAPTER VIII.	182
CHAPTER IX.	204
CHAPTER X.	210

	PAGE
CHAPTER XI.	220
CHAPTER XII.	229
CHAPTER XIII.	237
CHAPTER XIV.	242

THE ADVENTURES OF ÆNEAS.

CHAPTER I.	247
CHAPTER II.	265
CHAPTER III.	291
CHAPTER IV.	307
CHAPTER V.	331
CHAPTER VI.	342

NOTE.

IN "The Adventures of Æneas" the names of the gods are of the Latin form. As the story is taken from Virgil, this could not be avoided. The following table sets forth the correspondence of the Greek and Latin names:—

GREEK.	LATIN.
Zeus	Jupiter.
Heré	Juno.
Aphrodité	Venus.
Ares	Mars.
Hermes	Mercury.
Poseidon	Neptune.
Artemis	Diana.

THE STORY OF THE ARGO.

CHAPTER I.

THE son of Cretheus, Æson, bequeathed the kingdom of Thessaly to his brother Pelias, to keep for Jason, his son, whom he had sent to be taught by Chiron, the wise Centaur. Now when Jason was returning from Chiron he came to Anaurus, which is a river of Thessaly, and would have crossed it; but there was an old woman on the river bank, and she entreated of Jason that he would carry her over the river, for she feared herself, she said, to cross it. But the old woman was in truth the goddess Heré, who had taken upon herself the likeness of an old woman to try the young man's heart. Jason therefore carried her over, but in crossing he lost one of his sandals, for it cleaved to the sand that was in the river; and so he came to the dwelling of King Pelias, where they were preparing a great sacrifice and feast to Poseidon and the other gods. Now there had come an oracle aforetime to Pelias, saying, "Beware of him who shall come to thee with one sandal only, for it is thy doom to die by his means." Therefore, when Pelias saw Jason come in this plight, he was afraid; also he would fain keep the kingdom for himself. He dared not slay him; but he set him a task from which he might win great renown, hoping that he should never return therefrom; and the task was this: to fetch the fleece of gold from the land of the Colchians.

Now the story of the fleece is this: To Athamas, that was brother to Cretheus, were born two children of Nephele, his wife, and the names of these two were Phrixus and Helle. But Ino, whom Athamas had taken to wife when Nephele was dead, laid a plot against the children to cause them to be put to death, and the plot was this. She persuaded the women of the land to parch with fire the seed of the corn that their husbands sowed in the earth. And when the seed bare no increase, King Athamas sent to inquire of the oracle at Delphi what the cause might be. But Ino persuaded the messengers that they should bring back this message, as though it were the answer of the god, "Sacrifice the two children, Phrixus and Helle, if ye would be rid of this barrenness." So Athamas, being persuaded, brought the children to the altar to sacrifice them; but the gods had pity on them, and sent a winged ram with a fleece of gold to carry them away. So the ram carried them away; but Helle fell from it and was drowned (for which cause the sea in those parts is called the Sea of Helle to this day), but Phrixus came safe to the land of the Colchians. There he sacrificed the ram as a thankoffering to Zeus, and afterwards married the daughter of the king of that land, and then died. And now Pelias would have Jason fetch the fleece of gold as belonging of right to his own house. To this Jason consented, and he sent messengers through the land of Greece to gather the heroes, that they might be his companions in this labor; and the heroes hearkened to his word.

First there came Orpheus, the great singer of Thrace, who could cause rocks to move from their places, and rivers to stay their course, and trees to follow him, so sweetly he sang; and Polyphemus, who in his youth had fought with the Lapithæ against the Centaurs, and though his limbs were burdened with many years, he bare a brave heart within him; and Admetus of Thessaly, for whom his wife Alcestis was willing to die; and the two sons of Æacus of Ægina, Telamon and Peleus, of whom Telamon dwelt in Salamis, and Peleus in Phthia, for they had fled from Ægina, having slain Phocus, their brother, unwittingly. But Theseus, the bravest of the sons of Attica, came not, being imprisoned with Pirithoüs in the dwellings of the dead. Also there came Tiphys, who was the most skilful of men to foresee when the waves would rise, and the winds blow, and to guide a ship by sun and stars; and Hercules, who was newly come to Argos from Arcadia, whence he had brought alive the great Erymanthian boar, and put him down in the market-place of Mycenæ; and the twin brethren, Castor, the tamer of horses, and Pollux, the mighty boxer; and Lynceus, who was keener of sight than all other men, so that he could see even the things below the earth. With these came also two brethren, sons of Boreas, Prince of Thrace, whom men call also the North Wind. Wings had these two upon their feet,—a wonder to see, black, shining with scales of gold,—and their hair streamed behind them on either side as they ran. These, and many more heroes whom it needs not name, did Jason gather together.

As for the ship *Argo*, the goddess Athene devised it, but the hands of Argus, the son of Arestor, builded it.

Great was the wonder among the people to see such a gathering of heroes. "Surely," they said, "they will burn the house of Æetes with fire if he withhold from them the fleece." But the women lifted up their hands and prayed for a safe return; also they wept one to another, no one more bitterly than Alcimedé, the mother of Jason, casting her arms about her son, and bewailing the day when Pelias had sent him on this errand, seeing that he was her only son, and she would be left desolate and alone. But Jason comforted her, saying that Athene would help him in his quest, and that Apollo had prophesied good things for him; only he bade her abide within the house, lest she should speak some word of ill omen at their departure.

When the heroes were gathered together at the ship, Jason stood up in the midst, and spake: "My friends, seeing that all things are now ready for the voyage, and that there is nothing to hinder us from sailing, the wind being favorable, let us choose for our leader him whom we judge to be the best among us, for our going and our returning concerneth us all." Then the young men cast their eyes on Hercules, and cried out with one voice that he should be their leader. But the hero stretched forth his right hand from where he sat, and cried, "Not so; let no man seek to give me this honor, for I will not receive it. Let him that hath gathered us be also our leader." So spake Hercules, and they all were obedient to his word, and chose Jason to be their leader. Then said Jason, "First let us make a feast and a sacrifice to Apollo. But while the slaves fetch the oxen, let us drag down the ship to the sea, and when we have put all her tackling into her, let us cast lots for the benches whereon we shall sit." Then the heroes undergirded the ship with ropes, that she might be the stronger against the waves; and afterwards, standing on either side, pushed her with all their might; but Tiphys stood in the midst and gave the word, that they might do it with one heart and at one time. Quickly ran the *Argo* on the slips, and the heroes shouted as she ran. Then they fastened the oars in the rowlocks, and put a mast in the ship, and sails well woven. After this they divided the heroes among the benches, two heroes to a bench; and in the hindmost bench they set Hercules and Ancæus of Tegea, by choice and not by lot, considering the stature of the heroes, for there the ship was deepest. But for helmsman they chose Tiphys by common consent.

After this they built an altar of stones upon the shore. Then Jason prayed to Apollo, "O king, bring us again safe to Greece; so will we offer young bullocks on thy altars, both at Delphi and in Delos. And now let us raise our cable in peace, and give us favorable winds and a calm sea." Then Hercules smote one of the oxen with his fist between the horns and felled him to the earth; and Ancæus slew the other, smiting him on the neck with an axe. And the young men cut them in pieces, and they covered the thighs with fat, and burned them in the fire. But when Idmon, the seer, saw the blue smoke, how it arose in circles above the flames, he cried, by the inspiration of Apollo, "Truly ye shall come hither again, and bring the fleece of gold with you; but as for me, I must die far from my home in the land of Asia. This, indeed, I knew before, yet am I with you to-day, that I may share the glory of this voyage." And now the sun was setting, and the heroes sat in order on the shore, and drank the wine out of great cups, talking with each other as men are wont to talk at the banquet. But Jason sat apart, busy with many thoughts, which, when the hero Idas saw, he said, "What fearest thou, son of Æson? By this spear I swear—and in truth my spear helpeth me more than Zeus—thou shalt fail in nought if only Idas be with thee." And as he spake he raised with both his hands a mighty bowl of wine, and drenched his lips and bearded cheeks. Then the heroes murmured against him; but Idmon, the seer, spake aloud, "These are evil words that thou speakest against thyself. Hath the wine so wrought with thee that thou revilest the gods? Remember the sons of Aloeus, how mighty they were; but when they spake against the gods, Apollo slew them with his darts." Then Idas laughed aloud, and cried, "Thinkest thou, then, that the gods will slay me as Apollo slew the sons of Aloeus? Only take heed to thyself if thou shalt be found to have prophesied falsely concerning me." But Jason stayed them, that they should not strive together any more.

After this Orpheus took his harp and sang. He sang how the earth and heaven and sky, having had but one form before, were divided from each other; and how the stars are fixed in heaven; and of the moon and the courses of the sun. Also he sang how the mountains arose, and the rivers flowed; and how of old Chronos reigned in Olympus, ruling the Titan gods, while Zeus was yet a child, dwelling in the caves of Ida, before the Cyclopes had armed his hand with the thunderbolt. Then Orpheus ended his song; but the heroes sat awhile, after that he had ceased, with their heads bent forwards, so mighty was the spell upon them. After this they burnt the tongues of the beasts with fire, and poured wine upon them, and so lay down to sleep.

But when the morning shone on the top of Pelion, Tiphys first woke out of sleep, and roused the heroes, bidding them embark and prepare for rowing. But before they departed came Chiron down from the hills, and his wife with him, carrying in her arms the little Achilles, that Peleus, his father, might embrace him. And Chiron prayed aloud to the gods that the heroes might have a safe return.

Thus did the ship *Argo* depart upon her voyage. The heroes smote the sea with their oars in time to the music of Orpheus, and drave her on her course with a marvellous quickness. The tackling of the ship glistened like gold in the sun, and the waves were parted, foaming on either side of the prow, and their way was white behind them, plain to see as the path upon a meadow.

So soon as they were clear of the harbor's winding ways —and well did Tiphys guide them, holding the polished tiller in his hands—they set up the great mast in its socket, fastening it by ropes on either side; and upon the mast they spread out the sail, setting it duly with pulleys and sheets. Then, with the wind blowing fair behind them, they sped forward; and Orpheus sang the while of Artemis; and the fishes followed, leaping out of the sea about the ship, even as sheep when they are fed to the full follow back the shepherd to the sheepfold as he goes before them, making sweet music on his oaten pipe. Past the rocks of Pelion they sped, and Sciathos and Magnessa; and when they came to the tomb of Dolops, they drave their ship to the shore and did sacrifice by the tomb. There they abode for two days, for the sea was stormy; but on the third day they launched their ship and hoisted the great sail. Whereupon to this day they call this place "The Launching of the *Argo*." Then as they sailed they saw the valleys of Ossa and Olympus; all night the wind carried them on, and the next day there appeared Athos, the great mountain of Thrace; so great is it that its shadow falls on Myrina in Lemnos, though it be a half-day's journey for a fleet ship.

Then they came to Lemnos. There, but a year before,

had been wrought a dreadful deed; for the women had slain their husbands, aye, and every male throughout the land, lest the children, being grown to manhood, should avenge their fathers. Only Hypsipyle had spared the old man Thoas, her father, hiding him in a cave by the sea, that she might send him away alive. And now the women ploughed the fields, and donned the armor of men; nevertheless, they watched ever in fear lest the Thracians that dwelt on the shore over against them should come upon them. And now, when they saw the *Argo* and the band of heroes, they sallied forth from their city, duly armed, with Hypsipyle their Queen for their leader; for they thought that now indeed the Thracians were come. Speechless they were for fear, for all their brave show of war. But the heroes sent their herald to tell who they were, and whence they had come, and whither they went. For that day, therefore, they abode on the shore. But the Queen called the women to council; and when these were gathered together, she rose in the midst, and said: " Let us give gifts to these strangers, food and wine; but let them abide without the walls, for we have done a dreadful deed, and it is not well that they should know it. But if anyone have some better counsel, let her speak." Then Polyxo, that was nurse to the Queen, stood forth. Very old she was; she halted upon her feet, she leant upon her staff; and four young maidens, with long yellow hair, held her up. Yet could she scarce lift up her head, so bowed she was with age; nevertheless, age had not tamed her tongue. Thus she spake: " It is well, as saith the Queen, to send gifts to these strangers. Yet, bethink you, my daughters, what will ye do in the time to come? How will it fare with you, if these Thracians come, or other enemies? When ye are old, how will ye live? Will the oxen yoke themselves to the plough, or the harvests come without toil? As for me, though hitherto the Fates have passed me by, I shall surely die this year or the next, and escape from the evil to come. But what will ye do, my daughters? Wherefore my counsel is that ye make these men the partners of all that ye have." And the whole assembly gave their consent, and they sent Iphinoe as their herald to the heroes. And when these had heard the words of the daughter of Lemnos, the thing pleased them.

Then indeed had they dwelt in Lemnos to the end of their days, but Hercules called them apart and said: "Did ye come hither, my friends, to marry wives? Are there not maidens fair enough whom ye may wed at home? Will ye be content to plough and sow and reap in Lemnos? Think you that some god will put this fleece of gold into your hands while ye tarry here?" So did he rebuke them; but they answered him not again, nor dared so much as to lift their eyes from the ground. But the next day they climbed into their ship, and ranged themselves in order on the benches, and so departed. And after a while, the south wind blowing, they entered the Hellespont, and passing through it, came to the sea which men call the Propontis, and to a certain city of which Cyzicus was king, and now men call it by his name. Here were they entertained with all hospitality; for the King had been warned that if a ship of strangers should come, he should deal kindly with them, if haply he might so escape his fate. For his fate was this, that he should die by the hands of a stranger. Wherefore he gave them great store of flesh and wine. Now the next day some would climb the hill Dindymus, that they might behold the sea on which they should sail; and some rowed the *Argo* to a more convenient haven. But there were in an island hard by certain giants, of monstrous shape. Six hands had each of them,—two such as other men have, and four strangely growing from their sides. These sallied forth against the heroes, and would have blocked the mouth of the haven with rocks, as men block a wild beast in a cavern. But Hercules drew his bow against them, and slew many with arrows. And the heroes, when they saw what had befallen, left their journey and came to the help of their companions, and pursued the giants till they had destroyed them. But Queen Heré had reared these giants that they might do some harm to Hercules. After this the heroes set sail, and all that day they sped onward on their course; but at nightfall the wind blew contrary, and carried them back to the city of Cyzicus. Yet they knew not whither they were come; neither did any of the men of Cyzicus know the heroes for the darkness. Therefore they joined battle as though they had been enemies; and Jason smote King Cyzicus on the breast and slew him. Thus was his doom fulfilled. Many others also were slain; and the men of Cyzicus fled before the heroes, and shut themselves into their city. But when it was morning the heroes knew what they had done in their ignorance, and lamented. Also they set up a great tomb for the slain, and circled it thrice, clad in their armor, and celebrated funeral games in the meadow hard by. But Clite, that was the wife of Cyzicus, when she knew that her husband was dead, hanged herself; and the gods changed her tears into a fountain which is yet called Clite, after her name.

For twelve days the heroes tarried in this land, so stormy were the winds; but in the twelfth night a kingfisher flew with a shrill cry over the head of Jason as he slept; and Mopsus the seer knew what the kingfisher said, and cried, "Let us build an altar to Cybele, the mother of the gods, and do sacrifice to her. So shall we have an end of these stormy winds."

This therefore they did; and the next morning they departed. Quickly they sped, so that not even the chariot of Poseidon could have outstripped them. But towards the evening the wind blew more strongly, and the waves arose. Then indeed did Hercules, as he toiled with all his might in rowing, break his oar in the middle. One half he held in his hands and fell therewith, but the other half the sea carried with it. But when they were come to the land the people of Mysia entertained them with hospitality. And the next day Hercules went into the woods, seeking a pine-tree for an oar. And when he had found one that had but few branches or leaves upon it, but was tall and straight as a poplar, he laid his bow and his arrows and his lion-skin also on the ground, and first he smote the pine-tree with his club and loosened it, and then put his hands about the stem, and tare it by the roots from the earth, and so went back to the ship bearing it on his shoulders.

But in the meanwhile the youth Hylas had gone forth with his pitcher to fetch water from a spring; for he was page to Hercules, and would have all things ready for him against his coming back. Now all the Nymphs of the land, whether they dwelt in the water or on the hills, were wont to assemble at this fountain. And one of these saw the youth, how fair he was, for the moon was at her full and shone upon him as he went, and she loved him in her heart. And when the youth dipped his pitcher into the spring to fill it, she threw her arms about his neck and drew him down, and he fell into the fountain, but called aloud on Hercules as he fell. Now one of the heroes heard the cry of the youth, and hastened to the place, but found nothing. But as he returned from out of the wood, for he feared lest some wild beast or enemy should assail him, he met Hercules, and spake, saying, "These are sad tidings that I bring thee. For Hylas is gone to the spring and hath not returned, and either some beast hath slain him, or robbers have carried him away." So all that night Hercules wandered through the wood seeking for the youth, even as a bull which some gad-fly stings rusheth over the fields nor resteth anywhere. So Hercules hastened hither and thither, seeking for the youth, and calling him by his name, but found him not.

When it was now day, Tiphys, the helmsman, bade them depart, for that the wind favored them. But after a while they found that they had left the best of their company behind them unwittingly; and then arose great strife and contention among them. Then spake Telamon in his wrath: "Truly this is well, that we have left our bravest behind us! Thine is this counsel, O Jason, that thy glory might not be shadowed by his glory in the land of Greece, if so be that the gods shall bring us back." And he would have leapt on Tiphys, the helmsman, only the two sons of Boreas held him back; for which deed they suffered afterwards, seeing that Hercules slew them both as they returned from the funeral games of Pelias, because they had hindered the heroes from seeking for him. But in the midst of their anger there appeared to them the sea-god Glaucus. From the midst of the waves he lifted his shaggy head and breast, and laid hold of the ship, and spake: "Why do ye seek to take Hercules to the land of the Colchians against the will of Zeus? For it is his doom that he should fulfil his previous toils for Eurystheus, and afterwards be numbered with the gods. And as for Polyphemus, it is his fate to build a city in the land of the

Mysians. Neither mourn ye for Hylas, seeing that the Nymph of the fountain hath taken him for her husband." And when the god had so spoken he sank again into the sea, and was hidden from their sight. Then said Telamon to Jason, clasping him by the hand, " Pardon me, son of Æson, if I have wronged thee, and be not wroth for my hasty words. For indeed a great sorrow drave me to speak, and now let us be friends as before." To him answered Jason, "Thy words indeed were harsh when thou saidst that I had betrayed my friend, yet I bear no anger for them. For thy wrath was not for cattle or gold, but for a man whom thou lovest. And, indeed, I would have thee contend with me yet again for a like cause, if such should arise." So Telamon and Jason were made friends. And all that day and all that night the wind blew strong; but in the morning there was a calm; yet the heroes plied their oars, and at sunset they drave their ship on to the shore.

CHAPTER II.

Now the land whereunto they were come was the land of the Bebryces, whose King was one Amycus, the son of Poseidon. No man was more arrogant than he, for he made it a law that no stranger should depart from the land before he had made trial of him in boxing; and thus had he slain many. And coming down to the ship, when he had inquired of them the cause of their journey, he spake, saying, " Hearken to me, ye wanderers of the sea ; no man cometh to the land of the Bebryces but he must stand up against me in a fight of boxers. Choose me out, therefore, the best of your company, and set him to fight with me here; and if not, I will compel you." But the heroes were very wroth when they heard these words, and Pollux more than all. Wherefore he stood forth before his fellows, and said, "Talk not to us of compulsion. We will follow this custom of thine. Lo, I will meet thee myself." Then Amycus glared at him, even as a lion upon the hill glares at the man that wounded him at the first, caring not for the others that gird him about. Then Pollux laid aside his mantle, which one of the daughters of Lemnos had given him; and Amycus also stripped off his cloak, and put aside the great shepherd's crook made of a wild olive tree, that he bare. Very diverse were they to behold, for the King was like to Typhœus, or one of the giants, the sons of Earth; but Pollux was like a star of Heaven, so fair he was. And he tried his hands, whether they were supple as of old, or haply were grown stiff with toiling at the oar. But Amycus stood still, looking upon Pollux as thirsting for his blood. Then Lycoreus, the King's companion, threw down at Pollux's feet two pair of gauntlets covered with blood, and stiff, and marvellously hard. And Amycus said, "Take which thou wilt, stranger, that thou blame me not hereafter, and fit them to thine hands. So haply shalt thou learn that I can fell an ox or wound a man's cheek to bleeding." But Pollux answered him nothing, but smiled and took the gauntlets that lay nearest. Then came Castor and Talaus, and bound the gauntlets upon him, and bade him be of good courage. But Aretus and Orniptus bound them for King Amycus, and knew not that they should never bind them for him any more. Then the two stood up against each other. And Amycus came on as a wave of the sea comes upon a ship; which yet, by the skilful handling of the pilot, escapes from its might. Then did the King follow hard after Pollux, suffering him not to rest; but he, so skilful was he, escaped ever without a wound, for he knew wherein lay the strength of the King, and wherein also he failed. So the two strove together, and the sounds of their strokes was as the sound of shipwrights that build a ship. And after awhile they rested, wiping the sweat from their faces. Then they joined battle again, as bulls that fight for the mastery. But at the last Amycus, rising as one that fells an ox, smote with all his might. But Pollux leapt from under the blow, turning his head aside; yet did the King's arm graze his shoulder. Then he reached forward with his knee by the knee of the King, and smote him with all his might under the ear; and the giant fell to the earth with a groan, and all the heroes set up a shout when they saw it.

But the Bebryces were wroth to see that their King was slain, and they set themselves with their clubs and hunting-spears against Pollux; but the heroes drew their swords and stood by him. Then the battle waxed fierce, and many of the Bebryces were slain, and of the heroes certain were wounded; but at the last Ancæus and the two sons of Æacus and Jason rushed upon the enemy and scattered them. After this they feasted on the shore; and the next day they put into their ships so much of the spoil of the land as they would, and so departed; and on the morrow they came to the land of Phineus, the son of Agenor. Now Phineus, being skilled in divination beyond all other men, revealed to men all that Zeus prepared to do; for which reason the god smote him with old age and with blindness, and also sent the plague of the Harpies upon him, which, coming down suddenly upon him as he sat at the banquet, snatched away the meat from the table. And if they left somewhat, it stank so foully that a man might not touch it.

When Phineus heard that the heroes were come, he was glad, and came forth to meet them. Very feeble was he with old age and hunger; and when he saw them he said, "Welcome, ye heroes! Right glad I am to see you, for I know by the inspiration of Apollo that there shall come to this land the two sons of Boreas, who shall deliver me from this plague that I endure." And he told them what things he suffered from the Harpies. Then Zetes laid hold of the old man's hand, and said, "We pity thee, son of Agenor, and will help thee if it may be; but first thou must swear that we shall not anger the gods thereby; for, as thou knowest, these evils have come upon thee because thou hast revealed their will to men too plainly." And the old man swore that the thing was pleasing to the gods. Then they prepared a banquet for him, and as soon as the old man had reached his hand to the food, of a sudden the Harpies flew down, as lightning cometh out of the clouds, and carried off the meat. But the two sons of Boreas followed hard after them, and Zeus gave them strength; otherwise of a truth they had not caught them, for the winds themselves were not more fleet. And when they had caught them they would have slain them, only Iris, the messenger of Zeus, came down and said, "Slay not the Harpies, that are the hounds of Zeus. I will swear to you that they shall not come any more to the dwelling of Phineus, the son of Agenor." So they stayed from slaying them. After this Phineus and the heroes feasted together, and the King said, "I will expound to you things to come, yet so much only as the gods will have me tell; for they will not that men should know all things, but that they should yet need counsel and help. When ye have departed from this land ye shall see certain rocks, between the which ye must needs pass. Do ye therefore first send a dove before you, and if she pass through safely then may ye also follow. And row with all your might, for your hands rather than your prayers shall deliver you. But if the dove perish, then do ye go back, for it is not the will of the gods that ye should go further. After this ye shall see many places, as Helica, and the river of Halys, and the land of the Chalybes, the workers of iron, and at the last shall come to the river of Phasis, whereby ye shall see the town of Æætes and the grove of Æa, where the fleece of gold hangeth even on the top of a beech tree, and the dragon, a terrible monster to behold, watcheth it with eyes that turn every way." Then were the heroes much dismayed; but when Jason would have questioned him further, he said, "Seek ye for the help of Aphrodite, for the victory will be of her. And now ask me no more." And when he had ended his words, the two sons of Boreas came back, panting from their course, and told what things they had done. And the next morning many were gathered together to hear from him of things to come, among whom was a certain Parœbius, whom the King had delivered from great trouble; for the man's father had cut down an oak upon the mountains, not heeding the prayers of the Nymph that dwelt therein that he should spare it, for which reason the Nymph sent all manner of evil upon him and his children after him. Nor did they know the cause till Phineus expounded it to them.

After this they departed, and forgot not to take with them a dove, which Euphemus held bound to his hand by a cord; and Athene helped them on their way. And when they came to the rocks whereof Phineus had spoken, Euphemus let fly the dove, and it passed through, yet did the rocks, clashing together, touch the last feather of her tail. Then Tiphys shouted to them that they should row with all their might, for the rocks had parted again; but as they rowed a great terror came upon them, for they saw destruction hanging over them; and a great wave, like to a mountain, rose up against them. And when they saw it they turned their heads away, thinking it must overwhelm them; but Tiphys turned the helm, and the wave passed under the keel, lifting up the *Argo* to the top of the rocks. Then said Euphemus, "Row ye with all your might." And the heroes rowed till the stout oars were bent as bows. Athene, also, with one hand kept the ship from the rocks, and with the other drave it forward; and the rocks clashed together behind it, nor were divided any more; for it was the will of the gods that this should be so when the ship should pass through safely. But the heroes breathed again, being delivered from death. And Tiphys cried, "Fear not, son of Æson, for surely Athene hath delivered us, and now all things will be easy to thee, and thou wilt accomplish the command of the King." But Jason spoke, "Nay, my friend. Would that I had died before I took this task in hand, for there are perils by sea and perils by land, and I have no rest day or night. For myself I fear not, but for these, my companions, lest I should not take them back in safety." This he said, for he would try the temper of the heroes; and when they cried out that they feared not, he was glad at heart.

So the heroes passed on their way till they came to the land of the Mariandyni, of whom one Lycus was king. Here his doom came upon Idmon, the seer, that he should perish; for though he was a prophet, yet his prophecy availed him not against fate. Now there chanced to be in the marsh a great boar, that lay wallowing in the mud. Great white tusks had he, and even the Nymphs feared him. And as Idmon walked by the river side, the boar rushed on him of a sudden out of the reeds, and smote him on the thigh with his tusk, making a great wound. The hero fell not, indeed, but shouted aloud; and his companions ran thither at his voice. And first Peleus cast his javelin at the beast, but missed his aim; and afterwards Idas smote him, and he gnashed his teeth upon the spear. Then the heroes carried back their companion to the ship, but he died even as they carried him. Then they abode in that place for three days, and on the fourth they made a great funeral for him; and Lycus and his people came also to do honor to the dead man. But while they mourned for him it befell that Tiphys, the pilot, died also; for he could not endure his great sorrow for his companion. So they buried Tiphys also; and for each they built a great tomb, to be a memorial to them who should come after.

Sore dismayed were the heroes that their helmsman was dead, and they sat a long time in silence, and neither ate nor drank. Then Heré put courage into the heart of Ancæus, and he spake to Peleus, saying, "Is it well, son of Æacus, to abide here in the land of strangers? Here am I that know more of seamanship than of war, and others also as skilful; nor should we suffer loss if we set one of them at the helm." Then spake Peleus in the midst of the heroes, "Why waste we time in sorrow, my friends? There are skilful helmsmen; many are in this company, of whom let us choose us out the best." But Jason answered, "If there be such, why sit they here with the rest lamenting? I fear me much that we shall neither see the city of Æetes nor yet the land of Greece." But Ancæus stood forth, saying that he would be their helmsman; so also did Euphemus and other two; but the heroes chose Ancæus.

So on the morning of the twelfth day they set sail, and a strong west wind blew from behind and carried them quickly over the sea. But when they came to the tomb of Sthenelus they beheld a marvellous sight. Now this Sthenelus was companion to Hercules in battling with the Amazons, and had been wounded with an arrow, and so died. And he besought Persephone, that is Queen of the dead, that he might look upon the heroes; and when she consented, he stood upon the top of his tomb equipped as one that went forth to battle, with a fair four-crested helmet on his head. Much did the heroes marvel to behold him. But Mopsus, the seer, bade them tarry and make offerings to the dead. Wherefore they landed and built an altar, and offered sacrifices, and Orpheus also dedicated his harp for a gift. After this they departed, and sailed by the river of Parthenius, which is by interpretation the Virgin River; so men call it, because Artemis the Virgin, the daughter of Latona, is wont to bathe therein when she is weary with hunting. Also they passed the river of Thermodon, and tarried not, for such was the will of Zeus, that they might not join battle with the Amazons who dwelt in these parts, a fierce race and delighting in war. Surely not without much bloodshed and damage to both such battle had been. The next day they came to the land of the Chalybes. These care not to plough the land with oxen, or to plant seed or to reap harvests; nor have they flocks or herds; but they dig iron out of the earth, and change it with other men for food. Never doth morning come, but it seeth them at their toil, where they labor without ceasing in the midst of reek and smoke. But after the Chalybes they came to the Mossyni, a strange folk that are contrary to other men, doing abroad what others do at home, and at home what others do abroad. Their king also sitteth all day on his throne, and judgeth his people; nor, indeed, is he to be envied for all his royal state, seeing that if he err at all in his judgment the people shut him in prison till he die of hunger. Next they came to the island of Aretias, wherefrom as they sailed in the twilight there came a great bird flying over them, and shooting a sharp-pointed feather from its wing. And the feather struck Oileus on his left shoulder and wounded him, so that he dropped the oar from his hand. After this came other like birds also; and though the heroes shot at them with arrows and slew certain of them, yet could they not drive them away. Then said Amphidamas to his companions: "We are come to the island of Aretias, and I judge that we shall not prevail over these birds with our arrows. For Hercules prevailed not thus over the birds of the Lake Stymphalus, as I saw with my own eyes. Do ye, therefore, as I bid you. Put ye on your helmets, and let some of you row with the oars, and let the rest so order their spears and their shields that they may be a covering to the ship. Shout also with all your might; and when ye shall be come nigh unto the island, beat upon your shields, and make all the noise that ye may." And the heroes did so, and covered the ship, even as a house is covered from the rain by its roof; and they shouted and beat upon their shields; nor did they suffer further damage from the birds.

Now it chanced in these days that the sons of Phrixus sailed from the land of King Æætes to the city of Orchomenus, that they might get for themselves the possessions of their father. And coming near to this same island of Aretias, a mighty wind from the north brake their ship; and the men, being four in number, laid hold of a beam, and so were driven about by the waves, being in great peril of death, till, at the last, they were cast upon the shore of the island. Therefore, when the *Argo* came near, one of them spake to the heroes, saying, "We entreat you, whosoever ye be, to help us, seeing that the waves have broken our ship. Give us, I pray you, some clothing and a morsel of food." Then said Jason, "Tell us who you are, and whence ye are come, and whither ye go." Then the man made answer, "Doubtless ye have heard how Phrixus came to the city of King Æetes on a ram with the fleece of gold, and how the fleece hangeth to this day on a tree near to the city; how the King gave to this Phrixus his daughter Chalciope in marriage; and we are the children of these two. And our father being newly dead, we sailed to Orchomenus that we might get for ourselves the possessions of Athamas, our grandfather; for so Phrixus, our father, commanded us."

The heroes were right glad of this meeting, and Jason made answer, "Ye are my kinsmen, for Cretheus and Athamas were brothers, and I am grandson to Cretheus; and I sail with these my comrades to the city of King Æetes. But of these things we will talk hereafter. But now we will give you what ye need." So he gave them clothing, and afterwards they did sacrifice in the Temple of Ares that was hard by, and there feasted together. And after the feast Jason spake, saying, "It is manifest that Zeus hath a care both for you and for us; for us he hath brought safely through many perils to this place, and you he suffered not to perish in the sea. Ye shall sail hereafter in this ship whithersoever ye will; but now do ye help us in our quest, for we are come from the land of Greece seeking the fleece of gold, and we would gladly have you for our guides."

But the men were sore dismayed to hear these words,

knowing what manner of man King Æætes was. And he who had spoken at the first made answer, "O my friends, ye shall have such help as we can give you. But know that Æætes is fierce and savage beyond all other men, and that your voyage is perilous. Men say that he is of the race of the Sun, and he is mighty in battle as Ares himself. Nor will it be an easy thing to carry away the fleece, for a dragon watcheth it continually, and this dragon cannot be slain, and it sleepeth not." Then many of the heroes, when they heard these words, grew pale. But Peleus spake out boldly: "Fear not, my friend; we lack not strength to meet King Æætes in battle, if need be, for we are well used to war, and are, for the most part, of the race of the gods. Wherefore, if the King yield us not the fleece peaceably, I judge that his Colchians shall not help him."

After this the heroes slept. And the next day they departed, and sailing with a favorable wind, came near to the further end of the Euxine Sea; thence they could see the mountains of Caucasus, whereto the Titan Prometheus is bound. And indeed in the evening they beheld the great vulture which feedeth on his liver flying above their ship; and after a while they heard the Titan groaning with the bitterness of his pain, and then again the vulture returning by the same way when his feast was ended. That night, by skilful guidance of the sons of Phrixus, they came to the river of Phasis, and straightway they lowered the sails and the yardarms, and afterwards the mast, and so entered the river. And on their left hand was the mountain of Caucasus and the city of Æætes, and on the right the oak grove wherein the dragon watched continually the fleece of gold. And Jason poured a libation of wine from a cup of gold into the river, praying to the gods of the land and to the spirits of the dead heroes that they should help them in their quest. And when their prayers were ended they fastened the ship with anchors under cover of a wood that was hard by, and so slept.

CHAPTER III.

But while the heroes lay hidden among the reeds of the river, Heré and Athene sought a chamber where they might hold counsel apart from the other gods. And Heré first spake, saying, "Come now, daughter of Zeus, consider by what craft or device we may bring it to pass that the heroes may carry back the fleece of gold to the land of Greece." Then Athene made answer, "That which thou askest, O Heré, I had already in my thoughts; but though I have weighed many counsels, yet have I not found one that would serve this purpose." Then said Heré, "Come, let us go to Aphrodite, and when we have found her let us persuade her to command her son, if only he will hearken to her words, that he smite the daughter of King Æetes with an arrow, that she may love Prince Jason, for she is skilful in magic and drugs." This counsel pleased Athene mightily, and she said, "I know not anything of these matters, nor can I say what may work love in a maiden's heart. Yet thy counsel pleaseth me; only when we are come to Aphrodite do thou speak for us both."

So the two departed, and came to the palace of Aphrodite, which her husband, the halting god, had wrought for her when the first took her to wife, and they stood in the porch. Now Hephæstes was gone to his workshop, and the goddess sat alone over against the door; and she was combing her hair with a comb of gold, and weaving her tresses. But when she saw the two she rose from her seat, and gave them welcome, and spake, saying, "What is your errand, that ye are come now after these many years?"

To her Heré made answer, "We are in trouble, O Queen, for Jason and they that are with him are come to the river of Phasis, seeking the fleece of gold; and I fear for him. Yet would I serve him with all my strength, on whatever errand he might go, for he hath always honored me with sacrifices; and besides he did me good service at the river of Anaurus. For the mountains were white with snow, and the streams came down from the heights, and the river was swollen. And Jason came from his hunting, and when he saw me he had pity on me, for I had made myself like to an old woman, and he carried me over the river."

Then said Aphrodite, "It were ill done of me were I to deny such help as these weak hands can give."

And Heré spake again, "We want no help of hands, be they weak or strong. Only bid thy son smite with his arrows the daughter of King Æetes, for surely if she be willing to help him he will easily carry away the fleece of gold, and so come safe to Iolcos."

But Aphrodite made answer, "Surely he will hearken to you rather than to me. For to you, shameless though he be, he must needs pay some reverence; but me he heedeth not at all. I had well nigh broken in my wrath his arrows and his bows."

And when the goddesses laughed, she spake again, saying, "Yea, I know that others laugh at my sorrows But if ye are urgent for this thing, I will persuade him, and I doubt not but that he will hearken to me."

So the three went together to the halls of Olympus.

And they found Eros playing at dice with Ganymede, that was the cupbearer of Zeus; and he laughed aloud, for he had won at his playing, but the other was angry, having lost. And when Aphrodite saw him, she said, "Hast thou defrauded him, after thy wont, that thou laughest? But come, do now what I shall tell thee, and thou shalt have a fair plaything of Zeus that his nurse Adrastea made for him, a ball with two bands of gold about it; and none can see the seams of it; and when thou throwest it it will glitter like a star. And the thing is this: that thou make the maiden daughter of King Æætes to love Jason; and this thou must do without delay, or it profiteth nothing."

Then cried Eros, "Give me the ball straightway." But she caught him in her arms and kissed him, and said, "I will not deceive thee, only do my bidding." Then he took up his bow and passed his quiver on his back, and went his way to the land of Colchis.

Meanwhile Jason spoke to the heroes, "Hearken now, and I will unfold my counsel. I will go to the hall of Æætes, and the sons of Phrixus with me, and two heroes besides; and first I will make trial of him, whether he will yield the fleece of gold willingly, for it would be ill to seek to take it by force till we have seen what words can do." To this the heroes agreed; wherefore Jason departed, taking with him the sons of Phrixus, and Telamon and Augeas; and as they went Heré threw a mist about them till they had passed through the city, but when they came to the palace of the King, then was the mist scattered; and they stood in the porch marvelling at the things which they saw, even the mighty gates, and the walls set with pillars, and the cornice of brass above them. Round about the threshold grew great vines, and under the vines four fountains that ceased not to flow, whereof one was of milk, and one of wine, and one of sweet-smelling olive-oil, and of water the fourth; and the water was hot in the wintertide, and as cold as ice in the summer. In the midst stood the hall, with chambers on either side, two chambers being loftier than the rest, in one whereof dwelt the King and his wife, and in the other Absyrtus his son, whom the Colchians also called Phaeton, because he excelled all his equals of age. Now two of the chambers were of the King's daughters, Chalciope and Medea; and it chanced that Medea was now going to the chamber of her sister. Meanwhile came Eros unseen through the air, and stood behind a pillar in the porch, and bent his bow, fitting to it an arrow, the sharpest of all his quiver. And he came lightly into the hall, following close upon Jason, and drew his bow with both his hands, and shot the arrow at Medea, and smote her under the heart. And when he had so done he laughed, and departed from the palace. Then the servants prepared a meal for the sons of Phrixus and for Jason. And when they had bathed they sat down, and ate, and drank, and were merry.

Jason and the sons of Phrixus having eaten well, the King inquired of his grandsons, saying, "What brings you back? Did some misfortune overtake you on your journey? Surely it was not of my bidding that ye went; for I knew how perilous was the way, having seen it from the chariot of the Sun, my father, when he took Circe, my sister, to the land of Hesperia. But tell me now what befell you, and who are these your companions?" Then Argus made answer, " Our ship was broken and we scarcely were saved; and as for these men, they gave us food and raiment, treating us kindly when they heard thy name and the name of Phrixus our father; and they are come for the fleece of gold, for they say that the wrath of Zeus may not be turned away from the land of Greece till this be brought back. Never was such ship as theirs, for Athene built it; neither can storm break it, and it is swift alike with sails or with oars; and for a crew it hath all the heroes of the land of Greece. But their chief thinketh not to take the fleece by force, but will make thee due return, subduing under thee thy enemies, the Sauromatæ. And if thou wouldst hear his name, know that it is Jason, grandson to King Cretheus, whose brother was Athamas, father to Phrixus, and they that are with him are Augeas and Telamon."

But the King was very wroth when he heard these words, and cried, "Get you out of my sight! Ye are not come for the fleece, but to spy out the land, that ye may possess my kingdom. Surely, had ye not eaten at my table, I had cut out your tongues and lopped your hands."

Then Telamon was minded to give the King a fierce answer, but Jason held him back, and spake softly, "'Tis not as thou thinkest, O King; we do not desire thy kingdom, but are coming at the bidding of the gods. Also for what we seek we will make thee due recompense, subduing under thee the Sauromatæ, or whomsoever thou wilt."

Then the King doubted awhile whether he should not fall on them straightway with the sword, but afterwards spake again, " If ye be in truth of the race of the gods, I will give you the fleece, for I grudge nothing to brave men. But first I must make trial of your strength. There feed in the plain of Ares two bulls, having hoofs of brass and breathing fire from their nostrils. With these I plough the field of Ares, four acres and more; and, having ploughed it, I sow it with seed — not, indeed, with the seed of corn, but with the teeth of a serpent; and when these have sprung up into armed men, I slay the men and so finish my harvest. In the morning I yoke the bulls, and in the evening I rest from my reaping. And if ye will do this, ye shall have the fleece of gold; but if not, ye shall not have it."

Then the heroes stood for a while, with their eyes cast upon the ground, speechless, for they knew not what they should say. But afterwards Jason spake, " I will do this thing, even if I die for it." And the King answered, " If ye hold back from the ploughing or the reaping it shall be the worse for you." Then Jason and his companions departed from the palace; and Medea looked upon Jason, as he went, from behind her veil, and loved him. And when he was gone she thought to herself of his face, and of the garments wherewith he was clothed, and of the words which he had spoken. But when the heroes were now without the city, Argus spake to Jason saying, " There is a maiden, the priestess of Hecate, that is skilled in all manner of witchcraft; and, if she be willing to help you, ye need not fear this task. Only I doubt me much whether I shall prevail with her. Nevertheless, if thou art willing, I will speak with my mother, who is her sister, of the matter." And Jason said, " Speak to thy mother, if thou wilt; but, if we must trust in women, there is little hope of our return." Then they went back to the ship to the rest of the heroes, and told to them the words of the King. And for a while they sat speechless and sad, for the thing seemed greater than they could do. But then rose up Peleus, and cried, " If thou wilt give thyself to this task, son of Æson, it is well; but if not, and if there be none other of this company that will adventure upon it, yet will I not shrink from it, for a man can but die." And Telamon and the sons of Tyndarus, and Meleager the son of Œneus, said that they would follow him. Then said Argus, "This can ye do, my friends, if there be no other way. But hearken to me: abide ye yet in your ship, for there is a maiden in the palace of the King whom Hecate hath taught to use all the drugs that are in the earth, so that she can quench fire, and stay winds, and turn the stars from their courses. Maybe my mother will persuade her that she help you. If this counsel please you, I will go to her straightway."

And as he spake, the birds gave a favorable sign, for a dove that fled from a hawk fell into the bosom of Jason; and the hawk fell upon the hinder part of the ship. And when Mopsus saw it he prophesied saying, "Ye must make your supplication to the maiden. Nor do I doubt that she will hearken to you; for did not Phrixus prophesy that our help should be in Aphrodite? And did ye not see how the dove that is her bird hath escaped from death?" And all the heroes gave heed to his words; but Idas was very wroth, and cried with a terrible voice, "Will ye look at doves and hawks, and turn back from battle? Out on you, that ye think to cheat maidens with words, rather than to trust in your spears!" But Jason said, "We will send Argus as he hath said. Only we will not lie hidden here, as if we were afraid, but will go forth." So the heroes brought forth the ship.

Meanwhile, King Æætes held a council of the Colchians, to whom he said, "So soon as the oxen have killed, as surely they will kill, the man who shall seek to yoke them, then will I burn these fellows with their ship. For, verily, I had not received Phrixus with hospitality, but for the commands of Zeus; but as for these robbers, they shall not go unpunished."

But while he yet spake, Argus went to the palace to his

mother Chalciope, and besought her that she should persuade her sister Medea to help the heroes. And this the woman had herself thought to do; only she feared the anger of her father. And as they talked, it befell that Medea dreamed a dream, for she had fallen asleep for weariness. And in her dream she yoked the bulls right easily; but her father would not fulfil his promise, saying that he had given this task not to maidens but to men; and hereupon there arose great strife; but she took part with the strangers, and her parents cried shame upon her. After this she awoke, and leapt in great fear from her bed, saying to herself. "I fear me much lest this coming of the heroes should be the beginning of great sorrows. As for this Jason, let him wed a maiden of his own race; but I will keep my unmarried state, and abide in my father's house; yet, if my sister need help for her sons, I will not stand aloof." Then she made as if she would seek her sister, standing barefoot on the threshold of her chamber, yet went not, for shame. Thrice she essayed to go, and thrice she returned, for love drove her on, as shame kept her back; but one of her maidens spied her, and told the thing to her sister Chalciope. And Chalciope came to her and took her by the hand, saying, "Why weepest thou, Medea? Dost thou fear the wrath of thy father? As for me, would that I had perished before I saw this day!" And after long silence Medea made answer, speaking craftily, for love so taught her to speak, "My sister, I am troubled for thy sons, lest thy father slay them with these strangers; for, verily, I have seen terrible dreams in my sleep." So she spake, for she would have her sister pray to her for help for her sons. And when Chalciope heard these words she cried aloud, "O my sister, I beseech thee by the gods, and by thy father and mother, that thou help us in our strait. For, verily, if thou help us not, I will haunt thee as a Fury." Then the two lifted up their voices together and wept. But at the last Chalciope said, "Wilt thou not, for my children's sake, give help to this stranger? Verily, my son Argus is come to beg this thing of me, and he is even now in my chamber." When Medea heard these words she was glad at heart, and said, "My sister, I will surely help thy sons, for they are as brothers to me, and thou as my mother. Wherefore, so soon as it is dark, I will carry to the temple of Hecate such drugs as shall tame these oxen." Then Chalciope went to her chamber, and told the tidings to her son that Medea would help them; but Medea sat alone and lamented over herself, because she was minded to betray her father to do service to a stranger. Nor did she sleep when night came and all the world was at rest, doubting whether she should do this thing or no, and crying, "Would that Artemis had slain me with her arrows before this stranger came to the land!" And she rose from her bed, and looked into the chest wherein her drugs were stored, some being good and some evil. And now she was minded to take from it some deadly thing that she might end herewith her troubles, but there came upon her a great horror at death, for she thought of all the joys that the living possess, but the dead lose forever; and also, when she regarded her face in the glass, she seemed to herself fairer to look upon than before.

But in the morning she arose and adorned herself, and put a white veil about her head. Then she bade her maidens—twelve she had of like age with herself—to yoke the mules to her chariot, that she might go to the temple of Hecate. And while they yoked them, she took from the chest the medicine that is called the *Medicine of*

Prometheus, wherewith if a man anoint himself, water shall not hurt him, nor fire burn. This cometh, men say, from a certain flower which grew from the blood of Prometheus when it dropped from the vulture's beak, and the flower is of the color saffron, having a root like to flesh that is newly cut, but the juice of the root is black. Then she climbed into the chariot, and a maiden stood on either side, but she took the reins and the whip, and drove the horses through the city, and the other maidens ran behind, laying their hands on the chariot; and the people made way before them as they went.

And when they were come to the temple, Medea said to her maidens, "Argus and his brethren have besought me to help this stranger in his task, and I made as if I hearkened to their words. But the thing that I am minded to do is this: I will give him some medicine indeed, but it shall not be that which he needs, and we will divide his gifts between us. And now he cometh to have speech with me; do ye, therefore, depart, and leave us alone." And the counsel pleased the maidens well.

Now when Jason went his way to the temple, Argus and Mopsus, the soothsayer, were with him; and as they went Mopsus heard the speech of a raven that said, "Verily the prophet is a fool; if he knew what all men know, will a maid speak kind words to a youth if his companions be with us?" And Mopsus laughed when he heard it, and spake to Jason saying, "Go now to the temple of Hecate, and Aphrodite will help thee, but go alone; and I and Argus will abide where we are." So Jason went forward, and Medea saw him as he came, very beautiful and bright to behold, even as the star Sirius, when it riseth from the sea. But when she saw him her eyes were darkened with fear, and her cheeks burned with a blush, and her knees failed under her. But when Jason saw how she was troubled, he spake softly to her: "Fear me not, lady, for I am not of those who speak the thing that is false; but listen to my words, and give me this medicine that shall strengthen me for my work, as thou hast promised to Chalciope, thy sister. Verily thou shalt not miss thy reward. For thou shalt be famous in the land of Greece; and all the heroes shall tell of thee, and their wives and mothers, who now sit lamenting upon the shore for those who are far away. Did not Ariadne help King Theseus, and the gods loved her for her kindness, making her a star in the heavens? So shalt thou be loved of the gods, if thou wilt save this famous company of heroes. And, indeed, thou seemest to be both wise and of a kindly heart."

And when the maiden heard these words, she took the medicine from her bosom and gave it to Jason, who took it with great gladness of heart. Then spake Medea: "Hear, now, O Prince, what thou must do, so soon as my father shall give thee the serpent's teeth to sow. Wait till it be midnight; but have no companion with thee. Then dig a trench that shall be round of form; and build in it a pile of wood, and slay on it a ewe sheep, and pour over the sheep a libation of honey to Queen Hecate. After this, depart from the place, and turn not at any sound, or the barking of dogs. But in the morning thou shalt anoint thyself with the medicine; and it shall give thee the strength of the gods. Anoint also thy spear and thy shield. So the spears of the giants shall not harm thee, nor the fire that the bulls shall breathe. But remember that this strength endureth for the day only; wherefore slack not thy hand, but finish thy work. And I will tell thee another thing that shall be for thy help.

So soon as the giants shall begin to spring up from the furrows wherein thou shalt have sown the teeth, throw secretly among them a great stone; and it shall come to pass that they will fall upon each other and perish by their own hands. So wilt thou carry away the fleece of gold to the land of Greece, departing when it shall please thee to go." And when she had spoken these words she wept, thinking how he would depart and leave her. Then she spake again: "When thou art come to thy home, remember, I pray thee, Medea, even as I shall remember thee; and tell me whither thou art minded to go."

Then Jason made answer, "Surely, lady, I shall not cease to think of thee if only I return safe to my native country. And if thou wouldst fain hear what manner of land it is, know that it is girded about with the hills and feedeth many sheep. The name of him that founded the kingdom is Deucalion, and the name of the city is Iolcos." And Medea said, "I would that where thou shalt be there could come some tidings of thee by bird of the air or the like; or that the winds could carry me thither, that I may know for a certainty that thou hast not forgotten me." Then Jason said, "O lady, if thou wilt come to that land, surely all shall honor thee, and thou shalt be my wife, neither shall anything but death only divide us twain." And when the maiden heard these words she stood divided between fear and love. But Jason said, "Surely now the sun is setting, and it is time to go back, lest some stranger come upon us." So Medea went back to the city, and Jason to the heroes, to whom he showed the medicine that the maiden had given him. And they all rejoiced, save Idas only, who sat apart in great anger.

The next day Jason sent Telamon and another to fetch from the King the serpent's teeth; and the King gave them gladly, for he thought that if Jason should yoke the oxen, yet he should not overcome the giants in battle. And when the heroes slept, Jason went alone and did as Medea had commanded him. And when he had finished the sacrifice he departed; and Queen Hecate came, and there was a great shaking of the earth and a barking of dogs. But Jason looked not behind him, but departed to the heroes.

On the morrow King Æetes armed him for the battle, giving him a breastplate which Ares had given to him, and a helmet of gold with four crests, and a shield of bull's hide, many folds thick, and a spear such as none of the others but Hercules only could have borne. And Jason anointed them with the medicine; which when he had done, all the heroes made trial of the arms, but did them no damage; and when Idas smote with his sword on the butt of the spear, it bounded back as from an anvil. After this he anointed himself with the medicine, and it was as if his strength had been multiplied tenfold. Afterwards he took to himself a helmet and a sword, and so went forth to his labor. And there lay ready to his hand a brazen yoke of the bulls, and a great plough of iron. Then he fixed his spear in the earth, and laid down his helmet, but he himself went on with his shield. But when the bulls saw him, they ran forth from their stalls, and all the heroes trembled to behold them; but Jason stood firm, holding his shield before him. And the bulls drave their horns against the shield, but harmed him not. And though they breathed fire from their nostrils, for all this the medicine of Medea kept him safe. Then he took hold of the right-hand bull by the horns, and dragged it down to the yoke, and, kicking its hoof from under it, so brought it to the ground; and in like manner dealt with the other. And the King marvelled at his strength. Then the heroes helped him with the fastening of the bulls to the plough, for so much was permitted to him. Then he put his shield upon his shoulders and took the serpent's teeth, a helmet full, and drave the bulls before him, which went with a horrible bellowing; and as he made the furrow he threw the teeth into it. Now when the day was a third part spent he had finished the ploughing; and he loosed the bulls and went back to the ship, for as yet there had sprung nothing from the furrows. And he took of the water of the river in his helmet and drank, and while he drank the giants sprang up from the furrows.

Then Jason remembered the words of Medea, and took from the earth a great round stone — of such bigness it was that four youths could not lift it — and cast it into the midst of the giants. And straightway they fell upon each other with great rage, and Jason sat behind his shield and watched. But when they had been now fighting among themselves for a long while, and many were wounded and many dead, Jason drew his sword and ran among them till he had slain them all. So he finished his work that day; but the King and his people returned, sad at heart, to the city.

All that night the King sat with his nobles, meditating harm against Jason and the heroes; for he knew that the thing had been done by craft, and also that his daughter was concerned in the matter. And Medea also sat grievously troubled in her chamber, fearing the wrath of her father; and ofttime she thought that she had best kill herself with poison. But at last Heré put it into her heart that she should flee, taking the sons of Phrixus for companions. Then she arose from her bed, and took the medicines that she had from their chest, and hid them in her bosom.

And she kissed her bed and the posts of her chamber doors and the walls. Also she cut off a long lock of her hair, to be a memorial of her to her mother. And when she had done this, she cried with a lamentable voice, "Farewell, my mother, and thou, Chalciope, my sister! Would that this stranger had perished before he came to the land of the Colchians!" Then she went out from the house, the great gates opening before her of their own accord, for she had anointed them with a mighty drug; and, being come into the street, she ran very swiftly, holding her robe over her head, till she saw the light of the fires where the heroes sat feasting all the night in the joy of the victory that Jason had won. Then she came near, and, lifting up her voice, cried to the youngest of the sons of Phrixus, whose name was Phrontis. And Phrontis heard her, and knew the voice that it was the voice of Medea, and told the thing to Jason. Then Jason bade the heroes be silent; and they listened. Thrice she cried, and thrice did Phrontis answer her. And the heroes loosed the ship and rowed it across the river; but ere ever it came to the other shore, Jason and the sons of Phrixus leapt from the deck on to the land.

And when Medea saw the brothers, she ran to them, and caught them by the knees, and cried to them, "Save me now from King Æetes! yea, and save yourselves also, for all things are now known to him. Let us fly hence in the ship, before he come upon us with a great army. But first I will give the fleece into your hands, having laid to sleep the dragon that guardeth it. But do thou, Prince Jason, do as thou didst promise, calling the gods to witness." And Jason was glad when he saw her, and took her by the hand, and lifted her up, and spake kindly to her, saying, "Dearest of women, now may Zeus and Heré his wife, that is the goddess of marriage, be my witnesses that I will take thee to wife as soon as we shall have returned to the land of Greece." Then he bade the heroes row the ship to the sacred grove, for he was minded to take away the fleece that very night, before the King should know of the matter. Then the heroes rowed; and the *Argo* passed quickly over the waves till they came to the grove. Then Medea and Jason went forth from the ship, and followed the path, seeking for the great bush whereon the fleece was hung. And in no long space they found it; for it was like a cloud which the shining of the sun makes bright when he riseth in the East. But before the tree there lay a great serpent, with eyes that slept not night nor day. Horribly did it hiss as they came. But Medea cried aloud to Sleep, that is mightiest among the servants of the gods, that he should help her. Also she called to the Queen of Night, that their undertaking might prosper in their hands. And now the great serpent, being wrought upon by her charms, began to unloose his folds; yet his head was lifted up against them, and his dreadful jaws were opened. Therefore Medea took a bough that she had newly cut from a juniper tree, and put a mighty medicine upon it, and dropped the drops of the medicine into his mouth, singing her charms all the while. Then sleep came upon the beast, and he dropped his head upon the ground. When Jason saw this, he snatched the fleece of gold from the tree, for Medea had bidden him do it and delay not; but she stood the while and put the medicine on the head of the beast, fearing lest perchance he should awake. After this they both departed from the grove; and Jason carried the fleece with great gladness of heart.

A mighty fleece it was, hanging down from his shoulders even to his feet. And as he went the day dawned. And when he was come near to the ship the heroes marvelled to behold him, for the fleece was very bright to look upon. But when they would have touched it, Jason hindered them, and covered it with a covering which he had prepared for it.

Then Jason said to his companions, "Come now, my friends; we have accomplished this thing for the which we came to this land. Let us think, therefore, of our return. As to this maiden, I will take her to be my wife in the land of Greece. But do you remember that she has saved all our lives this day. Row, therefore, with all your might, the half of you; and let half hold forth your shields to be a defence against the spears of our enemies, if they should come upon us. For as ye shall quit yourselves this day, so shall it be whether or no we see again our native country and our homes." Then he cut with his sword the cable of the ship; bidding the maiden sit by the helmsman Ancæus. Then the heroes rowed with all their might, and were far away before the King had knowledge of their going.

Many things they suffered in their journey, and many lands they visited, for the gods suffered them not to return by the way by which they went, and some of them perished; but at the last they brought back the ship *Argo* to the land of Greece, and the Fleece of Gold for which Pelias had sent them. And when they were returned, Prince Jason took Medea to be his wife.

THE STORY OF THEBES.

CHAPTER I.

IT befell in times past that the Gods, being angry with the inhabitants of Thebes, sent into their land a very noisome beast which men called the Sphinx. Now this beast had the face and breast of a very fair woman, but the feet and claws of a lion; and it was wont to ask a riddle of such as encountered it; and such as answered not aright it would tear and devour. Now when it had laid waste the land many days, there chanced to come to Thebes one Œdipus, who had fled from the city of Corinth that he might escape the doom which the Gods had spoken against him. And the men of the place told him of the Sphinx, how she cruelly devoured the people, and that he who should deliver them from her should have the kingdom. So Œdipus, being very bold, and also ready of wit, went forth to meet the monster. And when she saw him she spake, saying:—

> "Read me this riddle right, or die:
> What liveth there beneath the sky,
> Four-footed creature that doth choose
> Now three feet and now twain to use,
> And still more feebly o'er the plain
> Walketh with three feet than with twain?"

And Œdipus made reply:—

> "'Tis man, who in life's early day
> Four-footed crawleth on his way;
> When time hath made his strength complete,
> Upright his form and twain his feet;
> When age hath bowed him to the ground,
> A third foot in his staff is found."

And when the Sphinx found that her riddle was answered, she cast herself from a high rock and perished. Now for a while Œdipus reigned in great power and glory; but afterwards his doom came upon him, so that in his madness he put out his own eyes. Then his two sons cast him into prison, and took his kingdom, making agreement between themselves that each should reign for the space of one year. And the elder of the two, whose name was Eteocles, first had the kingdom; but when his year was come to an end, he would not abide by his promise, but kept that which he should have given up, and drave out his younger brother from the city. Then the younger, whose name was Polynices, fled to Argos, to King Adrastus. And after a while he married the daughter of the King, who made a covenant with him that he would bring him back with a high hand to Thebes, and set him on the throne of his father. Then the King sent messengers to certain of the princes of Greece, entreating that they would help in this matter. And of these some would not, but others hearkened to his words, so that a great army was gathered together, and followed the King and Polynices to make war against Thebes. So they came and pitched their camp over against the city. And after that they had fought against it many days, and yet had prevailed nothing, Adrastus held a council of the chiefs, and it was agreed that next day, early in the morning, they should assault the city with all their might. And when the morning was come the chiefs were gathered together, being seven in number. And first of all they slew a bull, and caught the blood of the beast in the hollow of a shield, into which they dipped their hands, and sware a great oath that they would take the city of Thebes or die. And having sworn, they hung upon the chariot of Adrastus what should be memorials of them, each for his own father and mother, all weeping the while. After this they cast lots for the places which they should take, for there were seven gates to the city, that each chief might assault a gate.

But their purpose was known to the King, Eteocles, for he had heard the whole matter from Tiresias, the wise seer, who told beforehand all that should come to pass, discovering it from the voice of birds; for, being blind he could not judge from their flight, or from the tokens of fire, as other soothsayers are wont. Wherefore the King gathered together all that could bear arms, even youths not grown, and old men that were waxed feeble with age, and bade them fight for the land, for "she," he said, "gave you birth and reared you, and now asketh that ye help her in this her need. And though hitherto we have fared well in this war, know ye for certain, for Tiresias the soothsayer hath said it, that there cometh a great danger this day upon the city. Wherefore haste ye to the battlements, and to the towers that are upon the walls, and take your stand in the gates, and be of good courage, and quit you like men."

And as he made an end of speaking there ran in one who declared that even now the enemy was about to assault the city. And after him came a troop of maidens of Thebes, crying out that the enemy had come forth from the camp, and that they heard the tramp of many feet upon the earth, and the rattling of shields, and the noise of many spears. And they lifted up their voices to the Gods that they should help the city, to Ares, the God of the Golden Hemlet, that he should defend the land which in truth was his from old time, and to Father Zeus, and to Pallas, who was the daughter of Zeus, and to Poseidon, the great ruler of the sea, and to Aphrodité the Fair, for that she was the mother of their race, and to Apollo, the Wolf-king, that he would be as a devouring wolf to the enemy, and to Artemis, that she should bend her bow against them, and to Heré, the Queen of Heaven, even to all the dwellers in Olympus, that they should defend the city, and save it.

But the King was very wroth when he heard this outcry, and cried, "Think ye to make bold the hearts of our men by these lamentations? Now may the Gods save me from this race of women; for if they be bold no man can endure their insolence, and if they be afraid they vex both their home and their country. Even so now do ye help them that are without and trouble your own people. But hearken to this. He that heareth not my command, be he man or woman, the people shall stone him. Speak I plainly?"

"But, O son of Œdipus," the maidens made reply, "we hear the rolling of the chariot wheels, and the rattling of the axles, and the jingling of the bridle reins."

"What then?" said the King, "if the ship labor in the sea, and the helmsman leave the helm and fly to the prow that he may pray before the image, doeth he well?"

"Nay, blame us not that we came to beseech the Gods when we heard the hailstorm of war rattling on the gates."

"'Tis well," cried the King, "yet men say that the

Gods leave the city that is at the point to fall. And mark ye this, that safety is the child of obedience. But as for duty, 'tis for men to do sacrifice to the Gods, and for women to keep silence and to abide at home."

But the maidens made reply, "'Tis the Gods who keep this city, nor do they transgress who reverence them."

"Yea, but let them reverence them in due order. And now hearken to me. Keep ye silence. And when I have made my prayer, raise ye a joyful shout that shall gladden the hearts of our friends and put away all fear from them. And to the Gods that keep this city I vow that if they give us victory in this war I will sacrifice to them sheep and oxen, and will hang up in their houses the spoils of the enemy. And now, ye maidens, do ye also make your prayers, but not with vain clamor. And I will choose seven men, being myself the seventh, who shall meet the seven that come against the gates of our city."

Then the King departed, and the maidens made their prayer after this fashion: "My heart feareth as a dove feareth the serpent for her young ones, so cruelly doth the enemy come about this city to destroy it! Shall ye find elsewhere as fair a land, ye Gods, if ye suffer this to be laid waste, or streams as sweet? Help us then, for indeed it is a grievous thing when men take a city; for the women, old and young, are dragged by the hair, and the men are slain with the sword, and there is slaughter and burning, while they that plunder cry each man to his comrade, and the fruits of the earth are wasted upon the ground; nor is there any hope but in death."

And as they made an end, the King came back, and at the same time a messenger bringing tidings of the battle, how the seven chiefs had ranged themselves each against a gate of the city. And the man's story was this.

"First Tydeus, the Ætolian, standeth in great fury at the gate of Prœtus. Very wroth is he because the soothsayer, Amphiaraüs, suffereth him not to cross the Ismenus, for that the omens promise not victory. A triple crest he hath, and there are bells of bronze under his shield which ring terribly. And on his shield he hath this device: the heaven studded with stars, and in the midst the mightiest of the stars, the eye of night, even the moon. Whom, O King, wilt thou set against this man?"

Then the King made reply, "I tremble not at any man's adorning, and a device woundeth not. And, indeed, as for the night that thou tellest to be on his shield, haply it signifieth the night of death that shall fall upon his eyes. Over against him will I set the son of Astacus, a brave man and a modest. Also he is of the race of the Dragon's Teeth, and men call him Melanippus."

And the messenger said, "Heaven send him good fortune! At the gate of Electra standeth Capaneus, a man of great stature, and his boastings are above all measure, for he crieth out that he will destroy this city whether the Gods will or no, and that Zeus with his thunder shall not stay him, for that the thunder is but as the sun at noon. And on his shield he hath a man bearing a torch, and these words, 'I WILL BURN THIS CITY.' Who now shall stand against this boaster and fear not?"

Then the King said, "His boastings I heed not. They shall turn to his own destruction. For as he sendeth out swelling words against Zeus, so shall Zeus send against him the thunder, smiting him, but not of a truth as the sun smiteth. Him shall Polyphantus encounter, a valiant man and dear to Queen Artemis."

"He that is set against the gate of Neïs is called Eteoclus by name. He driveth a chariot with four horses, in whose nostrils are pipes making a whistling noise, after the fashion of barbarians. And on his shield he hath this device: a man mounting a ladder that is set against a tower upon a wall, and with it these words, 'NOT ARES' SELF SHALL DRIVE ME HENCE.' See that thou set a fit warrior against him."

"Megarius, son of Creon, of the race of the Dragon, shall fight against him, who will not leave the gate for any whistling noise of horses; for either he will die as a brave man dieth for his country, or will take a double spoil, even this boaster and him also that he beareth upon his shield."

"At the next gate to this, even the gate of Athené, standeth Hippomedon. A great shield and a terrible he hath, and on it this device, which no mean workman hath wrought: Typhon breathing out a great blast of black smoke, and all about it serpents twined together. And the man also is terrible as his shield, and seemeth to be inspired of Ares. Whom wilt thou set against this man, O King?"

"First shall Pallas stand against him and drive him from this city, even as bird driveth a snake from her young ones. And next I have set Hyperbius, son of Œneus, to encounter him, being inferior neither in form nor courage, nor yet in skill of arms, and also dear to Hermes. Enemies shall they be, bearing also on their shields gods that are enemies, for Hippomedon hath Typhon, but Hyperbius hath Zeus; and even as Zeus prevailed over Typhon, so also shall Hyperbius prevail over this man."

"So be it, O King. Know also that at the north gate is set Parthenopæus the Arcadian. Very young is he, and fair also to behold, and his mother was the huntress

Atalanta. This man sweareth by his spear, which he holdeth to be better than all the gods whatsoever, that he will lay waste this city. And on his shield he beareth a device, the Sphinx, which holdeth in her claws one of the sons of Cadmus."

"Against this Arcadian will I set Actor, brother to Hyperbius, no boaster but a man of deeds, who will not let this hateful monster, the Sphinx, pass thus into the city; but will rather make it ill content to have come hither, so many and fierce blows shall he deal it."

"Hear now of the sixth among the chiefs, the wise soothsayer, Amphiaraüs. Ill pleased is he with these things, for against Tydeus he uttereth many reproaches, that he is an evil counsellor to Argos and to King Adrastus, stirring up strife and slaughter. And to thy brother also he speaketh in like fashion, saying, 'Is this a thing that the Gods love, and that men shall praise in the days to come, that thou bringest a host of strangers to lay waste the city of thy fathers? Shall this land, if thou subduest it by the spear of the enemy, ever make alliance with thee? As for me I shall fall in this land, for am I not a seer? Be it so. I shall not die without honor!' No device hath this man on his shield, for he seeketh not to seem, but to be in very deed most excellent. Thou must need send some wise man to stand against him."

"It is an ill fate that bringeth a just man into company with the wicked. And of a truth there is not a worse thing upon the earth than ill companionship, wherein the sowing is madness and the harvest is death. For thus a godfearing man being on shipboard with godless companions perisheth with them; and one that is righteous, if he dwell in one city with the wicked, is destroyed with the same destruction. So shall it fare with this Amphiaraüs;

for though he be a good man and righteous, and that feareth God, yet shall he perish because he beareth these boasters company. And I think that he will not come near to the gates, so well knoweth he what shall befall him. Yet have I set Lasthenes to stand against him, young in years but old in counsel, very keen of eye, and swift of hand to cast his javelin from under his shield."

"And now, O King, hear how thy brother beareth himself, for he it is who standeth yonder at the seventh gate. For he crieth aloud that he will climb upon the wall and slay thee, even though he die with thee, or drive thee forth into banishment, even as thou, he saith, hast driven him. And on his shield there is this device: a woman leading an armed man, and while she leadeth him she saith, 'I AM JUSTICE, AND I WILL BRING BACK THIS MAN TO THE KINGDOM WHICH IS HIS OF RIGHT.'"

But when the King heard this he brake forth in much fury, "Now will the curse of this house be fulfilled to the uttermost. Yet must I not bewail myself, lest there should fall upon us an evil that is yet greater than this. And as for this Polynices, thinketh he that signs and devices will give him that which he coveteth? Thinketh he that Justice is on his side? Nay, but from the day that he came forth from the womb he hath had no converse with her, neither will she stand by him this day. I will fight against him. Who more fit than I? Bring forth my armor that I may make ready."

And though the maidens entreated with many words that he would not do this thing, but leave the place to some other of the chiefs, saying that there was no healing or remedy for a brother's blood shed in such fashion, he would not hearken, but armed himself and went forth to the battle. Thus ever doth the madness of men work out to the full the curses of the Gods.

Then the battle grew fierce about the wall, and the men of Thebes prevailed. For when Parthenopæus the Arcadian fell like a whirlwind upon the gate that was over against him, Actor the Theban smote him on the head with a great stone, and brake his head, so that he fell dead upon the ground. And when Capaneus assaulted the city, crying that not even the Gods should stay him, there came upon him the wrath which he defied; for when he had mounted the ladder and was now about to leap upon the battlements, Zeus smote him with the thunderbolt, and there was no life left in him, so fierce was the burning heat of the lightning. But the chiefest fight was between the two brothers; and this, indeed, the two armies stood apart to see. For the two came together in an open space before the gates; and first Polynices prayed to Heré, for she was the goddess of the great city of Argos, which had helped him in this enterprise, and Eteocles prayed to Pallas of the Golden Shield, whose temple stood hard by. Then they crouched, each covered with his shield, and holding his spear in his hand, if by chance his enemy should give occasion to smite him; and if one showed so much as an eye above the rim of his shield the other would strike at him. But after a while King Eteocles slipped upon a stone that was under his foot, and uncovered his leg, at which straightway Polynices took aim with his spear, piercing the skin. And the men of Argos shouted to see it. But so doing he laid his own shoulder bare, and King Eteocles gave him a wound in the breast; and then the men of Thebes shouted for joy. But he brake his spear in striking, and would have fared ill but that with a great stone he smote the spear of Polynices, and brake this also in the middle. And now were the two equal, for each had lost his spear. So they drew their swords and came yet closer together. But Eteocles used a device which he had learnt in the land of Thessaly; for he drew his left foot back, as if he would have ceased from the battle, and then of a sudden moved the right forward; and so smiting sideways, drave his sword right through the body of Polynices. But when, thinking that he had slain him, he set his weapons in the earth, and began to spoil him of his arms, the other, for he yet breathed a little, laid his hand upon his sword, and though he had scarce strength to smite, yet gave the King a mortal blow, so that the two lay dead together on the plain. And the men of Thebes lifted up the bodies of the dead, and bare them both into the city.

So was the doom of the house of Œdipus accomplished; and yet not all, as shall now be told.

CHAPTER II.

WHEN the two brothers, the sons of King Œdipus, had fallen each by the hand of the other, the kingdom fell to Creon their uncle. For not only was he the next of kin to the dead, but also the people held him in great honor because his son Menœceus had offered himself with a willing heart that he might deliver his city from captivity. Now when Creon was come to the throne, he made a proclamation about the two Princes, commanding that they should bury Eteocles with all honor, seeing that he died as beseemed a good man and a brave, doing battle for his country, that it should not be delivered into the hands of the enemy; but as for Polynices he bade them leave his body to be devoured by the fowls of the air and the beasts of the field, because he had joined himself to the enemy, and would have beaten down the walls of the city, and burned the temples of the Gods with fire, and led the people captive. Also he commanded that if any man should break this decree he should suffer death by stoning.

Now Antigone, who was sister to the two Princes, heard that the decree had gone forth, and chancing to meet her sister Ismené before the gates of the palace, spake to her, saying, "O my sister, hast thou heard this decree that the King hath put forth concerning our brethren that are dead?"

Then Ismené made answer, "I have heard nothing, my sister, only that we are bereaved of both of our brethren in one day, and that the army of the Argives is departed in this night that is now past. So much I know, but no more."

"Hearken then. King Creon hath made a proclamation that they shall bury Eteocles with all honor; but that Polynices shall lie unburied, that the birds of the air and the beasts of the field may devour him, and that whosoever shall break this decree shall suffer death by stoning."

"But if it be so, my sister, how can we avail to change it?"

"Think whether or no thou wilt share with me the doing of this deed."

"What deed? What meanest thou?"

"To pay due honor to this dead corpse."

"What? Wilt thou bury him when the King hath forbidden it?"

"Yea, for he is my brother and also thine, though perchance thou wouldst not have it so. And I will not play him false."

"O my sister, wilt thou do this when Creon hath forbidden it?"

"Why should he stand between me and mine?"

"But think now what sorrows are come upon our house. For our father perished miserably, having first put out his own eyes; and our mother hanged herself with her own hands; and our two brothers fell in one day, each by the other's spear; and now we two only are left. And shall we not fall into a worse destruction than any if we transgress these commands of the King. Think, too, that we are women and not men, and must of necessity obey them that are stronger. Wherefore, as for me, I will pray the dead to pardon me, seeing that I am thus constrained; but I will obey them that rule."

"I advise thee not, and if thou thinkest thus I would not have thee for helper. But know that I will bury my brother, nor could I better die than for doing such a deed. For as he loved me, so also do I love him greatly. And shall not I do pleasure to the dead rather than to the living, seeing that I shall abide with the dead forever? But thou, if thou wilt, do dishonor to the laws of the Gods."

"I dishonor them not. Only I cannot set myself against the powers that be."

"So be it: but I will bury my brother."

"O my sister, how I fear for thee!"

"Fear for thyself. Thine own lot needeth all thy care."

"Thou wilt at least keep thy counsel, nor tell the thing to any man."

"Not so: hide it not. I shall scorn thee more if thou proclaim it not aloud to all."

So Antigone departed; and after a while came to the same place King Creon, clad in his royal robes, and with his sceptre in his hand, and set forth his counsel to the elders who were assembled, how he had dealt with the two Princes according to their deserving, giving all honor to him that loved his country, and casting forth the other unburied. And he bade them take care that this decree should be kept, saying that he had also appointed certain men to watch the dead body.

But he had scarcely left speaking when there came one of these same watchers and said, "I have not come hither in haste, O King; nay, I doubted much while I was yet on the way whether I should not turn again. For now I thought, 'Fool, why goest thou where thou shalt suffer for it;' and then again, 'Fool, the King will hear the matter elsewhere, and then how wilt thou fare?' But at the last I came as I had purposed, for I know that nothing may happen to me contrary to fate."

"But say," said the King, "what troubles thee so much?"

"First hear my case. I did not the thing, and know not who did it, and it were a grievous wrong should I fall into trouble for such a cause."

"Thou makest a long preface excusing thyself, but yet hast, as I judge, something to tell."

"Fear, my lord, ever causeth delay."

"Wilt thou not speak out thy news and then begone?"

"I will speak it. Know then that some man hath thrown dust upon this dead corpse, and done besides such things as are needful."

"What sayest thou? Who hath dared to do this deed?"

"That I know not, for there was no mark as of spade or pickaxe; nor was the earth broken, nor had wagon passed thereon. We were sore dismayed when the watchman showed the thing to us; for the body we could not see.

Buried indeed it was not, but rather covered with dust. Nor was there any sign as of wild beast or of dog that had torn it. Then there arose a contention among us, each blaming the other, and accusing his fellows, and himself denying that he had done the deed or was privy to it. And doubtless we had fallen to blows but that one spake a word which made us all tremble for fear, knowing that it must be as he said. For he said that the thing must be told to thee, and in no wise hidden. So we drew lots, and by evil chance the lot fell upon me. Wherefore I am here, not willingly, for no man loveth him that bringeth ill tidings."

Then said the chief of the old men, "Consider, O King, for haply this thing is from the Gods."

But the King cried, "Thinkest thou that the Gods care for such an one as this dead man, who would have burnt their temples with fire, and laid waste the land which they love, and set at naught the laws? Not so. But there are men in this city who have long time had ill will to me, not bowing their necks to my yoke; and they have persuaded these fellows with money to do this thing. Surely there never was so evil a thing as money, which maketh cities into ruinous heaps, and banisheth men from their houses, and turneth their thoughts from good unto evil. But as for them that have done this deed for hire, of a truth they shall not escape, for I say to thee, fellow, if ye bring not here before my eyes the man that did this thing, I will hang you up alive. So shall ye learn that ill gains bring no profit to a man."

So the guard departed; but as he went he said to himself, "Now may the Gods grant the man be found; but however this may be, thou shalt not see me come again on such errand as this, for even now have I escaped beyond all hope." Notwithstanding, after a space he came back with one of his fellows; and they brought with them the maiden Antigone, with her hands bound together. And it chanced that at the same time King Creon came forth from the palace. Then the guard set forth the thing to him, saying, "We cleared away the dust from the dead body, and sat watching it. And when it was now noon, and the sun was at his height, there came a whirlwind over the plain, driving a great cloud of dust. And when this had passed, we looked, and lo! this maiden whom we have brought hither stood by the dead corpse. And when she saw that it lay bare as before, she sent up an exceeding bitter cry, even as a bird whose young ones have been taken from the nest. Then she cursed them that had done this deed; and brought dust and sprinkled it upon the dead man, and poured water upon him three times. Then we ran and laid hold upon her, and accused her that she had done this deed; and she denied it not. But as for me, 'tis well to have escaped from death, but it is ill to bring friends into the same. Yet I hold that there is nothing dearer to a man than his life."

Then said the King to Antigone, "Tell me in a word, didst thou know my decree?"

"I knew it. Was it not plainly declared?"

"How daredst thou to transgress the laws?"

"Zeus made not such laws, nor Justice that dwelleth with the Gods below. I judged not that thy decrees had such authority that a man should transgress for them the unwritten sure commandments of the Gods. For these, indeed, are not of to-day or yesterday, but they live for ever, and their beginning no man knoweth. Should I, for fear of thee, be found guilty against them? That I should die I knew. Why not? All men must die. And if I die before my time, what loss? He who liveth among many sorrows, even as I have lived, counteth it gain to die. But had I left my own mother's son unburied, this had been loss indeed."

Then said the King, "Such stubborn thoughts have a speedy fall, and are shivered even as the iron that hath been made hard in the furnace. And as for this woman and her sister, — for I judge her sister to have had a part in this matter, — though they were nearer to me than all my kindred, yet shall they not escape the doom of death. Wherefore let some one bring the other woman hither."

And while they went to fetch the maiden Ismené, Antigone said to the King, " Is it not enough for thee to slay me? What need to say more? For thy words please me not nor mine thee. Yet what nobler thing could I have done than to bury my own mother's son? And so would all men say but fear shutteth their mouths."

"Nay," said the King, "none of the children of Cadmus thinketh thus, but thou only. But, hold, was not he that fell in battle with this man thy brother also?"

"Yes, truly, my brother he was."

"And dost thou not dishonor him when thou honorest his enemy?"

"The dead man would not say it, could he speak."

"Shall then the wicked have like honor with the good?"

"How knowest thou but that such honor pleaseth the Gods below?"

"I have no love for them I hate, though they be dead."

"Of hating I know nothing; 'tis enough for me to love."

"If thou wilt love, go love the dead. But while I live no woman shall rule me."

Then those that had been sent to fetch the maiden

Ismené brought her forth from the palace. And when the King accused her that she had been privy to the deed, she denied not, but would have shared one lot with her sister. But Antigone turned from her, saying, "Not so; thou hast no part or lot in the matter. For thou hast chosen life, and I have chosen death; and even so shall it be." And when Ismené saw that she prevailed nothing with her sister, she turned to the King and said, "Wilt thou slay the bride of thy son?"

"Aye," said he, "there are other brides to win!"

"But none," she made reply, "that accord so well with him."

"I will have no evil wives for my sons," said the King.

Then cried Antigone, "O Hæmon, whom I love, how thy father wrongeth thee!"

Then the King bade the guards lead the two into the palace. But scarcely had they gone when there came to the palace the Prince Hæmon, the King's son, who was betrothed to the maiden Antigone. And when the King saw him, he said, "Art thou content, my son, with thy father's judgment?"

And the young man answered, "My father, I would follow thy counsels in all things."

Then said the King, "'Tis well spoken, my son. This is a thing to be desired, that a man should have obedient children. But if it be otherwise with a man, he hath gotten great trouble for himself, and maketh sport for them that hate him. And now as to this matter. There is nought worse than an evil wife. Wherefore I say, let this damsel wed a bridegroom among the dead. For since I have found her, alone of all this people, breaking my decree, surely she shall die. Nor shall it profit her to claim kinship with me, for he that would rule a city must first deal justly with his own kindred. And as for obedience, this it is that maketh a city to stand both in peace and in war!"

To this the Prince Hæmon made answer, "What thou sayest, my father, I do not judge. Yet bethink thee, that I see and hear on thy behalf what is hidden from thee. For common men cannot abide thy look if they say that which pleaseth thee not. Yet do I hear it in secret. Know then that all the city mourneth for this maiden, saying that she dieth wrongfully for a very noble deed, in that she buried her brother. And 'tis well, my father, not to be wholly set on thy own thoughts, but listen to the counsels of others."

"Nay," said the King; "shall I be taught by such an one as thou?"

"I pray thee regard my words, if they be well, and not my years."

"Can it be well to honor them that transgress? And hath not this woman transgressed?"

"The people of this city judgeth not so."

"The people, sayest thou! Is it for them to rule, or for me?"

"No city is the possession of one man only."

So the two answered one the other, and their anger waxed hot. And at the last the King cried, "Bring this accursed woman, and slay her before his eyes."

And the Prince answered, "That thou shalt never do. And know this also, that thou shalt never see my face again."

So he went away in a rage; and the old men would have appeased the King's wrath, but he would not hearken to them, but said that the two maidens should die. "Wilt thou then slay them both?" said the old men.

"'Tis well said," the King made answer. "Her that meddled not with the matter I harm not."

"And how wilt thou deal with the other?"

"There is a desolate place, and there I will shut her up alive in a sepulchre; yet giving her so much of food as shall quit us of guilt in the matter, for I would not have the city defiled. There let her persuade Death, whom she loveth so much, that he harm her not."

So the guards led Antigone away to shut her up alive in the sepulchre. But scarcely had they departed when there came the old prophet Tiresias, seeking the King. Blind he was, so that a boy led him by the hand; but the Gods had given him to see things to come. And when the King saw him he asked, "What seekest thou, wisest of men?"

Then the prophet answered, "Hearken, O King, and I will tell thee. I sat in my seat, after my custom, in the place whither all manner of birds resort. And as I sat I heard a cry of birds that I knew not, very strange and full of wrath. And I knew that they tare and slew each other, for I heard the fierce flapping of their wings. And being afraid, I made inquiry about the fire, how it burned upon the altars. And this boy, for as I am a guide to others so he guideth me, told me that it shone not at all, but smouldered and was dull, and that the flesh which was burnt upon the altar spluttered in the flame, and wasted away into corruption and filthiness. And now I tell thee, O King, that the city is troubled by thy ill counsels. For the dogs and the birds of the air tear the flesh of this dead son of Œdipus, whom thou sufferest not to have due burial, and carry it to the altars, polluting them therewith. Wherefore the Gods receive not from us prayer or sacrifice; and the cry of the birds hath an evil sound, for they are full of the flesh of a man. Therefore I bid thee be wise in time. For all men may err; but he that keepeth not his folly, but repenteth, doeth well; but stubbornness cometh to great trouble."

Then the King answered, "Old man, I know the race of prophets full well, how ye sell your art for gold. But, make thy trade as thou wilt, this man shall not have burial; yea, though the eagles of Zeus carry his flesh to their master's throne in heaven, he shall not have it."

And when the prophet spake again, entreating him, and warning, the King answered him after the same fashion, that he spake not honestly, but had sold his art for money. But at the last the prophet spake in great wrath, saying, "Know, O King, that before many days shall pass, thou shalt pay a life for a life, even one of thine own children, for them with whom thou hast dealt unrighteously, shutting up the living with the dead, and keeping the dead from them to whom they belong. Therefore the Furies lie in wait for thee, and thou shalt see whether or no I speak these things for money. For there shall be mourning and lamentation in thine own house; and against thy people shall be stirred up all the cities, whose sons thou hast made to lie unburied. And now, my child, lead me home, and let this man rage against them that are younger than I."

So the prophet departed, and the old men were sore afraid, and said, "He hath spoken terrible things, O King; nor ever since these gray hairs were black have we known him say that which was false."

"Even so," said the King, "and I am troubled in heart, and yet am loath to depart from my purpose."

"King Creon," said the old men, "thou needest good counsel."

"What, then, would ye have done?"

"Set free the maiden from the sepulchre, and give this dead man burial."

Then the King cried to his people that they should bring bars wherewith to loosen the doors of the sepulchre, and hasted with them to the place. But coming on their way to the body of Prince Polynices, they took it up, and washed it, and buried that which remained of it, and raised over the ashes a great mound of earth. And this being done, they drew near to the place of the sepulchre; and as they approached, the King heard within a very piteous voice, and knew it for the voice of his son. Then he bade his attendants loose the door with all speed; and when they had loosed it, they beheld within a very piteous sight. For the maiden Antigone had hanged herself by the girdle of linen which she wore, and the young man Prince Hæmon stood with his arms about her dead corpse, embracing it. And when the King saw him, he cried to him to come forth; but the Prince glared fiercely upon him, and answered him not a word, but drew his two-edged sword. Then the King, thinking that his son was minded in his madness to slay him, leapt back, but the Prince drave the sword into his own heart, and fell forward on the earth, still holding the dead maiden in his arms. And when they brought the tidings of these things to Queen Eurydice, that was the wife of King Creon and mother to the Prince, she could not endure the grief, being thus bereaved of her children, but laid hold of a sword, and slew herself therewith.

So the house of King Creon was left desolate unto him that day, because he despised the ordinances of the Gods.

THE STORY OF TROY.

CHAPTER I.

PRINCE Paris that was son to Priam, King of Troy, carried away the Fair Helen, wife of Menelaüs, King of Sparta. Now all the kings and princes of Greece had bound themselves by an oath that they would avenge Menelaüs on any man that should rob him of his wife. But first of all they sent ambassadors to Troy, who should demand the Fair Helen of Priam and his people. So the ambassadors came and made their demand; and the King himself was willing that she should be given back, and the wisest of the princes gave like counsel. But there stood up certain evil men, whom Paris had persuaded with his gold, and said, "Fear not, men of Troy, to suffer Prince Paris to keep the Fair Helen for his wife. For verily these words of the ambassadors, that the Greeks will come with an army and fetch her away, are but idle talk. Think ye that they will indeed journey so far and endure such trouble for the sake of a woman? Not so. It standeth not to reason. And if indeed they come, how shall they take the city? Were not these walls builded of gods, and shall any man that is born of a woman avail to overthrow them?" And the men of Troy gave ear to this counsel, and sent away the ambassadors empty, for the Gods would destroy them.

Then King Agamemnon, that was brother to Menelaüs, being the greatest lord in the land of Greece, gathered together an army, not without great pains and trouble, because many of the princes were loath to go. Thus the wise Ulysses feigned that he was mad, and, for proof of his madness, ploughed the sand upon the sea-shore. But when a certain counsellor of the King put his son, being an infant of a few days old, before the plough, Ulysses turned away his plough lest he should hurt him, and so betrayed himself. Also Thetis, that was mother to Achilles, knowing that if her son should go to the land of Troy he would die before his time, put upon him women's garments and hid him in the palace of the King of Scyros. Then Ulysses disguised himself as a merchant and journeyed to Scyros. And when he was come into the hall of the palace, he opened his wares, goodly robes of purple, and earrings, and necklaces, and divers other ornaments, both of jewels and gold. And when the maidens gathered about him, and chose such things as women love, then of a sudden he opened another bale in which were a hand spear, and a sword, and a shield. And when Achilles saw them, he sprang forth and laid his hands upon them with great joy. So he also betrayed himself.

Thus King Agamemnon at the last gathered his army of the Greeks together, and sailed to the land of Troy. For nine years and more he besieged the city and pressed it hard, so that they that were within scarce dared to go without their walls. And doubtless he had taken it without more delay, but that there arose a deadly quarrel between him and Achilles, who was the bravest and most valiant man of all the host. Now the strife chanced in this wise.

The Greeks, having been away from home now many years, were in great want of things needful. Wherefore it was their custom to leave a part of their army to watch the city, and to send a part to spoil such towns in the country round about as they knew to be friendly to the men of Troy, or as they thought to contain good store of provision or treasure. "Are not all these," they were wont to say, "towns of the barbarians, and therefore lawful prey to men that are Greeks?" Now among the towns with which they dealt in this fashion was Chrysa, which was sacred to Apollo, who had a great temple therein and a priest. The temple and the priest the Greeks, fearing the anger of the god, had not harmed; but they had carried off with other prisoners the priest's daughter, Chryseïs by name. These and the rest of the spoil they divided among the kings, of whom there were many in the army, ruling each his own people. Now King Agamemnon, as being sovereign lord, went not commonly with the army at such times, but rather stayed behind, having charge of the siege that it should not be neglected. Yet did he always receive, as indeed was fitting, a share of the spoil. This time the Greeks gave him, with other things, the maiden Chryseïs. But there came to the camp next day the priest Chryses, wishing to ransom his daughter. Much gold he brought with him, and he had on his head the priest's crown, that all men might reverence him the more. He went to all the chiefs, making his prayer that they would take the gold and give him back his daughter. And they all spake him fair, and would have done what he wished. Only Agamemnon would not have it so.

"Get thee out, graybeard!" he cried in great wrath. "Let me not find thee lingering now by the ships, neither coming hither again, or it shall be the worse for thee, for all thy priesthood. And as for thy daughter, I shall carry her away to Argos, when I shall have taken this city of Troy."

Then the old man went out hastily in great fear and trouble. And he walked in his sorrow by the shore of the sounding sea, and prayed to his god Apollo.

"Hear me, God of the silver bow. If I have built thee a temple, and offered thee the fat of many bullocks and rams, hear me, and avenge me on these Greeks!"

And Apollo heard him. Wroth he was that men had so dishonored his priest, and he came down from the top of Olympus, where he dwelt. Dreadful was the rattle of his arrows as he went, and his presence was as the night coming over the sky. Then he shot the arrows of death, first on the dogs and the mules, and then on the men; and soon all along the shore rolled the black smoke from the piles of wood on which they burnt the bodies of the dead.

On the tenth day Achilles, who was the bravest and strongest of all the Greeks, called the people to an assembly. When they were gathered together he stood up among them and spake to Agamemnon.

"Surely it were better to return home, than that we should all perish here by the plague. But come, let us ask some prophet, or priest, or dreamer of dreams, why it is that Apollo is so wroth with us."

Then stood up Calchas, best of seers, who knew what had been, and what was, and what was to come, and spake.

"Achilles, thou biddest me tell the people why Apollo is wroth with them. Lo! I tell thee, but thou must first swear to stand by me, for I know that what I shall say will anger King Agamemnon, and it goes ill with common men when kings are angry."

"Speak out, thou wise man!" cried Achilles; "for I swear by Apollo that while I live no one shall lay hands on thee, no, not Agamemnon's self, though he be sovereign lord of the Greeks."

Then the prophet took heart and spake. "It is on behalf of his priest that Apollo is wroth, for he came to ransom his daughter, but Agamemnon would not let the maiden go. Now, then, ye must send her back to Chrysa without ransom, and with her a hundred beasts for sacrifice, so that the plague may be stayed."

Then Agamemnon stood up in a fury, his eyes blazing like fire.

"Never," he cried, "hast thou spoken good concerning me, ill prophet that thou art, and now thou tellest me to give up this maiden! I will do it, for I would not that the people should perish. Only take care, ye Greeks, that there be a share of the spoil for me, for it would ill beseem the lord of all the host that he alone should be without his share."

"Nay, my lord Agamemnon," cried Achilles, "thou art too eager for gain. We have no treasures out of which we may make up thy loss, for what we got out of the towns we have either sold or divided; nor would it be fitting that the people should give back what has been given to them. Give up the maiden, then, without conditions, and when we shall have taken this city of Troy, we will repay thee three and four fold."

"Nay, great Achilles," said Agamemnon, "thou shalt not cheat me thus. If the Greeks will give me such a share as I should have, well and good. But if not, I will take one for myself, whether it be from thee, or from Ajax, or from Ulysses; for my share I will have. But of this hereafter. Now let us see that this maiden be sent back. Let them get ready a ship, and put her therein, and with her a hundred victims, and let some chief go with the ship, and see that all things be rightly done."

Then cried Achilles, and his face was black as a thunder-storm, "Surely thou art altogether shameless and greedy, and, in truth, an ill ruler of men. No quarrel have I with the Trojans. They never harried oxen or sheep of mine. But I have been fighting in thy cause, and that of thy brother Menalaüs. Naught carest thou for that. Thou leavest me to fight, and sittest in thy tent at ease. But when the spoil is divided, thine is always the lion's share. Small indeed is my part — 'a little thing, but dear.' And this, forsooth, thou wilt take away! Now am I resolved to go home. Small booty wilt thou get then, methinks!"

And King Agamemnon answered, "Go, and thy Myrmidons with thee! I have other chieftains as good as thou art, and ready, as thou art not, to pay me due respect. I hate thee, with thy savage, bloodthirsty ways. And as for the matter of the spoil, know that I will take thy share, the girl Briseïs, and fetch her myself, if need be, that all may know that I am sovereign lord here in the host of the Greeks."

Then Achilles was mad with anger, and he thought in his heart, "Shall I arise and slay this caitiff, or shall I keep down the wrath in my breast?" And as he thought he laid his hand on his sword-hilt, and had half drawn his sword from the scabbard, when lo! the goddess Athené stood behind him (for Heré, who loved both this chieftain and that, had sent her), and caught him by the long locks of his yellow hair. But Achilles marvelled much to feel the mighty grasp, and turned, and looked, and knew the goddess, but no one else in the assembly might see her.

Then his eyes flashed with fire, and he cried, "Art thou come, child of Zeus, to see the insolence of Agamemnon? Of a truth, I think that he will perish for his folly."

But Athené said, "Nay, but I am come to stay thy wrath. Use bitter words, if thou wilt, but put up thy sword in its sheath, and strike him not. Of a truth, I tell thee that for this insolence of to-day he will bring thee hereafter splendid gifts, threefold and fourfold for all that he may take away."

Then Achilles answered, "I shall abide by thy command, for it is ever better for a man to obey the immortal gods." And as he spake he laid his heavy hand upon the hilt, and thrust back the sword into the scabbard, and Athené went her way to Olympus.

Then he turned him to King Agamemnon, and spake again. "Drunkard, with the eyes of a dog and the heart of a deer! never fighting in the front of the battle, nor daring to lie in the ambush! 'Tis a puny race thou rulest, or this had been thy last wrong. And as for me, here is this sceptre: once it was the branch of a tree, but a cunning craftsman bound it with bronze to be the sign of the lordship which Zeus gives to kings; as surely as it shall never again have bark or leaves or shoot, so surely shall the Greeks one day miss Achilles, when they fall in heaps before the dreadful Hector, and thou shalt eat thy heart to think that thou hast wronged the bravest of thy host."

And as he spake he dashed his sceptre on the ground and sat down. And on the other side Agamemnon sat in furious anger. Then Nestor rose, an old man of a hundred years and more, and counselled peace. Let them listen, he said, to his counsel. Great chiefs in the old days, with whom no man now alive would dare to fight, had listened. Let not Agamemnon take away from the bravest of the Greeks the prize of war; let not Achilles, though he was mightier in battle than all other men, contend with Agamemnon, who was sovereign lord of all the hosts of Greece. But he spake in vain. For Agamemnon answered, —

"Nestor, thou speakest well, and peace is good. But this fellow would lord it over all, and he must be taught that there is one here, at least, who is better than he."

And Achilles said, "I were a slave and a coward if I owned thee as my lord. Not so: play the master over others, but think not to master me. As for the prize which the Greeks gave me, let them do as they will. They gave it; let them take it away. But if thou darest to touch aught that is mine own, that hour thy life-blood shall redden on my spear."

Then the assembly was dismissed. Chryseïs was sent to her home with due offerings to the god, the wise Ulysses going with her. And all the people purified themselves, and the plague was stayed.

But King Agamemnon would not go back from his purpose. So he called to him the heralds, Talthybius and Eurybates, and said, —

"Heralds, go to the tents of Achilles and fetch the maiden Briseïs. But if he will not let her go, say that I will come myself with many others to fetch her; so will it be the worse for him."

Sorely against their will the heralds went. Along the sea-shore they walked, till they came to where, amidst the Myrmidons, were the tents of Achilles. There they found him sitting, but stood silent in awe and fear. But Achilles spied them, and cried aloud, "Come near, ye heralds, messengers of gods and men. 'Tis no fault of yours that ye are come on such an errand."

Then he turned to Patroclus (now Patroclus was his dearest friend) and said, "Bring the maiden from her tent, and let the heralds lead her away. But let them be witnesses before gods and men, and before this evil-minded king, against the day when he shall have sore need of me to save his host from destruction. Fool that he is, who thinks not of the past nor of the future, that his people may be safe!"

Then Patroclus brought forth the maiden from her tent and gave her to the heralds. And they led her away, but it was sorely against her will that she went. But Achilles went apart from his comrades and sat upon the sea-shore, falling into a great passion of tears, and stretching out his hands with loud prayer to his mother, who indeed was a goddess of the sea, Thetis by name. She heard him where she sat in the depths by her father, the old god of the sea, and rose — you would have thought it a mist rising — from the waves, and came to where he sat weeping, and stroked him with her hand and called him by his name.

"What ails thee, my son?" she said.

Then he told her the story of his wrong, and when he had ended he said, —

"Go, I pray thee, to the top of Olympus, to the palace of Zeus. Often have I heard thee boast how, long ago, thou didst help him when the other gods would have bound him, fetching Briareus of the hundred hands, who sat by him in his strength, so that the gods feared to touch him. Go now and call these things to his mind, and pray him that he help the sons of Troy and give them victory in the battle, so that the Greeks, as they flee before them, may have joy of this king of theirs, who has done such wrong to the bravest of his host."

And his mother answered him, "Surely thine is an evil

lot, my son! Thy life is short, and it should of right be without tears and full of joy; but now it seems to me to be both short and sad. But I will go as thou sayest to Olympus, to the palace of Zeus, but not now, for he has gone, and the other gods with him, to a twelve days' feast with the pious Ethiopians. But when he comes back I will entreat and persuade him. And do thou sit still, nor go forth to battle."

When the twelve days were past Thetis went to the top of Olympus, to the palace of Zeus, and made her prayer to him. He was loath to grant it, for he knew it would anger his wife, Heré, who loved the Greeks and hated the sons of Troy. Yet he could not refuse her, but promised that it should be as she wished. And to make his word the surer, he nodded his awful head, and with the nod all Olympus was shaken.

That night Zeus took counsel with himself how he might best work his will. And he called to him a dream, and said, "Dream, go to the tent of Agamemnon, and tell him to set his army in array against Troy, for that the gods are now of one mind, and the day of doom is come for the city, so that he shall take it, and gain eternal glory for himself."

So the dream went to the tent of Agamemnon, and it took the shape of Nestor, the old chief, whom the king honored more than all beside.

Then the false Nestor spake: "Sleepest thou, Agamemnon? It is not for kings to sleep all through the night, for they must take thought for many, and have many cares. Listen now to the words of Zeus: 'Set the battle in array against Troy, for the gods are now of one mind, and the day of doom is come for the city, and thou shall take it, and gain eternal glory for thyself.'"

And Agamemnon believed the dream, and knew not the purpose of Zeus in bidding him go forth to battle, how that the Trojans should win the day, and great shame should come to himself, but great honor to Achilles, when all the Greeks should pray him to deliver them from death. So he rose from his bed and donned his tunic, and over it a great cloak, and fastened the sandals on his feet, and hung from his shoulders his mighty silver-studded sword, and took in his right hand the great sceptre of his house, which was the token of his sovereignty over all the Greeks. Then he went forth, and first took counsel with the chiefs, and afterwards called the people to the assembly. And after the assembly the shrill-voiced heralds called the host to the battle. As is the flare of a great fire when a wood is burning on a hill-top, so was the flash of their arms and their armor as they thronged to the field. And as the countless flocks of wild geese or cranes or swans now wheel and now settle in the great Asian fen by the stream of Caÿster, or as the bees swarm in the spring, when the milk-pails are full, so thick the Greeks thronged to the battle in the great plain by the banks of the Scamander. Many nations were there, and many chiefs. But the most famous among them were these: Agamemnon, King of Mycenæ, and his brother, the yellow-haired Menelaüs, King of Sparta, and husband of the beautiful Helen; Ajax Oïleus, or, as men called him, the lesser Ajax, King of the Locri, swiftest of foot among the Greeks after the great Achilles; Ajax Telamon, from Salamis; Diomed, son of Tydeus, King of Argos, and with him Sthenelus; Nestor, King of Pylos, oldest and wisest among the Greeks; Ulysses, King of Ithaca, than whom there was no one more crafty in counsel; Idomeneus, grandson of the great judge Minos, King of Crete, and with him Meriones;

Tlepolemus, son of Hercules, from Rhodes; Eumelus from Pheræ, son of that Alcestis who died for her husband and was brought back from death by Hercules. All these were there that day, and many more; and the bravest and strongest of all was Ajax, son of Telamon, and the best horses were the horses of Eumelus; but there was none that could compare with Achilles and the horses of Achilles, bravest man and swiftest steeds. Only Achilles sat apart, and would not go to the battle.

And on the other side the sons of Troy and their allies came forth from the gates of the city and set themselves in array. The most famous of their chiefs were these: Hector, son of King Priam, bravest and best of all; Æneas, son of Anchises and the goddess Aphrodité; Pandarus, from Mount Ida, with the bow which Apollo gave him; Asius, the son of Hyrtacus, who came from the broad salt river, the Hellespont; Pylæmenes, King of Paphlagonia; and Sarpedon from Lycia, whom men affirmed to be the son of Zeus himself, and with him Glaucus.

So the battle was set in array, and the two hosts stood over against each other.

They were now about to fight, when from the ranks of the Trojans Paris rushed forth. He had a panther's skin over his shoulders, and a bow and a sword, and in either hand a spear, and he called aloud to the Greeks that they should send forth their bravest to fight with him. But when Menelaüs saw him he was glad, for he said that now he should avenge himself on the man who had done him such wrong. So a lion is glad when, being sorely hungered, he finds a stag or a wild goat; he devours it, and will not be driven from it by dogs or hunters. He leapt from his chariot and rushed to meet his enemy; but Paris, having done evil, and being therefore a coward in his heart, was afraid when he saw Menelaüs, and fled back into the ranks of his comrades, just as a man steps back in haste when unawares in a mountain glen he comes upon a snake. But Hector saw him and rebuked him. "Fair art thou to look upon, Paris, but nothing worth. Surely the Greeks will scorn us if they think that thou art our bravest warrior, because thou art of stately presence. But thou art a coward; and yet thou daredst to go across the sea and carry off the fair Helen. Why dost thou not stand and abide the onset of her husband, and see what manner of man he is? Little, I ween, would thy harp and thy long locks and thy fair face avail when thou wert lying in the dust! A craven race are the sons of Troy, or they would have stoned thee ere this."

Then Paris answered, "Thou speakest well, Hector, and thy rebuke is just. As for thee, thy heart is like iron, ever set on battle; yet are beauty and love also the gifts of the gods, and not to be despised. But now set Menelaüs and me in the midst, and let us fight, man to man, for the fair Helen and for all her possessions. And if he prevail over me, let him take her and them and depart, and the Greeks with him, but ye shall dwell in peace; but if I prevail they shall depart without her."

Then Hector was glad, and going before the Trojan ranks, holding his spear by the middle, he kept them back. But the Greeks would have thrown spears and stones at him, only Agamemnon cried aloud and said, "Hold: Hector has somewhat to say to us."

Then Hector said, "Hear, Trojans and Greeks, what Paris saith: Let all besides lay their arms upon the ground, and let Menelaüs and me fight for the fair Helen and all her wealth. And let him that is the better keep her and them, but the rest shall dwell in peace."

Then Menelaüs said, "The word pleaseth me well; let us fight together, and let us make agreement with oath and sacrifice. And because the sons of Priam are men of fraud and violence, let Priam himself come."

So they sent a herald to King Priam, but he sat on the wall with the old men. And as they talked, the fair Helen came near, and they said, "What wonder that men should suffer much for such a woman, for indeed she is divinely fair. Yet let her depart in the ships, nor bring a curse on us and our children."

But Priam called to her, "Come near, my daughter; tell me about these old friends of thine. For 'tis not thou, 'tis the gods who have brought about all this trouble. But tell me, who is this warrior that I see, so fair and strong? There are others even a head taller than he, but none of such majesty."

And Helen answered, "Ah, my father! would that I had died before I left husband and child to follow thy son. But as for this warrior, he is Agamemnon, a good king and brave soldier, and my brother-in-law in the old days."

"Happy Agamemnon," said Priam, "to rule over so many! Never saw I such an army gathered together, not even when I went to help the Phrygians when they were assembled on the banks of the Sangarus against the Amazons. But who is this that I see, not so tall as Agamemnon, but of broader shoulders? His arms lie upon the ground, and he is walking through the ranks of his men just as some great ram walks through a flock of sheep."

"This," said Helen, "is Ulysses of Ithaca, who is better in craft and counsel than all other men."

"'Tis well spoken, lady," said Antenor. "Well I remember Ulysses when he came hither on an embassy about thee with the brave Menelaüs. My guests they were, and I knew them well. And I remember how, in the assembly of the Trojans, when both were standing, Menelaüs was the taller, but when they sat, Ulysses was the more majestic to behold. And when they rose to speak, Menelaüs said few words, but said them wisely and well; and Ulysses — you had thought him a fool, so stiffly he held his sceptre and so downcast were his eyes; but as soon as he began, oh! the mighty voice, and the words thick as the falling snow!"

Then Priam said, "Who is that stalwart hero, so tall and strong, overtopping all by head and shoulders?"

"That," said Helen, "is mighty Ajax, the bulwark of the Greeks. And next to him is Idomeneus. Often has Menelaüs had him as his guest in the old days, when he came from Crete. As for the other chiefs, I see and could name them all. But I miss my own dear brothers, Castor, tamer of horses, and Pollux, the mighty boxer. Either they came not from Sparta, or, having come, shun the meeting of men for shame of me."

So she spake, and knew not that they were sleeping their last sleep far away in their dear fatherland. And when they had ended talking, the heralds came and told King Priam how that the armies called for him. So he went, and Antenor with him. And he on the one side, for the Trojans, and King Agamemnon for the Greeks, made a covenant with sacrifice that Paris and Menelaüs should fight together, and that the fair Helen, with all her treasures, should go with him who should prevail. And afterwards Hector and Ulysses marked out a space for the fight, and Hector shook two pebbles in a helmet, looking away as he shook them, that he whose pebble leapt forth the first should be the first to throw his spear. And it so befell that the lot of Paris leapt forth first. Then the two warriors armed themselves and came forth into the space, and stood over against each other, brandishing their spears, with hate in their eyes. Then Paris threw his spear. It struck the shield of Menelaüs, but pierced it not, for the spear point was bent back. Then Menelaüs prayed to Zeus, "Grant, father Zeus, that I may avenge myself on Paris, who has done me this wrong: so shall men in after time fear to do wrong to their host." So speaking, he cast his long-shafted spear. It struck the shield of Paris and pierced it through, and passed through the corselet, and through the tunic, close to the loin; but Paris shrank aside, and the spear wounded him not. Then Menelaüs drew his silver-studded sword and struck a mighty blow on the top of the helmet of Paris, but the sword broke in four pieces in his hand. Then he cried in his wrath, "O Zeus, most mischief-loving of the gods, my spear I cast in vain, and now my sword is broken." Then he rushed forward and seized Paris by the helmet, and dragged him towards the host of the Greeks. And truly he had taken him, but Aphrodité loosed the strap that was beneath the chin, and the helmet came off in his hand. And Menelaüs whirled it among the Greeks and charged with another spear in his hand. But Aphrodité snatched Paris away, covering him with a mist, and put him down in his chamber in Troy. Then Menelaüs looked for him everywhere, but no one could tell him where he might be. No son of Troy would have hidden him out of kindness, for all hated him as death.

Then King Agamemnon said, "Now, ye sons of Troy, it is for you to give back the fair Helen and her wealth, and to pay me besides so much as may be fitting for all my cost and trouble."

But it was not the will of the gods that the sons of Troy should do this thing, but rather that their city should perish. So Athené took upon herself the shape of Laodocus, son of Antenor, and went to Pandarus, son of Lycaon, where he stood among his men. Then the false Laodocus said, "Pandarus, darest thou aim an arrow at Menelaüs? Truly the Trojans would love thee well, and Paris best of all, if they could see Menelaüs slain by an arrow from thy bow. Aim then, but first pray to Apollo, and vow that thou wilt offer a hundred beasts when thou returnest to thy city, Zeleia." Now Pandarus had a bow made of the horns of a wild goat which he had slain; sixteen palms long they were, and a cunning workman had made them smooth, and put a tip of gold whereon to fasten the bowstring. And Pandarus strung his bow, his comrades hiding him with their shields. Then he took an arrow from his quiver, and laid it on the bow-string, and drew the string to his breast, till the arrow-head touched the bow, and let fly. Right well aimed was the dart, but it was not the will of heaven that it should slay Menelaüs. It struck him, indeed, and passed through the belt and through the corselet and through the girdle, and pierced the skin. Then the red blood rushed out and stained the white skin, even as some Lycian or Carian woman stains the white ivory with red to adorn the war-horse of a king.

Sore dismayed was King Agamemnon to see the blood; sore dismayed also was the brave Menelaüs till he spied the barb of the arrow, and knew that the wound was not deep. But Agamemnon cried,—

"It was in an evil hour for thee, my brother, that I made a covenant with these false sons of Troy. Right well, indeed, I know that oath and sacrifice are not in vain, but will have vengeance at the last. Troy shall fall; but woe is me if thou shouldst die, Menelaüs. For the Greeks will straight go back to their fatherland, and the fair Helen will be left a boast to the sons of Troy, and I shall have great shame when one of them shall say, as he leaps on the tomb of the brave Menelaüs, 'Surely the great Agamemnon has avenged himself well; for he brought an army hither, but now is gone back to his home, but left Menelaüs here.' May the earth swallow me up before that day!"

"Nay," said Menelaüs, "fear not, for the arrow has but grazed the skin."

Then King Agamemnon bade fetch the physician. So the herald fetched Machaon, the physician. And Machaon came, and drew forth the arrow, and when he had wiped away the blood he put healing drugs upon the wound, which Chiron, the wise healer, had given to his father.

CHAPTER II.

But while this was doing, King Agamemnon went throughout the host, and if he saw anyone stirring himself to get ready for the battle he praised him and gave him good encouragement; but whomsoever he saw halting and lingering and slothful, him he blamed and rebuked whether he were common man or chief. The last that he came to was Diomed, son of Tydeus, with Sthenelus, son of Capaneus, standing by his side. And Agamemnon spake, "How is this, son of Tydeus? Shrinkest thou from the battle? This was not thy father's wont. I never saw him indeed, but I have heard that he was braver than all other men. Once he came to Mycenæ with great Polynices to gather allies against Thebes. And the men of Mycenæ would have sent them, only Zeus showed evil signs from heaven and forbade them. Then the Greeks sent Tydeus on an embassy to Thebes, where he found many of the sons of Cadmus feasting in the palace of Eteocles; but Tydeus was not afraid, though he was but one among many. He challenged them to contend with him in sport, and in everything he prevailed. But the sons of Cadmus bare it ill, and they laid an ambush for Tydeus as he went back, fifty men with two leaders — Mæon and Lycophon. But Tydeus slew them all, leaving only Mæon alive, that he might carry back the tidings to Thebes. Such was thy father; but his son is worse in battle, but better, it may be, in speech."

Nothing said Diomed, for he reverenced the king; but Sthenelus cried out, "Why speakest thou false, King Agamemnon, knowing the truth? We are not worse but better than our fathers. Did not we take Thebes, though we had fewer men than they, who indeed took it not?" But Diomed frowned and said, "Be silent, friend. I blame not King Agamemnon that he rouses the Greeks to battle. Great glory will it be to him if they take the city, and great loss if they be worsted. But it is for us to be valiant."

So he passed through all the host. And the Greeks went forward to the battle, as the waves that curl themselves and then dash upon the shore, throwing high the foam. In order they went after their chiefs; you had thought them dumb, so silent were they. But the Trojans were like a flock of ewes which wait to be milked, and bleat hearing the voice of their lambs, so confused a cry went out from their army, for there were men of many tongues gathered together. And on either side the gods urged them on, but chiefly Athené the Greeks, and Ares the sons of Troy. Then, as two streams in flood meet in some chasm, so the armies dashed together, shield on shield and spear on spear.

Antilochus, son of Nestor, was the first to slay a man of Troy, Echepolus by name, smiting him through the helmet into the forehead. Like a tower he fell, and Elphenor the Eubœan sought to drag him away that he might strip him of his arms. But Agenor smote him with his spear as he stooped, so baring his side to a wound. Dreadful was the fight around his body. Like wolves the Trojans and the Greeks rushed upon each other. And Ajax Telamon slew Simoisius (so they called him, because he was born on the banks of Simois). He fell as a poplar falls, and Antiphon, son of King Priam, aimed at Ajax, but, missing him, slew Leucus, the valiant comrade of Ulysses. And Ulysses, in great anger, stalked through the foremost fighters, brandishing his spear, and the sons of Troy gave way, and when he hurled it he slew Democoön, a son of Priam. Then Hector and the foremost ranks of Troy were borne backward, till Apollo cried from the heights of Pergamos, "On, Trojans! The flesh of these Greeks is not stone or iron, that ye cannot pierce it. Know, too, that the mighty Achilles does not fight to-day." But on the other side Athené urged on the Greeks to battle. Then Peiros the Thracian slew Diores, first striking him to the ground with a huge stone, and then piercing him with his spear; and him in turn Thoas of Ætolia slew, but could not spoil of his arms, so strongly did the men of Thrace defend the body. Then Athené roused Diomed to battle, making a fire shine from his helmet, bright as Orion shines in the vintage time. First there met him two warriors, sons of Dares, priest of Hephæstus, Phegeus and Idæus, the one fighting on foot and the other from his chariot. First Phegeus threw his spear and missed his aim; but Diomed missed not, smiting him through the breast. And Idæus, when he saw his brother fall, fled, Hephæstus saving him, lest the old man should be altogether bereaved. And each of the chiefs slew a foe; but there was none like Diomed, who raged through the battle so furiously that you could not tell with which host he was, whether with the Greeks or with the sons of Troy. Then Pandarus aimed an arrow at him, and smote him in the right shoulder as he was rushing forward, and cried aloud, "On, great-hearted sons of Troy, the bravest of the Greeks is wounded! Soon, methinks, will his strength fail him, unless Apollo has deceived me."

But Diomed cared not for the arrow. Only he leapt down from the chariot and spake to Sthenelus, his charioteer, "Come down and draw this arrow from my shoulder." Then Sthenelus drew it, and the blood spirted out from the wound. And Diomed prayed to Athené, "O goddess, if ever thou hast helped me, be with me now, and grant me to slay this boaster whose arrow has wounded me!" So speaking, he rushed into the ranks of the Trojans, slaying a man at every stroke. Æneas saw him, and thought how he might stay him in his course. So he passed through the host till he found Pandarus. "Pandarus," he said, "where are thy bow and arrows? See how this man deals death through the ranks. Send a shaft at him, first making thy prayer to Zeus."

Then Pandarus answered, —

"This man, methinks, is Diomed. The shield and the

helmet and the horses are his. And yet I know not whether he is not a god. Some god, at least, stands by him and guards him. But now I sent an arrow at him and smote him on the shoulder, right through the corselet, and thought that I had slain him; but lo! I have harmed him not at all. And now I know not what to do, for here I have no chariot. Eleven, indeed, there are at home, in the house of my father Lycaon, and the old man was earnest with me that I should bring one of them; but I would not, fearing for my horses, lest they should not have provender enough. So I came, trusting in my bow, and lo! it has failed me these two times. Two of the chiefs I have hit, Menelaüs and Diomed, and from each have seen the red blood flow, yet have I not harmed them. Surely, if ever I return safe to my home, I will break this useless bow."

"Nay," said Æneas, "talk not thus. Climb into my chariot, and see what horses we have in Troy. They will carry us safe to the city, even should Diomed prevail against us. But take the rein and the whip, and I will fight; or, if thou wilt, fight thou, and I will drive."

"Nay," said Pandarus, "let the horses have the driver whom they know. It might lose us both, should we turn to flee, and they linger or start aside, missing their master's voice."

So Pandarus mounted the chariot and they drove together against Diomed. And Sthenelus saw them coming, and said to his comrades — "I see two mighty warriors, Lycaon and Æneas. It would be well that we should go back to our chariot."

But Diomed frowned and said, "Talk not of going back. Thou wilt talk in vain to me. As for my chariot, I care not for it. As I am will I go against these men. Both shall not return safe, even if one should escape. But do thou stay my chariot where it is, tying the reins to the rail; and if I slay these men, mount the chariot of Æneas and drive into the hosts of the Greeks. There are no horses under the sun such as these, for they are of the breed which Zeus himself gave to King Tros."

Meanwhile Pandarus and Æneas were coming near, and Pandarus cast his spear. Right through the shield of Diomed it passed, and reached the corselet, and Pandarus cried, —

"Thou art hit in the loin. This, methinks, will lay thee low."

"Nay," said Diomed, "thou hast missed and not hit at all."

And as he spake he threw his spear. Through nose and teeth and tongue it passed, and stood out below the chin. Headlong from the chariot he fell, and his armor clashed about him. Straightway Æneas leapt off with spear and shield to guard the body of his friend, and stood as a lion stands over a carcase. But Diomed lifted a great stone, such as two men of our day could scarcely carry, and cast it. It struck Æneas on the hip, crushing the bone. The hero stooped on his knee, clutching the ground with his hand, and darkness covered his eyes. That hour he had perished, but his mother Aphrodité caught him in her white arms and threw her veil about him. But even so Diomed was loath to let his foe escape, and knowing that the goddess was not of those who mingle in the battle, he rushed on her and wounded her on the wrist, and the blood gushed out — such blood (they call it *ichor*) as flows in the veins of the immortal gods, who eat not the meat and drink not the drink of men. With a loud shriek she dropped her son, but Apollo caught him up and covered him with a dark mist, lest perchance one of the Greeks should spy him and slay him. And still Diomed pursued. Thrice he rushed on, and thrice Apollo pushed back his shining shield; but the fourth time the god cried to him, —

"Be wise, son of Tydeus, and give way, nor think to match the gods."

And Diomed gave way, fearing the wrath of the far-shooting bow. But Apollo carried Æneas out of the battle, and laid him down in his own temple in the citadel of Troy, and there Artemis and Latona healed him of his wound. And all the while the Trojans and the Greeks were fighting, as they thought, about his body, for Apollo had made a likeness of the hero and thrown it down in their midst. Then Sarpedon the Lycian spake to Hector with bitter words, —

"Where are thy boasts, Hector? Thou saidst that thou couldst guard thy city, without thy people or thy allies, thou alone, with thy brothers and thy brothers-in-law. But I cannot see even one of them. They go and hide themselves, as dogs before a lion. It is we, your allies, who maintain the battle. I have come from far to help thy people, — from Lycia, where I left wife and child and wealth, — nor do I shrink from the fight, but thou shouldst do thy part."

And the words stung Hector to the heart. He leapt from his chariot and went through the host, urging them to the battle. And on the other side the Greeks strengthened themselves. But Ares brought back Æneas whole from his wound, and gave him courage and might. Right glad were his comrades to see him, nor did they ask him any question; scant leisure was there for questions that day. Then were done many valiant deeds, nor did any bear himself more bravely than Æneas. Two chieftains of the Greeks he slew, Crethon and Orsilochus, who came from the banks of Alpheüs. Sore vexed was Menelaüs to see them fall, and he rushed to avenge them, Ares urging him on, for he hoped that Æneas would slay him. But Antilochus, Nestor's son, saw him go, and hasted to his side that he might help him. So they went and slew Pylæmenes, King of the Paphlagonians, and Medon, his charioteer. Then Hector rushed to the front, and Ares was by his side. Diomed saw him, and the god also, for his eyes were opened that day, and he fell back a space and cried, —

"O my friends! here Hector comes; nor he alone, but Ares is with him in the shape of a mortal man. Let us give place, still keeping our faces to the foe, for men must not fight with gods."

Then drew near to each other Sarpedon the Lycian and Tlepolemus, the son of Hercules, the one a son and the other a grandson of Zeus. First Tlepolemus spake, —

"What art thou doing here, Sarpedon? Surely 'tis a false report that thou art a son of Zeus. The sons of Zeus in the old days were better men than thou art, such as my father Hercules, who came to this city when Laomedon would not give him the horses which he had promised, and brake down the walls and wasted the streets. No help, methinks, wilt thou be to the sons of Troy, slain here by my hands."

But Sarpedon answered, "He indeed spoiled Troy, for Laomedon did him grevious wrong. But thou shalt not fare so, but rather meet with thy death."

Then they both hurled their spears, aiming truly, both of them. For Sarpedon smote Tlepolemus in the neck, piercing it through so that he fell dead, and Tlepolemus smote Sarpedon in the left thigh, driving the spear close to the bone, but slaying him not, his father Zeus warding off the doom of death. And his comrades carried him out of the battle, sorely burdened with the spear, which no one had thought to take out of the wound. And as he was borne along, Hector passed by, and Sarpedon rejoiced to see him, and cried, —

"Son of Priam, suffer me not to become a prey to the Greeks; let me at least die in your city, for Lycia I may see no more, nor wife, nor child."

But Hector heeded him not, so eager was he for the battle. So his comrades carried him to the great beech-tree and laid him down, and one of them drew the spear out of his thigh. When it was drawn out he fainted, but the cool north wind blew and revived him, and he breathed again.

But all the while Hector, with Ares at his side, dealt death and destruction through the ranks of the Greeks. Heré and Athené saw him where they sat on the top of Olympus, and were wroth. So they went to Father Zeus, and prayed that it might be lawful to them to stop him in his fury. And Zeus said, "Be it as you will." So they yoked the horses to the chariot of Heré and passed down to earth, the horses flying at every stride over so much space as a man sees who sits upon a cliff and looks across the sea to where it meets the sky. They alighted on the spot where the two rivers Simoïs and Scamander join their streams. There they loosed the horses from the yoke, and then sped like doves to where the bravest of the Greeks stood round King Diomed. There Heré took the shape of Stentor with the lungs of bronze, whose voice was as the voice of fifty men, and cried, "Shame, men of Greece! When Achilles went to the battle, the men of Troy came not beyond the gates, but now they fight far from the city, even by the ships." But Athené went to Diomed where he stood wiping away the blood from the wound where Pandarus had struck him with the arrow. And she spake, "Surely the son of Tydeus is little like to his sire. Small of stature was he, but a keen fighter. But thou — whether it be weariness or fear that keeps thee back I know not — canst scarcely be a true son of Tydeus."

But Diomed answered, "Nay, great goddess, for I know thee who thou art, daughter of Zeus, it is not weariness or fear that keeps me back. 'Tis thy own command that I heed. Thou didst bid me fight with none other of the immortal gods but only with Aphrodité, should she come to the battle. Therefore I give place, for I see Ares lording it through the ranks of war."

"Heed not Ares; drive thy chariot at him, and smite him with the spear. This very morning he promised that he would help the Greeks, and now he hath changed his purpose."

And as she spake she pushed Sthenelus, who drove the chariot, so that he leapt out upon the ground, and she mounted herself and caught the reins and lashed the horses. So the two went together, and they found Ares where he had just slain Periphas the Ætolian. But Athené had donned the helmet of Hades, which whosoever puts on straightway becomes invisible, for she would not that Ares should see her who she was. The god saw Diomed come near, and left Periphas, and cast his spear over the yoke of the chariot, eager to slay the hero. But Athené caught the spear in her hand, and turned it aside, so that it flew vainly through the air. Then Diomed in turn thrust forward his spear, and Athené leant upon it, so that it pierced the loin of Ares where his girdle was clasped. And Ares shouted with the pain, loud as a host of men, thousands nine or ten, shouts when it joins in battle. And the Greeks and Trojans trembled as they heard. And Diomed saw the god go up to Olympus as a thundercloud goes up when the wind of the south blows hot.

But when Ares had departed the Greeks prevailed again, slaying many of the sons of Troy and of their allies. But at last Helenus, the wise seer, spake to Hector and Æneas, —

"Cause the army to draw back to the walls, and go through the ranks and give them such strength and courage as ye may. And do thou, Hector, when thou hast so done, pass into the city, and bid thy mother go with the daughters of Troy, and take the costliest robe that she hath, and lay it on the knees of Athené in her temple, vowing therewith to sacrifice twelve heifers, if perchance she may have pity upon us, and keep this Diomed from our walls. Surely there is no Greek so strong as he; we did not fear even Achilles' self so much as we fear this man to-day, so dreadful is he and fierce. Go, and we will make such stand meanwhile as we can."

Then Hector passed through the ranks, bidding them be of good heart, and so departed to the city.

But when he was gone, Glaucus the Lycian and Diomed met in the space between the two hosts. And Diomed said, —

"Who art thou that meetest me thus? for never have I seen thee before. If thou art a man, know that luckless are the fathers whose sons meet my spear. But if thou art a god, I will not fight with thee. It fares ill with them that fight with gods."

Then Glaucus answered, "Diomed, why askest thou of my race? The races of men are as the leaves of the forest which the wind blows to the earth, and lo! in the spring they shoot forth again. Yet, if thou wouldst know it, hearken to my words. There is a city Ephyra in the land of Argos, where Sisyphus dwelt, who was the craftiest of men; and Sisyphus begat Glaucus, and Glaucus, Bellerophon. Now Bellerophon was the fairest and most valiant of men. And Queen Antea accused him falsely to her husband, King Prœtus. Whereupon the king sent him to his father-in-law, who was king of Lycia, and gave him a tablet, whereon were written letters of death, so that the king having read them should cause him to be slain. So Bellerophon came to Lycia. And for nine days the king feasted him, but on the tenth he asked for the tablet. And when he had read it, he sought how he might slay him. For first he sent him to subdue the Chimæra. Now the Chimæra was a marvellous thing, having the forepart of a lion, and the body of a goat, and the tail of a snake. And afterwards he sent him against the Solymi, who are the fiercest warriors of all that dwell on the earth. And his third labor was that he slew the Amazons. And as he was returning the king set an ambush for him, yet harmed him not, for Bellerophon slew all the men that lay in wait for him. Then the king knew him to be a good man and of the race of the gods. Wherefore he kept him, and gave him his daughter to wife, and with her the half of his kingdom; and the Lycians gave him a fair domain of orchard and plough-land. Now Bellerophon had three children — Laodamia, who bare Sarpedon to Zeus; and Isander, whom Ares slew in battle against the Solymi; and Hippolochus, my father, who sent me hither, bidding me ever bear myself bravely, nor shame the race of my fathers."

This Diomed was right glad to hear, and cried, "Nay, but thou art a friend by inheritance. For in former times

Œneus, my grandfather, feasted Bellerophon for twenty days, and gave him a belt broidered with purple, and Bellerophon gave him a great cup with two mouths, which indeed I left behind me when I came hither. And now let us two make agreement that we fight not with each other, for there are Trojans enough whom I may slay, and there are Greeks enough for thee. And let us also exchange our armor, that these men may know us to be friends by inheritance."

So they leapt down from their chariots and exchanged their armor. And Zeus took away all wise counsel from the heart of Glaucus, so that he gave golden armor for armor of bronze, the worth of a hundred oxen for the worth of nine.

Hector came into the city by the Scæan gates, and as he went wives and mothers crowded about him, asking how it had fared with their husbands and sons. But he said nought, save to bid them pray; and indeed there was sore news for many if he had told that which he knew. Then he came to the palace of King Priam, and there he saw Hecuba, his mother, and with her Laodicé, fairest of her daughters. She caught him by the hand and said, —

"Why hast thou come from the battle, my son? Do the Greeks press thee hard, and art thou minded to pray to Father Zeus from the citadel? Let me bring thee honey-sweet wine, that thou mayest pour out before him, aye, and that thou mayest drink thyself, and gladden thy heart."

But Hector said, "Give me not wine, my mother, lest thou weaken my knees and make me forget my courage. Nor must I pour out an offering with Zeus thus, with unwashed hands. But do thou gather the mothers of Troy together, and go to the temple of Athené, and take a robe, the one that is the most precious and beautiful in thy stores, and lay it on the knees of the goddess, and pray her to keep this dreadful Diomed from the walls of Troy; and forget not to vow therewith twelve heifers as a sacrifice. As for me, I will go and seek Paris, if perchance he will come with me to the war. Would that the earth might open and swallow him up, for of a truth he is a curse to King Priam and to Troy."

So Queen Hecuba and the mothers of Troy did as Hector had bidden them. But when they laid the robe on the knees of the goddess she would not hear them.

And Hector went to the house of Paris, where it stood on the citadel, near to his own dwelling and the dwelling of Priam. He found him busy with his arms, and the fair Helen sat near him and gave their tasks to her maidens.

But Hector spake: "Be not wroth, my brother. The people perish about the wall, and the war burns hot round the city, and all for thy sake. Rouse thee, lest it be consumed."

And Paris answered, "Brother, thou hast spoken well. It was not in wrath that I sat here. I was vexed at my sore defeat. But now my wife has urged me to join the battle, and truly it is well, for victory comes now to one and now to another. Wait thou, then, till I don my arms, or if thou wouldst depart, I will overtake thee."

So Hector departed and went to his own home, seeking his wife Andromaché, but found her not, for she was on a tower of the wall with her child and her child's nurse, weeping sore for fear. And Hector spake to the maids,—

"Tell me, whither went the white-armed Andromaché; to see some sister-in-law, or to the temple of Athené with the mothers of Troy?"

"Nay," said an aged woman, keeper of the house. "She

went to one of the towers of the wall, for she had heard that the Greeks were pressing our people hard. She hasted like as she were mad, and the nurse carried the child."

So Hector ran through the city to the Scæan gates, and there Andromaché spied him, and hasted to meet him — Andromaché, daughter of King Eëtion, of Thebé-under-Placus. And with her was the nurse, bearing the young child on her bosom — Hector's only child, beautiful, headed as a star. His father called him Scamandrius, after the river, but the sons of Troy called him Astyanax, the "City-King," because it was his father who saved the city. Silently he smiled when he saw the child, but Andromaché clasped his hand and wept, and said, —

"O Hector, thy courage will bring thee to death. Thou hast no pity on thy wife and child, but sparest not thyself, and all the Greeks will rush on thee and slay thee. It were better for me, losing thee, to die; for I have no comfort but thee. My father is dead, for Achilles slew him in Thebé — slew him but spoiled him not, so much he reverenced him. With his arms he burnt him, and the mountain-nymphs planted poplars about his grave. Seven brethren I had, and lo! they all fell in one day by the hand of the great Achilles. And my mother, she is dead, for when she had been ransomed, Artemis smote her with an arrow in her father's house. But thou art father to me, and mother and brother and husband also. Have pity, then, and stay here upon the wall, lest thou leave me a widow and thy child an orphan. And set the people here in array by this fig-tree, where the city is easiest to be taken; for there come the bravest of the Greeks, Ajax the Greater, and Ajax the Less, and Idomeneus, and the two sons of Atreus, and the son of Tydeus."

But Hector said, "Nay, let these things be my care

I would not that any son or daughter of Troy should see me skulking from the war. And my own heart loathes the thought, and bids me fight in the front. Well I know, indeed, that Priam, and the people of Priam, and holy Troy, will perish. Yet it is not for Troy, or for the people, or even for my father or my mother that I care so much, as for thee in the day when some Greek shall carry thee away captive, and thou shalt ply the loom or carry the pitcher in the land of Greece. And some one shall say when he sees thee, 'This was Hector's wife, who was the bravest of the sons of Troy.' May the earth cover me before that day!"

Then Hector stretched out his arms to his child. But the child drew back into the bosom of his nurse with a loud cry, fearing the shining bronze and the horse-hair plume which nodded awfully from his helmet top. Then father and mother laughed aloud. And Hector took the helmet from his head and laid it on the ground, and caught his child in his hands, and kissed him and dandled him, praying aloud to Father Zeus and all the gods.

"Grant, Father Zeus and all ye gods, that this child may be as I am, great among the sons of Troy; and may they say some day, when they see him carrying home the bloody spoils from the war, 'A better man than his father, this,' and his mother shall be glad at heart."

Then he gave the child to his mother, and she clasped him to her breast and smiled a tearful smile. And her husband had pity on her, and stroked her with his hand, and spake, —

"Be not troubled over much. No man shall slay me against the ordering of fate; but as for fate, that, I trow, no man may escape, be he coward or brave. But go, ply thy tasks, the shuttle and the loom, and give their tasks to thy maidens, and let men take thought for the battle."

Then Hector took up his helmet from the ground, and Andromaché went her way to her home, oft turning back her eyes. And when she was come, she and all her maidens wailed for the living Hector as though he were dead, for she thought that she should never see him any more returning safe from the battle.

And as Hector went his way, Paris came running, clad in shining arms, like to some proud steed which has been fed high in his stall, and now scours the plain with head aloft and mane streaming over his shoulders. And he spake to Hector, —

"I have kept thee, I fear, when thou wast in haste, nor came at thy bidding."

But Hector answered, "No man can blame thy courage, only thou wilfully heldest back from the battle. Therefore do the sons of Troy speak shame of thee. But now let us go to the war."

So they went together out of the gates, and fell upon the hosts of the Greeks and slew many chiefs of fame, and Glaucus the Lycian went with them.

Now when Athené saw that the Greeks were perishing by the hand of Hector and his companions, it grieved her sore. So she came down from the heights of Olympus, if haply she might help them. And Apollo met her and said, —

"Art thou come, Athené, to help the Greeks whom thou lovest? Well, let us stay the battle for this day; hereafter they shall fight till the doom of Troy be accomplished."

But Athené answered, "How shall we stay it?"

And Apollo said, "We will set on Hector to challenge

the bravest of the Greeks to fight with him, man to man."

So they two put the matter into the mind of Helenus the seer. Then Helenus went near to Hector:—

"Listen to me, for I am thy brother. Cause the rest of the sons of Troy and of the Greeks to sit down, and do thou challenge the bravest of the Greeks to fight with thee, man to man. And be sure thou shalt not fall in the battle, for the will of the immortal gods is so."

Then Hector greatly rejoiced, and passed to the front of the army, holding his spear by the middle, and kept back the sons of Troy; and King Agamemnon did likewise with his own people. Then Hector spake:—

"Hear me, sons of Troy, and ye men of Greece. The covenant that we made one with another hath been broken, for Zeus would have it so, purposing evil to both, till either you shall take our high-walled city, or we shall conquer you by your ships. But let one of you who call yourselves champions of the Greeks come forth and fight with me, man to man. And let it be so that if he vanquish me he shall spoil me of my arms but give my body to my people, that they may burn it with fire; and if I vanquish him, I will spoil him of his arms but give his body to the Greeks, that they may bury him and raise a great mound above him by the broad salt river of Hellespont. And so men of after days shall see it, sailing by, and say, 'This is the tomb of the bravest of the Greeks, whom Hector slew.' So shall my name live for ever."

But all the Greeks kept silence, fearing to meet him in battle, but shamed to hold back. Then at last Menelaüs leapt forward and spake:—

"Surely now ye are women and not men. Foul shame it were should there be no man to stand up against this

Hector. Lo! I will fight with him my own self, for the issues of battle are with the immortal gods."

So he spake in his rage rashly, courting death, for Hector was much stronger than he. Then King Agamemnon answered:—

"Nay, but this is folly, my brother. Seek not in thy anger to fight with one that is stronger than thou; for as for this Hector, even Achilles was loath to meet him. Sit thou down among thy comrades, and the Greeks will find some champion who shall fight with him."

And Menelaüs hearkened to his brother's words, and sat down. Then Nestor rose in the midst and spake:—

"Woe is me to-day for Greece! How would the old Peleus grieve to hear such a tale! Well I remember how he rejoiced when I told him of the house and lineage of all the chieftains of the Greeks, and now he would hear that they cower before Hector, and are sore afraid when he calls them to the battle. Surely he would pray this day that he might die! Oh that I were such as I was in the old days, when the men of Pylos fought with the Arcadians by the stream of Iardanus! Now the leader of the Arcadians was Ereuthalion, and he wore the arms of Areïthous, whom men called 'Areïthous of the club,' because he fought not with bow or spear, but with a club of iron. Him Lycurgus slew, not by might but by craft, taking him in a narrow place where his club of iron availed him not, and smiting him with his spear. He slew him, and took his arms. And when Lycurgus grew old he gave the arms to Ereuthalion to wear. So Ereuthalion wore them, and challenged the men of Pylos to fight with him. But they feared him. Only I, who was the youngest of all, stood forth, and Athené gave me glory that day, for I slew him, though he was the strongest and tallest among the sons of men. Would that I were such to-day! Right soon would I meet this mighty Hector."

Then rose up nine chiefs of fame. First of all, King Agamemnon, lord of many nations, and next to him Diomed, son of Tydeus, and Ajax the Greater and Ajax the Less, and then Idomeneus and Meriones, who was his companion in arms, and Eurypylus, and Thoas, son of Andræmon, and the wise Ulysses.

Then Nestor said, "Let us cast lots who shall do battle with the mighty Hector."

So they threw the lots into the helmet of King Agamemnon, a lot for each. And the people prayed, "Grant, ye gods, that the lot of Ajax the Greater may leap forth, or the lot of Diomed, or the lot of King Agamemnon." Then Nestor shook the lots in the helmet, and the one which they most wished leapt forth. For the herald took it through the ranks and showed it to the chiefs, but none knew it for his own till he came to where Ajax the Greater stood among his comrades. But Ajax had marked it with his mark, and put forth his hand for it, and claimed it, right glad at heart. On the ground by his feet he threw it, and said,—

"Mine is the lot, my friends, and right glad I am, for I think that I shall prevail over the mighty Hector. But come, let me don my arms; and pray ye to Zeus, but silently, lest the Trojans hear, or aloud, if ye will, for no fear have we. Not by force or craft shall any one vanquish me, for not such are the men that Salamis breeds."

So he armed himself and moved forwards, dreadful as Ares, smiling with grim face. With mighty strides he came, brandishing his long-shafted spear. And all the Greeks were glad to behold him, but the knees of the Trojans were loosened with fear, and great Hector's heart beat fast; but he trembled not, nor gave place, seeing that he had himself called him to battle. So Ajax came near, holding before the great shield, like a wall, which Tychius, best of craftsmen, had made for him. Seven folds of bull's hide it had, and an eighth of bronze. Threateningly he spake : —

"Now shalt thou know, Hector, what manner of men there are yet among our chiefs, though Achilles the lion-hearted is far away, sitting idly in his tent, in great wrath with King Agamemnon. Do thou, then, begin the battle."

"Speak not to me, Zeus-descended Ajax," said Hector, "as though I were a woman or a child, knowing nothing of war. Well I know all the arts of battle, to ply my shield this way and that, to guide my car through the tumult of steeds, and to stand fighting hand to hand. But I would not smite so stout a foe by stealth, but openly, if it so befall."

And as he spake he hurled his long shafted spear, and smote the great shield on the rim of the eighth fold, that was of bronze. Through six folds it passed, but in the seventh it was stayed. Then Ajax hurled his spear, striking Hector's shield. Through shield it passed and corselet, and cut the tunic close against the loin; but Hector shrank away and escaped the doom of death. Then, each with a fresh spear, they rushed together like lions or wild boars of the wood. First Hector smote the middle of the shield of Ajax, but pierced it not, for the spear-point was bent back; then Ajax, with a great bound, drove his spear at Hector's shield and pierced it, forcing him back, and grazing his neck so that the black blood welled out. Yet did not Hector cease from the combat. A great stone and rough he caught up from the ground, and hurled it at the boss of the seven-fold shield. Loud rang the bronze, but the shield brake not. Then Ajax took a stone heavier by far, and threw it with all his might. It brake the shield of Hector, and bore him backwards, so that he fell at length with his shield above him. But Apollo raised him up. Then did both draw their swords; but ere they could join in close battle came the heralds, and held their sceptres between them, and Idæus, the herald of Troy, spake:—

"Fight no more, my sons; Zeus loves you both, and ye are both mighty warriors. That we all know right well. But now the night bids you cease, and it is well to heed its bidding."

Then said Ajax, "Nay, Idæus, but it is for Hector to speak, for he called the bravest of the Greeks to battle. And as he wills it, so will I."

And Hector said, "O Ajax, the gods have given thee stature and strength and skill, nor is there any better warrior among the Greeks. Let us cease then from the battle; we may yet meet again, till the gods give the victory to me or thee. And now let us give gifts the one to the other, so that Trojans and Greeks may say — Hector and Ajax met in fierce fight and parted in friendship."

So Hector gave to Ajax a silver-studded sword with the scabbard and the sword-belt, and Ajax gave to Hector a buckler splendid with purple. So they parted. Right glad were the sons of Troy when they saw Hector returning safe. Glad also were the Greeks, as they led Ajax rejoicing in his victory to King Agamemnon. Whereupon the king called the chiefs to banquet together, and bade slay an ox of five years old, and Ajax he honored most of all, giving him the chine. And when the feast was ended, Nestor said, —

"It were well that we should cease awhile from war and burn the dead, for many, in truth, are fallen. And we will build a great wall, and dig a trench about it, and we will make gates, wide that a chariot may pass through, so that our ships may be safe, if the sons of Troy should press us hard."

But the next morning came a herald from Troy to the chiefs, as they sat in council by the ship of King Agamemnon, and said, —

"This is the word of Priam and the men of Troy: Paris will give back all the treasures of the fair Helen, and many more besides; but the fair Helen herself he will not give. But if this please you not, grant us a truce that we may bury our dead."

Then Diomed spake, "Nay, we will not take the fair Helen's self, for a man may know, even though he be a fool, that the doom of Troy is come."

And King Agamemnon said, "Herald, thou hast heard the word of the Greeks, but as for the truce, be it as you will."

So the next day they burnt their dead, and the Greeks made a wall with gates and dug a trench about it. And when it was finished, even at sunset, they made ready a meal, and lo! there came ships from Lemnos bringing wine, and Greeks bought thereof, some with bronze, and some with iron, and some with shields of ox hide. All night they feasted right joyously. The sons of Troy also feasted in their city. But the dreadful thunder rolled through the night, for Zeus was counselling evil against them.

CHAPTER III.

THE WOUNDING OF THE CHIEFS.

THE next day the battle was set in array as before. And all the morning the armies fought without advantage to the one or the other; but at noon, at the hour when one who cuts wood upon the hills sits down to his meal, the Greeks prevailed and drove back the sons of Troy. Nor was there one of all the chiefs who fought so bravely as King Agamemnon. Many valiant men he slew, and among them the two sons of Antimachus. These, indeed, he took alive in their chariot, for they had dropped the reins, and stood helpless before him, crying out that he should spare them and take ransom, for that Antimachus their father had much gold and bronze and iron in his house, and would gladly buy them back alive. Now Antimachus had taken a bribe from Prince Paris, and had given counsel to the Trojans that they should not give back the fair Helen. So when King Agamemnon heard them, he said, "Nay, but if ye be sons of Antimachus, who counselled the men of Troy that they should slay Menelaüs when he came an ambassador to their city, ye shall die for your father's sin." So he slew them both, and leaving them he still rushed on, driving back the Trojans even to the walls of their city. Nor did Hector himself dare to meet him, for Zeus had sent him a message saying that he should hold himself back till King Agamemnon should chance to be wounded. And indeed this chance happened presently, for the king had slain Iphidamas, son to Antenor, and Coön, his brother, the eldest born, was very wroth to see it. So standing sideways he aimed with his spear, Agamemnon not knowing, and smote the king in the hand near the wrist. Then he seized the body of his brother, and shouted to his comrades that they should help him; but Agamemnon dealt him a deadly blow underneath his shield. So he fell; and for a while, while the wound was warm, the king fought as before; but when it grew cold and stiff great pain came upon him, and he leapt into his chariot and bade the charioteer drive him to the ships, for that he could fight no more.

Then again the battle went for the Trojans, though Diomed and Ulysses, who fought very valiantly, stayed it awhile, Diomed coming very near to slay Hector. But Paris, who was in hiding behind the pillar on the tomb of Ilus, drew his bow, and smote him with an arrow through the ankle of the right foot. Loud he boasted of his aim. "Only," he said, "I would that I had pierced thee in the loin; then hadst thou troubled the sons of Troy no more."

But Diomed answered, "Small good were thy bow to thee, cowardly archer, if thou shouldst dare to meet me face to face. And as for this graze on my foot, I care no more than if a woman or child had smitten me. Not such the wounds I deal; as for those that meet my spear in the battle, I trow that they are dearer to the fowls of the air than to women in the chamber."

Then Ulysses stood before him while he drew the arrow out of his foot. Grievous was the smart of the wound, for all his brave words. Wherefore he leapt into his chariot, and bade drive in haste to the ships. So Ulysses was left alone, and the Trojans came about him as men with dogs come about a wild boar who stands at bay gnashing his white teeth. Fiercely he stood at bay, and slew five chiefs of fame. But one of them, Socus by name, before he fell, wounded him on the side, scraping the flesh from the ribs. High spurted the blood from the wound, and the Trojans shouted to see it. Then Ulysses shouted for help; three times he shouted, and Menelaüs heard him and called to Ajax that it was the voice of Ulysses, and that they should help him. So they went together and made head awhile against the Trojans. But soon Paris wounded with an arrow another brave chieftain, even the physician Machaon. Then Ajax himself was affrighted and gave way, but slowly, and sore against his will. Just so a lion is driven off from a herd of oxen by dogs and men. Loath he is to go, so hungry is he, but the spears and the burning torches affright him. So Ajax gave way. Now he would turn and face the sons of Troy, and now he would flee, and they sought how to slay him, but harmed him not. Then once more Paris loosed his bow and wounded a chief, Eurypylus, striking him on the right thigh. So the battle went sorely against the Greeks.

Now Achilles was standing on the stern of his ship, looking at the war, and he saw Nestor carrying Machaon in his chariot to the ships. Then he called to Patroclus, and Patroclus, who was in the tent, came forth; but it was an evil hour for him. Then said Achilles, —

"Now will the Greeks soon come, methinks, praying for help, for their need is sore. But go and see who is this whom Nestor is taking to the ships. His shoulders are the shoulders of Machaon, but I saw not his face, so swift the horses passed me by."

Then Patroclus ran. And as he stood in the tent door, old Nestor saw him, and went and took him by the hand, and would have had him sit down. But Patroclus would not, saying, —

"Stay me not. I came but to see who is this that thou hast brought wounded from the battle. And now I see that it is Machaon. Therefore I will return, for thou knowest what manner of man is Achilles, that he is hasty and swift to blame."

Then said Nestor, "But what cares Achilles for the Greeks? or why does he ask who are wounded? But, O Patroclus, dost thou mind the day when I and Ulysses came to the house of Peleus, and how thy father Menætius was there, and how we feasted in the hall; and when the feast was finished told our errand, for we were gathering the heroes for the war against the sons of Troy? Right willing were ye two to come, and many counsels did the old men give you. Then to Achilles Peleus said that he should always be foremost in the host, but to thee thy father Menætius spake, 'Achilles is nobler born than thou, and stronger far; but thou art older. Do thou therefore counsel him well, when there is need.' But this thou forgettest, Patroclus. Hear, then, what I say. It may be that Achilles will not go forth to the battle. But let him send thee forth, and the Myrmidons with thee, and let him put his arms upon thee, so that the sons of Troy be affrighted, thinking that he is in the battle, and we shall have breathing space."

Then Patroclus turned to run to Achilles, but as he ran he met Eurypylus, who spake to him, —

"Small hope is there now for the Greeks, seeing that all their bravest chiefs lie wounded at the ships. But do thou help me, for thou knowest all the secrets of healing, seeing that the wise Chiron himself taught thee."

Then Patroclus answered, "I am even now on my way to tell these things to Achilles, but thee I may not leave in thy trouble."

So he took him to his tent, and cut out the arrow from his thigh, washing the wound with water, and putting on it a bitter healing root, so that the pain was stayed and the blood stanched.

Now by this time the Trojans were close upon the trench. But the horses stood on the brink, fearing to leap it, for it was broad and deep, and the Greeks had put great stakes therein. Thus said Polydamas, —

"Surely, Hector, this is madness that we strive to cross the trench in our chariots, for it is broad and deep, and there are great stakes therein. Look, too, at this: even if we should be able to cross it, how will the matter stand? If indeed it be the pleasure of Zeus that the Greeks should perish utterly, — it will be well. But if they turn upon us and pursue us, driving us back from the ships, then shall we not be able to return. Wherefore let us leave our chariots here upon the brink, and go on foot against the wall."

So they went in five companies, of whom Hector led that which was bravest and largest, and with him were Polydamas and Cebriones. And the next Paris commanded. And of the third Helenus and Deïphobus were leaders, and with them was Asius, the son of Hyrtacus, from Arisbê. And the fourth followed Æneas, the valiant son of Anchises. But of the allies Sarpedon was the leader, and with him were Glaucus and Asteropæus. And in each company they joined shield to shield, and so went against the Greeks. Nor was there one of them but hearkened to the counsel of Polydamas when he bade them leave their chariots by the trench, save Asius only. But Asius drove his chariot right up to that gate which was on the left hand in the wall. Now the gates chanced to be open, for the warders had opened them, if so any of the Greeks that fled might save themselves within them. Now the warders were two mighty heroes of the race of the Lapithæ, Polypœtes and Leonteus; and these, when they saw Asius and his company coming, went without and stood in front of the gates, just as two wild boars stand at bay against a crowd of men and dogs. And all the while they that stood on the wall threw heavy stones which fell, thick as the snow-flakes fall in the winter, on the men of Troy, and loud rang the helmets and the shields. And many fell wounded to the death, nor could Asius, for all his fury, win his way into the walls. But where, at another of the gates, Hector led the way, there appeared a strange marvel in the skies, for an eagle was bearing in his claws a great snake, which it had taken as a prey. But the snake fought fiercely for its life, and writhed itself about, even till it bit the eagle on the breast. Whereupon the eagle dropped it into the midst of the host, and fled with a loud cry. Then Polydamas, the wise counsellor, came near to Hector, and said,—

"Now it will be well that we should not follow these Greeks to their ships. For I take that this marvel that we have seen is a sign to us. For as this eagle had caught in his claws a snake, but held it not, dropping it before it could bear it to her young, so shall it fare with us. For we shall drive the Greeks to their ships, but shall not subdue them, but shall return in disorder by the way that we came, leaving full many of our comrades behind us."

But Hector frowned and answered, "Nay, but this is ill counsel, Polydamas. For if thou sayest this from thy heart, surely the gods have changed thy wisdom into foolishness. Dost thou bid me forget the command of Zeus the Thunderer, and take heed to birds, how they fly? Little care I whether they go to the east or to the west, to the right or to the left. Surely there is but one sign for a brave man, that he is fighting for his fatherland. Wherefore take thou heed; for if thou holdest back from the war, or holdest back any other, lo! I will smite thee with my spear."

Then he sprang forward, and the men of Troy followed him with a shout. And Zeus sent down from Ida a great blast of wind which bore the dust of the plain straight to the ships, troubling the hearts of the Greeks. Then the Trojans sought to drag down the battlements from the wall, and to wrench up the posts which had been set to strengthen it. Nor did the Greeks give way, but they joined shield to shield and fought for the wall. And foremost among them were Ajax the Greater and Ajax the Less. Just as the snow falls in mid-winter, when the winds are hushed, and the mountain-tops are covered, and the plains and the dwellings of men and the very shores of the sea, up to the waves' edge, so thickly fell the stones which the Greeks showered from the wall against the men of Troy, and which these again threw upon the Greeks. But still Hector and his men availed not to break through the gate. But at the last Zeus stirred up the heart of his own son, Sarpedon. Holding his shield before him he went, and he shook in either hand a spear. As goes a lion, when hunger presses him sore, against a stall of oxen or a sheepfold, and cares not though he find men and dogs keeping watch against him, so Sarpedon went against the wall. And first he spake to stout Glaucus, his comrade, —

"Tell me, Glaucus, why is it that men honor us at home with the chief rooms at feasts, and with fat portions of flesh and with sweet wine, and that we have a great domain of orchard and plough land by the banks of Xanthus? Surely it is that we may fight in the front rank. Then shall some one who may behold us say, 'Of a truth these are honorable men, these princes of Lycia, and not without good right do they eat the fat and drink the sweet, for they fight ever in the front.' Now, indeed, if we might live for ever, nor know old age nor death, neither would I fight among the first, nor would I bid thee arm thyself for the battle. But seeing that there are ten thousand fates above us which no man may avoid, let us see whether we shall win glory from another, or another shall take it from us."

And Glaucus listened to his words and charged at his side, and the great host of the Lycians followed them. Sore dismayed was Menestheus the Athenian when he saw them. All along the wall of the Greeks he looked, spying out for help; and he saw Ajax the Greater and Ajax the Less, and with them Teucer, who had just come forth from his tent. Close to him they were, but it was of no avail to shout, so loud was the clash and din of arms, of shield and helmets, and the thundering at the gates, for each one of these did the men of Troy assail.

Wherefore he called to him Thoas, the herald, and said, "Run, Thoas, and call Ajax hither, — both of the name if that may be, — for the end is close upon us in this place, so mightily press on the chiefs of the Lycians, who were ever fiery fighters. But if there is trouble there also, let at the least Ajax the Greater come, and with him Teucer of the bow."

Then the herald ran, and said as he had been bidden.

And Ajax Telamon spake to the son of Oïleus: "Stand thou here with Lycomedes and stay the enemy. But I will go thither, and come again when I have finished my work."

So he went, and Teucer his brother went with him, with

Pandion carrying his bow. And even as they went the Lycians came up like a tempest on the wall. But Ajax slew Epicles, a comrade of Sarpedon, smiting him on the head with a mighty stone, and crushing all the bones of his head. And Teucer smote Glaucus on the shoulder and wounded him sore. Silently did Glaucus leap down from the wall, for he would not that any of the Greeks should see that he was wounded. But Sarpedon saw that he had departed, and it grieved him. Nevertheless, he ceased not from the battle, but first slew Alcmaon, the son of Mestor, and next caught one of the battlements in his hands and dragged it down. So the wall was laid open, and a way was made for the Trojans to enter. Then did both Ajax and Teucer aim at him together. And Teucer smote the strap of the shield, but harmed him not, and Ajax drove his spear through his shield and stayed him, so that he fell back a space from the battlement, yet would not cease from the fight. Loud he shouted to the Lycians that they should follow him, and they came crowding about their king. Then fierce and long was the fight, for the Lycians could not break down the wall of the Greeks and make a way to the ships, and the Greeks could not drive away the Lycians from the wall where they stood. Just so two men contend for the boundary in some common field. Small is the space, and they stand close together. So close stood the Lycians and the Greeks, on this side of the battlement, and on that, and all the wall was red with blood. But not to Sarpedon and the men of Lycia, but to Hector, did Zeus give the glory that day. Now, in front of the gate there lay a great stone, broad at the base and sharp at the top. Scarce could two men of the strongest, such as are men in these days, move it with levers on to a wagon; but Hector lifted it easily, easily as a shepherd carries in one hand the fleece of a sheep. Two folding doors there were in the gates, held by bolts and a key, and at these he hurled the great stone, planting his feet apart, that his aim might be the surer and stronger. With a mighty crash it came against the gates, and the bolts held not against it, and the hinges were broken, so that the folding doors flew back. Then Hector leapt into the space, holding a spear in either hand, and his eyes flashed as fire. And the men of Troy came after him, some mounting the wall, and some pouring through the gates.

Now Poseidon was watching the battle from the wooded height of Samothrace, whence he could see Ida and Troy and the ships. And he pitied the Greeks when he saw how they fled before Hector, and purposed in his heart to help them. So he left the height of Samothrace, and came with four strides to Ægæ, where his palace was in the depths of the sea. There he harnessed the horses to his chariot and rode, passing over the waves, and the great beasts of the sea gambolled about him as he went, knowing their king. But when he came to the camp of the Greeks, he took upon him the shape of Calchas, the herald, and went through the host strengthening the heroes for the battle — Ajax the Greater, and Ajax the Less, and others also — so that they turned their faces again to the enemy. But not the less did the men of Troy press on, Hector leading the way.

Then first of all Teucer slew a Trojan, Imbrius by name, wounding him under the ear. He fell as some tall poplar falls which a woodman fells with axe of bronze. Then Teucer rushed to seize his arms, but Hector cast his spear. Teucer it struck not, missing him by a little, but Amphimachus it smote on the breast so that he fell dead. Then Hector seized the dead man's helmet, seeking to drag the body among the sons of Troy. But Ajax stretched forth his great spear against him, and struck the boss of his shield mightily, driving him backwards, so that he loosed hold of the helmet of Amphimachus. And him his comrades bore to the rear of the host, and the body of Imbrius also they carried off. Then did Idomeneus the Cretan, son of Minos, the wise judge, perform many valiant deeds, going to the left-hand of the battle-line, for he said, —

"The Greeks have stay enough where the great Ajax is. No man that eats bread is better than he; no, not Achilles' self, were the two to stand man to man, but Achilles indeed is swifter of foot."

And first of all he slew Othryoneus, who had but newly come, hearing the fame of the war. For Cassandra's sake he had come, that he might have her to wife, vowing that he would drive the Greeks from Troy, and Priam had promised him the maiden. But now Idomeneus slew him, and cried over him, —

"This was a great thing that thou didst promise to Priam, for which he was to give thee his daughter. Thou shouldst have come to us, and we would have given thee the fairest of the daughters of Agamemnon, bringing her from Argos, if thou wouldst have engaged to help us to take this city of Troy. But come now with me to the ships, that we may treat about this marriage: thou wilt find that we have open hands."

So he spake, mocking the dead. Then King Asius charged, coming on foot with his chariot behind him. But ere he could throw his spear, Idomeneus smote him that he fell, as falls an oak, or an alder, or a pine, which men fell upon the hills. And the driver of his chariot stood dismayed, nor thought to turn his horses and flee, so that Antilochus, the son of Nestor, struck him down, and took the chariot and horses for his own. Then Deïphobus in great wrath came near to Idomeneus, and would have slain him with a spear, but could not, for he covered himself with his shield, and the spear passed over his head. Yet did it not fly in vain, for it lighted on Hypsenor, striking him on the right side. And as he fell, Deïphobus cried aloud, —

"Now is Asius avenged; and though he go down to that strong porter who keeps the gates of hell, yet will he be glad, for I have sent him a companion."

But scarce had he spoken when Idomeneus the Cretan slew another of the chiefs of Troy, Alcathoüs, son-in-law of old Anchises. And having slain him, he cried, —

"Small reason hast thou to boast, Deïphobus, for we have slain three for one. But come thou and meet me in battle, that thou mayest know me who I am, son of Deucalion, who was the son of Minos, who was the son of Zeus."

Then Deïphobus thought within himself, should he meet this man alone, or should he take some brave comrade with him? And it seemed to him better that he should take a brave comrade with him. Wherefore he went for Æneas, and found him in the rear of the battle, vexed at heart because King Priam did not honor him among the princes of Troy. Then said he, —

"Come hither, Æneas, to fight for Alcathoüs, who was wont to care for thee when thou wast young, and now he lies dead under the spear of Idomeneus."

So they two went together; and Idomeneus saw them, but yielded not from his place, only called to his comrades that they should gather themselves together and help him. And on the other side Æneas called to Deïphobus, and

Paris, and Agenor. So they fought about the body of Alcathoüs. Then did Æneas cast his spear at Idomeneus, but struck him not; but Idomeneus slew Œnomaüs, only when he would have spoiled him of his arms he could not, for the men of Troy pressed him hard, so that perforce he gave way. And as he turned, Deïphobus sought to slay him with his spear, but smote in his stead Ascalaphus, son of Ares. But when he would have spoiled him of his arms, Meriones struck him through the wrist with a spear. Straightway he dropped the helmet which he had seized, and Polites, his brother, led him out of the battle. And he climbed into his chariot and went back to the city. But the rest stayed not their hands from fighting, and many valiant heroes fell, both on this side and on that. For on the left the sons of Greece prevailed, so fiercely fought Idomeneus the Cretan, and Meriones, his comrade, and Antilochus, the son of Nestor, and Menelaüs; but on the right the Locrians and the Bœotians and the men of Athens could scarce keep Hector from the ships. Yet here for a while the battle went with them, for the Locrians, who were mighty archers, bent their bows against the men of Troy and dismayed them, so thick flew the arrows, dealing wounds and death. Then said Polydamas to Hector, —

"O Hector, thou art ever loath to hear counsel from others. Yet think not that because thou art stronger than other men, therefore Zeus hath also made thee wiser. For truly he gives diverse gifts to diverse men — strength to one and counsel to another. Hear, then, my words. Thou seest that the Trojans keep not all together, for some stand aloof, while some fight, being few against many. Do thou therefore call the bravest together. Then shall we see whether we shall burn the ships, or, it may be, win our way back without harm to Troy; for indeed I forget not that there is a warrior here whom no man may match, nor will he, I trow, always keep aloof from the battle."

And the saying pleased Hector. So he went through the host looking for the chiefs — for Deïphobus, and Helenus, and Asius, and Acamas, son of Asius, and others, who were the bravest among the Trojans and allies. And some he found, and some he found not, for they had fallen in the battle, or had gone sorely wounded to the city. But at last he spied Paris, where he stood strengthening the hearts of his comrades.

"O Paris, fair of face, cheater of the hearts of women, where is Deïphobus, and Helenus, and Asius, and Acamas, son of Asius?"

But Paris answered him, "Some of these are dead, and some are sorely wounded. But we who are left fight on. Only do thou lead us against the Greeks, nor wilt thou say that we are slow to follow."

So Hector went along the front of the battle, leading the men of Troy. Nor did the Greeks give way when they saw him, but Ajax the Greater cried, —

"Friend, come near, nor fear the men of Greece. Thou thinkest in thine heart to spoil the ships, but we have hands to keep them, and ere they perish Troy itself shall fall before us. Soon, I trow, wilt thou wish that thy horses were swifter than hawks, when they bear thee fleeing before us across the plain to the city."

But Hector answered, "Nay, thou braggart Ajax, what words are these? I would that I were as surely one of the Immortals as this day shall surely bring woe to the Greeks. And thou, if thou darest to meet my spear, shalt be slain among the rest, and feed with thy flesh the beasts of the field and the fowls of the air."

So he spake, and from this side and from that there went up a great cry of battle.

So loud was the cry that it roused old Nestor where he sat in his tent, tending the wounded Machaon. Whereupon he said, "Sit thou here and drink the red wine till the fair Hecamedé shall have got ready the bath to wash the blood from thy wound, but I will ask how things fare in the battle."

So he went forth from the tent, seeking King Agamemnon. And lo! as he went the king met him, and with him were Diomed and Ulysses, who also had been wounded that day. So they held counsel together. And Agamemnon — for it troubled him sore that the people were slain — would that they should draw down the ships into the sea, and should flee homewards, as soon as the darkness should cover them, and the Trojans should cease from the battle.

But Ulysses would have none of such counsel, saying, "Now, surely, son of Atreus, thou art not worthy to rule over us, who have been men of war from our youth. Wilt thou leave this city, for the taking of which we have suffered so much? That may not be; let not any one of the Greeks hear thee say such words. And what is this, that thou wouldst have us launch our ships now, whilst the hosts are fighting? Surely, so doing, we should perish altogether, for the Greeks would not fight any more, seeing that the ships were being launched, and the men of Troy would slay us altogether.

Then King Agamemnon said, "Thou speakest well." And he went through the host, bidding the men bear themselves bravely, and all the while Poseidon put courage and strength into their hearts. Then Hector cast his spear against Ajax Telamon. The shield kept it not off, for it passed beneath, but the two belts, of the shield and of the sword, stayed it, so that it wounded not his body. Then Hector in wrath and fear went back into the ranks of his comrades; but as he went Ajax took a great stone — now were there many such which they had as props for the ships — and smote him above the rim of his shield, on the neck. As an oak falls, stricken by the thunder of Zeus, so he fell, and the Greeks rushed with a great cry to drag him to them, but could not, for all the bravest of the sons of Troy held their shields before him — Polydamas, and Æneas, and Sarpedon, and Glaucus. Then they carried him to the Xanthus, and poured water upon him. And after a while he sat up, and then again his spirit left him, for the blow had been very grievous. But when the Greeks saw that Hector had been carried out of the battle, they pressed on the more, slaying the men of Troy, and driving them back even out of the camp and across the trench. But when they came to their chariots, where they had left them on the other side of the trench, there they stood trembling and pale with fear. But Apollo, at the bidding of Zeus, went to Hector, where he lay, and healed him of his wound, pouring strength and courage into his heart, so that he went back to the battle whole and sound. Then great fear came upon the Greeks when they saw him, and Thoas the Ætolian spake, saying, —

"Surely this is a great marvel that I see with mine eyes. For we thought that Hector had been slain by the hand of Ajax, son of Telamon, and now, behold! he is come back to the battle. Many Greeks have fallen before him, and many, I trow, will fall, for of a truth some god has raised him up and helps him. But come, let all the bravest stand together. So, mighty though he be, he shall fear to enter our array."

And all the bravest gathered together and stood in the front, but the multitude made for the ships. But Hector came on, and Apollo before him, with his shoulders wrapped in cloud and the ægis shield in his hand. And many of the Greeks fell slain before the sons of Troy, as Iäsus of Athens, and Arcesilaüs the Bœotian, and Medon, who was brother to Ajax the Less, and many more. Thus the battle turned again, and came near to the trench; and now Apollo made it easy for the men of Troy to pass, so that they left not their chariots, as before, upon the brink, but drave them across.

Meanwhile Patroclus sat in the tent of Eurypylus dressing his wound and talking with him. But when he saw what had chanced, he struck his thigh with his hand and cried, —

"Now must I leave thee, Eurypylus, for I must haste to Achilles, so dreadful is now the battle. Perchance I may persuade him that he go forth to the fight."

So he ran to the tent of Achilles. And now the men of Troy were at the ships. And Hector and Ajax were fighting for one of them, and Ajax could not drive him back, and Hector could not burn the ship with fire. Then sprang forward Caletor with a torch in his hand, and Ajax smote him on the heart with a sword, so that he fell close by the ship. Then Hector cried, —

"Come now, Trojans and allies, and fight for Caletor, that the Greeks spoil him not of his arms."

So saying he cast his spear at Ajax. Him he struck not, but Cytherius, his comrade, he slew. Then was Ajax sore dismayed, and spake to Teucer his brother, —

"See now, Cytherius, our dear comrade, is dead, slain by Hector. But where are thy arrows and thy bow?"

So Teucer took his bow and laid an arrow on the string,

and smote Clitus, who was charioteer to Polydamas. And then he aimed an arrow at Hector's self; but ere he could loose it, the bowstring was broken in his hands, and the arrow went far astray, for Zeus would not that Hector should so fall. Then Teucer cried aloud to his brother, —

"Surely some god confounds our counsels, breaking my bowstring, which this very day I tied new upon my bow."

But Ajax said, "Let be thy bow, if it please not the gods, but take spear and shield and fight with the men of Troy. For though they master us to-day, they shall not take our ships for nought."

So Teucer armed himself afresh for the battle. But Hector, when he saw the broken bow, cried out, —

"Come on, ye men of Troy, for Zeus is with us. Even now he broke the bow of Teucer, the great archer. And they whom Zeus helps prevail, and they whom he favors grow not weak. Come on; for even though a man fall, it is well that he fall fighting for his fatherland; and his wife and his children are safe, nor shall his glory cease, if so be that we drive the Greeks in their ships across the sea."

And on the other side Ajax, the son of Telamon, called to the Greeks, and bade them quit themselves like men. Then the battle grew yet fiercer, for Hector slew Schedius, who led the men of Phocis, and Ajax slew Laodamas, son of Antenor, and Polydamas Otus of Cyllene. Then Meges thought to slay Polydamas; but his spear went astray, smiting down Cræsmus; and Dolops, who was grandson to Laomedon, cast his spear at Meges, but the corselet stayed the point, though it pierced the shield. But Dolops' self Menelaüs smote through the shoulder, but could not spoil him of his arms, for Hector and his brothers hindered him. So they fought, slaying one another; but Hector still waxed greater and greater in the battle, and still the men of Troy came on, and still the Greeks gave way. So they came again, these pushing forward and these yielding ground, to the ships. And Hector caught hold of one of them, even the ship of Protesilaüs: him indeed it had brought from Troy, but it took him not back, for he had fallen, slain by the hand of Hector, as he leapt, first of all the Greeks, upon the shore of Troy. This Hector caught, and the battle raged like fire about it; for the men of Troy and the Greeks were gathered round, and none fought with arrows or javelins from afar, but man to man, with battle-axe and sword and great spears pointed at either end. And many a fair weapon lay shattered on the ground, and the earth flowed with blood as with a river. But still Hector held the stem of the ship with his hand, and called to the men of Troy that they should bring fire, for that Zeus had given them the victory that day. Then even Ajax himself gave way, so did the spears of the Trojans press him; for now he stood no longer upon the stern deck, but on the rowers' bench, thrusting thence with his spear at any one who sought to set fire to the ship. And ever he cried to the Greeks with a terrible voice, —

"O ye Greeks, now must ye quit yourselves like men. For have ye any helpers behind? or have ye any walls to shelter you? No city is here, with well-built battlements, wherein ye might be safe, while the people should fight for you. For we are here in the plain of Troy, and the sea is close behind us, and we are far from our country. Wherefore all our hope is in valor, and not in shrinking back from the battle."

And still he thrust with his spear, if any of the men of Troy, at Hector's bidding, sought to bring fire against the ship. Full twelve he wounded where he stood.

CHAPTER IV.

THE DEEDS AND DEATH OF PATROCLUS.

PATROCLUS stood by Achilles, weeping bitterly. Then said Achilles, "What ails thee, Patroclus, that thou weepest like a girl-child that runs along by her mother's side and would be taken up, holding her gown, and looking at her with tearful eyes till she lift her in her arms? Hast thou heard evil news from Phthia? Menœtius yet lives, they say, and Peleus. Or art thou weeping for the Greeks, because they perish for their folly?"

Then said Patroclus, "Be not wroth with me, great Achilles, for indeed the Greeks are in grievous straits, and all their bravest are wounded, and still thou cherishest thy wrath. Surely Peleus was not thy father, nor Thetis thy mother; but the rocks begat thee, and the sea brought thee forth. Or if thou goest not to the battle, fearing some warning from the gods, yet let me go, and thy Myrmidons with me. And let me put thy armor or me; so shall the Greeks have breathing space from the war."

So he spake, entreating, nor knew that for his own doom he entreated. And Achilles made reply, —

"It is no warning that I heed, that I keep back from the war. But these men took from me my prize, which I won with my own hands. But let the past be past. I said that I would not rise up till the battle should come nigh to my own ships. But thou mayest put my armor upon thee, and lead my Myrmidons to the fight. For in truth the men of Troy are gathered as a dark cloud about the ships, and the Greeks have scarce standing-ground between them and the sea. For they see not the gleam of my helmet. And Diomed is not there with his spear; nor do I hear the voice of Agamemnon, but only the voice of Hector, as he calls the men of Troy to battle. Go, therefore, Patroclus, and drive the fire from the ships. And then come thou back, nor fight any more with the Trojans, lest thou take my glory from me. And go not near, in the delight of battle, to the walls of Troy, lest one of the gods meet thee to thy hurt; and, of a truth, the keen archer Apollo loves them well."

But as they talked the one to the other, Ajax could hold out no longer. For swords and javelins came thick upon him, and clattered on his helmet, and his shoulder was weary with the great shield which he held; and he breathed heavily and hard, and the great drops of sweat fell upon the ground. Then at the last Hector came near and smote his spear with a great sword, so that the head fell off. Then was Ajax sore afraid, and gave way, and the men of Troy set torches to the ship's stem, and a great flame shot up to the sky. And Achilles saw it, and smote his thigh and spake, —

"Haste thee, Patroclus, for I see the fire rising up from the ships. Put thou on the armor, and I will call my people to the war." So Patroclus put on the armor — corselet and shield and helmet — and bound upon his shoulder the silver-studded sword, and took a mighty spear in his hand. But the great Pelian spear he took not, for that no man but Achilles might wield. Then Automedon yoked the horses to the chariot, Bayard and Piebald, and with them in the side harness, Pedasus; and they two were deathless steeds, but he was mortal.

Meanwhile Achilles had called the Myrmidons to battle.

Fifty ships had he brought to Troy, and in each there were fifty men. Five leaders they had, and the bravest of the five was Pisander.

Then Achilles said, "Forget not, ye Myrmidons, the bold words that ye spake against the men of Troy during the days of my wrath, making complaint that I kept you from the battle against your will. Now, therefore, ye have that which you desired."

So the Myrmidons went to the battle in close array, helmet to helmet and shield to shield, close as the stones with which a builder builds a wall. And in front went Patroclus, and Automedon in the chariot beside him. Then Achilles went to his tent and took a great cup from the chest which Thetis his mother had given him. Now no man drank of that cup but he only, nor did he pour out of it libations to any of the gods but only to Zeus. This first he cleansed with sulphur, and then with water from the spring. And after this he washed his hand, and stood in the midst of the space before his tent, and poured out of it to Zeus, saying, —

"O Zeus, I send my comrade to this battle; make him strong and bold, and give him glory, and bring him home safe to the ships, and my people with him."

So he prayed, and Father Zeus heard him, and part he granted and part denied.

But when Patroclus with the Myrmidons had come to where the battle was raging about the ship of Protesilaüs, and when the men of Troy beheld him, they thought that Achilles had forgotten his wrath, and was come forth to the war. And first Patroclus slew Pyræchmes, who was the chief of the Pæonians who live on the banks of the broad Axius. Then the men of Troy turned to flee, and many chiefs of fame fell by the spears of the Greeks. So the battle rolled back to the trench, and in the trench many chariots of the Trojans were broken, but the horses of Achilles went across it at a stride, so nimble were they and strong. And the heart of Patroclus was set to slay Hector; but he could not overtake him, so swift were his horses. Then did Patroclus turn his chariot, and keep back those that fled, that they should not go to the city, and rushed hither and thither, still slaying as he went.

But Sarpedon, when he saw the Lycians dismayed and scattered, called to them that they should be of good courage, saying that he would himself make trial of this great warrior. So he leapt down from his chariot, and Patroclus also leapt down, and they rushed at each other as two eagles rush together. Then first Patroclus struck down Thrasymelus, who was the comrade of Sarpedon; and Sarpedon, who had a spear in either hand, with the one struck the horse Pedasus, which was of mortal breed, on the right shoulder, and with the other missed his aim, sending it over the left shoulder of Patroclus. But Patroclus missed not his aim, driving his spear into Sarpedon's heart. Then fell the great Lycian chief, as an oak, or a poplar, or a pine falls upon the hills before the axe. But he called to Glaucus, his companion, saying,—

"Now must thou show thyself a good warrior, Glaucus. First call the men of Lycia to fight for me, and do thou fight thyself, for it would be foul shame to thee, all thy days, if the Greeks should spoil me of my arms."

Then he died. But Glaucus was sore troubled, for he could not help him, so grievous was the wound where Teucer had wounded him. Therefore he prayed to Apollo, and Apollo helped him and made him whole. Then he went first to the Lycians, bidding them fight for their king, and then to the chiefs of the Trojans, that they should save the body of Sarpedon. And to Hector he said, —

"Little carest thou for thy allies. Lo! Sarpedon is dead, slain by Patroclus. Suffer not the Myrmidons to carry him off and do dishonor to his body."

But Hector was troubled to hear such news, and so were all the sons of Troy, for Sarpedon was the bravest of the allies, and led most people to the battle. So with a great shout they charged and drove the Greeks back a space from the body; and then again the Greeks did the like. And so the battle raged, till no one would have known the great Sarpedon, so covered was he with spears and blood and dust. But at last the Greeks drave back the men of Troy from the body, and stripped the arms, but the body itself they harmed not. For Apollo came down at the bidding of Zeus and carried it out of the midst of the battle, and washed it with water, and anointed it with ambrosia, and wrapped it in garments of the gods. And then he gave it to Sleep and Death, and these two carried it to Lycia, his fatherland.

Then did Patroclus forget the word which Achilles had spoken to him, that he should not go near to Troy, for he pursued the men of the city even to the wall. Thrice he mounted on the angle of the wall, and thrice Apollo himself drove him back, pushing his shining shield. But the fourth time the god said, "Go thou back, Patroclus. It is not for thee to take the city of Troy; no, nor for Achilles, who is far better than thou art."

So Patroclus went back, fearing the wrath of the archer-god. Then Apollo stirred up the spirit of Hector, that he should go against Patroclus. Therefore he went, with his brother Cebriones for driver of his chariot. But when they came near, Patroclus cast a great stone which he had in his hand, and smote Cebriones on the forehead, crushing it in, so that he fell headlong from the chariot. And Patroclus mocked him, saying, —

"How nimble is this man! how lightly he dives! What spoil he would take of oysters, diving from a ship, even in a stormy sea! Who would have thought that there were such skilful divers in Troy!"

Then again the battle waxed hot about the body of Cebriones, and this too, at the last, the Greeks drew unto themselves, and spoiled it of the arms. And this being accomplished, Patroclus rushed against the men of Troy. Thrice he rushed, and each time he slew nine chiefs of fame. But the fourth time Apollo stood behind him and struck him on the head and shoulders, so that his eyes were darkened. And the helmet fell from off his head, so that the horsehair plumes were soiled with dust. Never before had it touched the ground, for it was the helmet of Achilles. And also the god brake the spear in his hand, and struck the shield from his arms, and loosed his corselet. All amazed he stood, and then Euphorbus, son of Panthoüs, smote him on the back with his spear, but slew him not. Then Patroclus sought to flee to the ranks of his comrades. But Hector saw him, and thrust at him with his spear, smiting him in the groin, so that he fell. And when the Greeks saw him fall, they sent up a terrible cry. Then Hector stood over him and cried, —

"Didst thou think to spoil our city, Patroclus, and to carry away our wives and daughters in the ships? But, lo! I have slain thee, and the fowls of the air shall eat thy flesh; nor shall the great Achilles help thee at all — Achilles, who bade thee, I trow, strip the tunic from my breast, and thou thoughtest in thy folly to do it."

But Patroclus answered, "Thou boasteth much, Hector.

Yet *thou* didst not slay me, but Apollo, who took from me my arms, for had twenty such as thou met me, I had slain them all. And mark thou this: death and fate are close to thee by the hand of the great Achilles."

And Hector answered, but Patroclus was dead already,—

"Why dost thou prophesy death to me? May be the great Achilles himself shall fall by my hand."

Then he drew his spear from the wound, and went after Automedon, to slay him, but the swift horses of Achilles carried him away.

Fierce was the fight about the body of Patroclus, and many heroes fell, both on this side and on that, and first of them all Euphorbus, who, indeed, had wounded him. For as he came near to strip the dead man of his arms, Menelaüs slew him with his spear. He slew him, but took not his arms, for Hector came through the battle; nor did Menelaüs dare to abide his coming, but went back into the ranks of his own people. Then did Hector strip off the arms of Patroclus, the arms which the great Achilles had given him to wear. Then he laid hold of the body, and would have dragged it into the host of the Trojans, but Ajax Telamon came forth, and put his broad shield before it, as a lion stands before its cubs when the hunters meet it in the woods, drawing down over its eyes its shaggy brows. Then Hector gave place, but Glaucus saw him and said,—

"Now is this a shame to thee, that thou darest not to stand against Ajax. How wilt thou and thy countrymen save the city of Troy? For surely no more will thy allies fight for it. Small profit have they of thee. Did not Sarpedon fall, and didst thou not leave him to be a prey to the dogs? And now, if thou hadst stood firm and carried off Patroclus, we might have made exchange, and gained from the Greeks Sarpedon and his arms. But it may not be, for thou fearest Ajax, and fleest before him."

But Hector said, "I fear him not, nor any man. Only Zeus gives victory now to one man and now to another. But wait thou here, and see whether I be a coward, as thou sayest."

Now he had sent the armor of Patroclus to the city. But now he ran after those that were carrying it, and overtook them, and put on the armor himself (but Zeus saw him doing it, and liked it not), and came back to the battle; and all who saw him thought that it had been the great Achilles himself. Then they all charged together, and fiercer grew the battle and fiercer as the day went on. For the Greeks said one to another, "Now had the earth better yawn and swallow us up alive, than we should let the men of Troy carry off Patroclus to their city"; and the Trojans said, "Now if we must all fall by the body of this man, be it so, but we will not yield." But the horses of Achilles stood apart from the battle, when they knew that Patroclus was dead, and wept. Nor could Automedon move them with the lash, nor with gentle words, nor with threats. They would not return to the ships, nor would they go into the battle; but as a pillar stands on the tomb of some dead man, so they stood, with their heads drooped to the ground, with the big tears dropping to the earth, and their long manes trailing in the dust.

But Father Zeus beheld them, and pitied them, and said, —

"It was not well that we gave you, immortal as ye are, to a mortal man; for of all things that move on earth, mortal man is the fullest of sorrow. But Hector shall not possess you. It is enough for him, yea, and too much, that he has the arms of Achilles."

Then did the horses move from their place and obey their charioteer as before. Nor could Hector take them, though he desired them very much. And all the while the battle raged about the dead Patroclus. And at last Ajax said to Menelaüs (now these two had borne themselves more bravely in the fight than all others),—

"See if thou canst find Antilochus, Nestor's son, that he may carry the tidings to Achilles, how that Patroclus is dead."

So Menelaüs went and found Antilochus on the left of the battle, and said to him, "I have ill news for thee. Thou seest, I trow, that the men of Troy have the victory to-day. And also Patroclus lies dead. Run, therefore, to Achilles, and tell him, if haply he may save the body; but as for the arms, Hector has them already."

Sore dismayed was Antilochus to hear such tidings, and his eyes were filled with tears and his voice was choked. Yet did he give heed to the words of Menelaüs, and ran to tell Achilles of what had chanced. But Menelaüs went back to Ajax, where he had left him by Patroclus, and said,—

"Antilochus, indeed, bears the tidings to Achilles. Yet I doubt whether he will come, for all his wrath against Hector, seeing that he has no armor to cover him. Let us think, then, how we may best carry Patroclus away from the men of Troy."

Then said Ajax, "Do thou and Meriones run forward and raise the body in your arms, and I and the son of Oïleus will keep off meanwhile the men of Troy."

So Menelaüs and Meriones ran forward and lifted up the body. And the Trojans ran forward with a great shout when they saw them, as dogs run barking before the hunters when they chase a wild boar; but when the beast turns to bay, lo! they flee this way and that. So did the men of Troy flee when Ajax the Greater and Ajax the Less turned to give battle. But still the Greeks gave way, and still the Trojans came on, and ever in the front were Hector, the son of Priam, and Æneas, the son of Anchises. But in the meantime Antilochus came near to Achilles, who, indeed, seeing that the Greeks fled and the men of Troy pursued, was already sore afraid. And he said, weeping as he spake, —

"I bring ill news, — Patroclus lies low. The Greeks fight for his body, but Hector has his arms."

Then Achilles took of the dust of the plain in his hands, and poured it on his head, and lay at his length upon the ground, and tare his hair. And all the women wailed. And Antilochus sat weeping; but ever he held the hands of Achilles, lest he should slay himself in his great grief.

Then came his mother, hearing his cry, from where she sat in the depths of the sea, and laid her hand on him and said, —

"Why weepest thou, my son? Hide not the matter from me, but tell me."

And Achilles answered, "All that Zeus promised thee for me he hath fulfilled. But what profit have I, for lo! my friend Patroclus is dead, and Hector has the arms which I gave him to wear. And as for me, I care not to live, except I can avenge me upon him."

Then said Thetis, "Nay, my son, speak not thus. For when Hector dieth, thy doom also is near."

And Achilles spake in great wrath: "Would that I might die this hour, seeing that I could not help my friend, but am a burden on the earth — I, who am better in battle than all the Greeks besides. Cursed be the wrath that sets men to strive the one with the other, even as it set me to strive with King Agamemnon! But let the past be past. And as for my fate,—let it come when it may, so that I first avenge myself on Hector. Wherefore seek not to keep me back from the battle."

Then Thetis said, "Be it so; only thou canst not go without thy arms, which Hector hath. But to-morrow will I go to Hephæstus, that he may furnish thee anew."

But while they talked the men of Troy pressed the Greeks more and more, and the two heroes, Ajax the Greater and Ajax the Less, could no longer keep Hector back, but that he should lay hold of the body of Patroclus. And indeed he would have taken it, but that Zeus sent Iris to Achilles, who said,—

"Rouse thee, son of Peleus, or Patroclus will be a prey for the dogs of Troy!"

But Achilles said, "How shall I go?—for arms have I none, nor know I whose I might wear. Haply I could shift with the shield of Ajax, son of Telamon, but he, I know, is carrying it in the front of the battle."

Then answered Iris, "Go only to the trench and show thyself; so shall the men of Troy tremble and cease from the battle, and the Greeks shall have breathing space."

So he went, and Athené put her ægis about his mighty shoulders, and a golden halo about his head, making it shine as a flame of fire, even as the watch-fires shine at night from some city that is besieged. Then went he to the trench; with the battle he mingled not, heeding his mother's commands, but he shouted aloud, and his voice was as the sound of a trumpet. And when the men of Troy heard, they were stricken with fear, and the horses backed with the chariots, and the drivers were astonished when they saw the flaming fire above his head which Athené had kindled. Thrice across the trench the great Achilles shouted, and thrice the men of Troy fell back. And that hour there perished twelve chiefs of fame, wounded by their own spears or trampled by their own steeds, so great was the terror among the men of Troy.

Right gladly did the Greeks take Patroclus out of the press. Then they laid him on a bier and carried him to the tent, Achilles walking with many tears by his side.

But on the other side the men of Troy held an assembly. Standing they held it, for none dared to sit, lest Achilles should be upon them.

Then spake Polydamas: "Let us not wait here for the morning. It was well for us to fight at the ships while Achilles yet kept his wrath against Agamemnon. But now it is not so. For to-morrow he will come against us in his anger, and many will fall before him. Wherefore let us go back to the city, for high are the walls and strong the gates, and he will perish before he pass them."

Then said Hector, "This is ill counsel, Polydamas. Shall we shut ourselves up in the city, where all our goods are wasted already, buying meat for the people? Nay, let us watch to-night, and to-morrow will we fight with the Greeks. And if Achilles be indeed come forth from his tent, be it so. I will not shun to meet him, for Ares gives the victory now to one man and now to another."

So he spake, and all the people applauded, foolish, not knowing what the morrow should bring forth.

Meanwhile in the camp of the Greeks they mourned for Patroclus. And Achilles stood among his Myrmidons and said, —

"Vain was the promise that I made to Menœtius that I would bring back his son with his portion of the spoils of

Troy. But Zeus fulfils not the thoughts of man. For he lies dead, nor shall I return to the house of Peleus, my father, for I, too, must die in this land. But thee, O Patroclus, I will not bury till I bring hither the head and the arms of Hector, and twelve men of Troy to slay at thy funeral pile."

So they washed the body of Patroclus and anointed it, putting ointment into the wounds, and laid it on a bed, and covered it with a veil from the head to the feet.

Then went Thetis to the palace of Hephæstus, to pray him that he would make arms for her son. And the lady his wife, whose name was Grace, bade her welcome, and said, —

"Why comest thou, Thetis? for thou art not wont to come hither, though thou art dear to us."

Then she called to her husband that Thetis sought him, and he answered from his forge where he wrought, —

"Dear is Thetis to me, for she saved me in the old time, when my mother would have put me away because that I was lame. Greet her therefore for me; right willingly will I pay her what she deserves at my hands." Then he came from his forge and sat down by the goddess, and asked her, "What wantest thou?"

Then did Thetis tell him of her son Achilles, and of the wrong that had been done to him, and of his wrath, and of how Patroclus was dead, and the arms that he had had were lost.

Then said Hephæstus, "Be of good cheer: I will make what thou askest. Would that I could as easily keep from him the doom of death."

Then Hephæstus wrought at his forge. And first of all he made a mighty shield. On it he wrought the earth, and the sky, and the sea, and the sun, and the moon, and all the stars. He wrought also two cities. In the one there was peace, and about the other there was war. For in the first they led a bride to her home with music and dancing, and the women stood in the doors to see the show, and in the market-place the judges judged about one that had been slain, and one man said that he had paid the price of blood, and the other denied. But about the other city there sat an army besieging it, and the men of the city stood upon the wall, defending it. These had also set an ambush by a river where the herds were wont to drink. And when the herds came down, they rose up and took them, and slew the herdsmen. But the army of the besiegers heard the cry, and came swiftly on horses, and fought by the bank of the river. Also he wrought one field where many men drove the plough, and another where reapers reaped the corn, and boys gathered it in their arms to bind into sheaves, while the lord stood glad at heart beholding them. Also he wrought a vineyard, wherein was a path, and youths and maidens bearing baskets of grapes, and in the midst a boy played on a harp of gold and sang a pleasant song. Also he made a herd of oxen going from the stables to the pastures, and herdsmen and dogs, and in the front two lions had caught a mighty bull and were devouring it, while the dogs stood far off and barked. Also he made a sheepfold; also a marvellous dance of men and maidens, and these had coronets of gold, and those daggers of gold hanging from belts of silver. And round about the shield he wrought the great river of ocean. Besides the shield, he also made a corselet brighter than fire, and a great helmet with a crest of gold, and greaves of tin.

But all the while Achilles sat mourning for Patroclus, and his comrades wept about him. And at dawn Thetis brought him the arms and laid them before him. Loud they rattled on the ground, and all the Myrmidons trembled to hear; but when Achilles saw them his eyes blazed with fire, and he rejoiced in his heart. Only he said to his mother that he feared lest the body should decay, but she answered, —

"Be not troubled about this, for I will see to it. Make thy peace with Agamemnon, and go to the battle."

Then Achilles went along the shore and called the Greeks to an assembly, shouting mightily; and all, even those who were wont to abide in the ships, listened to his voice and came. So the assembly was gathered, and Achilles stood up in the midst, saying that he had put away his wrath; and King Agamemnon, sitting on his throne (for his wound hindered him from standing), said that he repented him of the wrong which he had done, only that Zeus had turned his thoughts to folly; but now he would give to Achilles all that Ulysses had promised on his behalf. And Achilles would have led the Greeks straightway to battle, but the wise Ulysses hindered him, saying that it was not well that he should send them to the fight fasting. Then did Agamemnon send to the tents of Achilles all the gifts that he had promised, and with them the maiden Briseïs. But she, when she came and saw Patroclus, beat her breast and her fair neck and face, and wailed aloud, for he had been gentle and good, she said. And all the women wailed with her, thinking each of her own sorrows.

Then the chiefs would have Achilles feast with them; but he hearkened not, for he would neither eat nor drink till he had had vengeance for the dead. And he spake, saying, —

"Often, Patroclus, hast thou ordered the feast when we

were hastening to the war. And now thou liest slain, and for grief for thee I cannot eat nor drink. For greater sorrow could not have come to me, not though Peleus himself were dead, or my young son Neoptolemus. Often did I think that I only should perish here, but that thou shouldst return and show him all that was mine — goods and servants and palace."

And as he wept the old men wept with him, thinking each of what he had left at home.

But after this the Greeks were gathered to the battle, and Achilles shone in the midst with the arms of Hephæstus upon him, and he flashed like fire. Then he spake to his horses, —

"Take heed, Bayard and Piebald, that you save your driver to-day, nor leave him dead on the field, as you left Patroclus."

Then Heré gave to the horse Bayard a voice, so that he spake: "Surely we will save thee, great Achilles; yet, for all that, doom is near to thee, nor are we the cause, but the gods and mastering Fate. Nor was it of us that Patroclus died, but Apollo slew him, and gave the glory to Hector. So shalt thou, too, die by the hands of a god and of a mortal man."

And Achilles said, "What need to tell me of my doom? Right well I know it. Yet will I not cease till I have made the Trojans weary of battle."

Then with a shout he rushed to the battle. And first there met him Æneas. Now Achilles cared not to fight with him, but bade him go back to his comrades. But Æneas would not, but told him of his race, how that he came from Zeus on his father's side, and how that his mother was Aphrodité, and that he held himself a match for any mortal man. Then he cast his spear, which struck the shield of Achilles with so dreadful a sound that the hero feared lest it should pierce it through, knowing not that the gifts of the gods are not easy for mortal man to vanquish. Two folds indeed it pierced that were of bronze, but in the gold it was stayed, and there were yet two of tin within. Then Achilles cast his spear. Through the shield of Æneas it passed, and though it wounded him not, yet was he sore dismayed, so near it came. Then Achilles drew his sword and rushed on Æneas, and Æneas caught up a great stone to cast at him. But it was not the will of the gods that Æneas should perish, seeing that he and his sons after him should rule over the men of Troy in the ages to come. Therefore Poseidon lifted him up and bore him over the ranks of men to the left of the battle, but first he drew the spear out of the shield and laid it at the feet of Achilles. Much the hero marvelled to see it, crying,—

"This is a great wonder that I see with mine eyes. For, lo! the spear is before me, but the man whom I sought to slay I see not. Of a truth Æneas spake truth, saying that he was dear to the immortal gods."

Then he rushed into the battle, slaying as he went. And Hector would have met him, but Apollo stood by him and said, "Fight not with Achilles, lest he slay thee." Therefore he went back among the men of Troy. Many did Achilles slay, and among them Polydorus, son of Priam, who, because he was the youngest and very dear, his father suffered not to go to the battle. Yet he went, in his folly, and being very swift of foot, he trusted in his speed, running through the foremost of the fighters. But as he ran Achilles smote him and wounded him to the death. But when Hector saw it he could not bear any more to stand apart, Therefore he rushed at Achilles, and Achilles rejoiced to see him, saying, "This is the man who slew my comrade." But they fought not then, for when Hector cast his spear, Athené turned it aside, and when Achilles charged, Apollo bore Hector away.

Then Achilles turned to the others, and slew multitudes of them, so that they fled, part across the plain, and part to the river, the eddying Xanthus. And these leapt into the water as locusts leap into a river when the fire which men light drives them from the fields. And all the river was full of horses and men. Then Achilles leapt into the stream, leaving his spear on the bank, resting on the tamarisk trees. Only his sword had he, and with this he slew many; and they were as fishes which fly from some great dolphin in the sea. In all the bays of a harbor they hide themselves, for the great beast devours them apace. So did the Trojans hide themselves under the banks of the river. And when Achilles was weary of slaying he took twelve alive, whom he would slay on the tomb of Patroclus. Nor was there but one who dared to stand up against him, and this was Asteropæus, who was the grandson of the river-god Axius, and led the men of Pæonia. And Achilles wondered to see him, and said,—

"Who art thou, that standest against me?"

And he said, "I am the grandson of the river-god Axius, fairest of all the streams on the earth, and I lead the men of Pæonia."

And as he spake he cast two spears, one with each hand, for he could use either alike; and the one struck the shield, nor pierced it through, for the gold stayed it, and the other grazed the right hand so that the blood spurted forth. Then did Achilles cast his spear, but missed his aim, and the great spear stood fast in the bank. And thrice Asteropæus strove to draw it forth. Thrice he strove in vain, and the fourth time he strove to break the spear. But as he strove Achilles smote him that he died. Yet had he some glory, for that he wounded the great Achilles.

But Priam stood on a tower of the wall and saw the people. Sore troubled was he, and he hastened down to the gates and said to the keepers, "Keep the wicket-gates in your hands open, that the people may enter in, for they fly before Achilles." So the keepers held the wicket-gates in their hands, and the people hastened in, wearied with toil and thirst, and covered with dust, and Achilles followed close upon them. And that hour would the Greeks have taken the city of Troy, but that Apollo saved it. For he put courage into the heart of Antenor's son Agenor, standing also by him, that he should not be slain. Therefore Agenor stood, thinking within himself, —

"Shall I now flee with these others? Nay, for not the less will Achilles take me and slay me, and I shall die as a coward dies. Or shall I flee across the plain to Ida, and hide me in the thickets, and come back at nightfall to the city? Yet should he see me he will overtake me and smite me, so swift of foot is he and strong. But what if I stand to meet him before the gates? Well, he, too, is a mortal man, and his flesh may be pierced by the spear."

Therefore he stood till Achilles should come near. And when he came he cast his spear, striking the leg below the knee, but the greave turned off the spear, so strong was it. But when Achilles would have slain him, lo! Apollo lifted him up and set him within the city. And that the men of Troy might have space to enter, he took upon him Agenor's shape. And the false Agenor fled, and Achilles pursued. But meanwhile the men of Troy flocked into the city, nor did they stay to ask who was safe and who was dead, in such haste and fear did they flee.

CHAPTER V.

THE DEATH OF HECTOR.

THE Trojans were now safe in the city, refreshing themselves after all their grievous toil. Only Hector remained outside the walls, standing in front of the great Scæan gates. But all the while Achilles was fiercely pursuing the false Agenor, till at last Apollo turned and spake to him, —

"Why dost thou pursue me, swift-footed Achilles? Hast thou not yet found out that I am a god, and that all thy fury is in vain? And now all the sons of Troy are safe in their city, and thou art here, far out of the way, seeking to slay me, who cannot die."

In great wrath Achilles answered him, "Thou hast done me wrong in so drawing me away from the wall, great archer, most mischief-loving of all the gods that are. Had it not been for this, many a Trojan more had bitten the ground. Thou hast robbed me of great glory, and saved thy favorites. O that I had the power to take vengeance on thee! Thou hadst paid dearly for thy cheat!"

Then he turned and rushed towards the city, swift as a racehorse whirls a chariot across the plain. Old Priam spied him from the walls, with his glittering armor, bright as that brightest of the stars — men call it Orion's dog — which shines at vintage-time, a baleful light, bringing the fevers of autumn to men. And the old man groaned aloud when he saw him, and stretching out his hands, cried to his son Hector, where he stood before the gates, eager to do battle with this dread warrior, —

"Wait not for this man, dear son, wait not for him, lest thou die beneath his hand, for indeed he is stronger than thou. Wretch that he is! I would that the gods bare such love to him as I bear! Right soon would the dogs and vultures eat him. Of many brave sons has he bereaved me. Two I miss to-day — Polydorus and Lycaon. May be they are yet alive in the host of the Greeks, and I shall buy them back with gold, of which I have yet great store in my house. And if they are dead, sore grief will it be to me and to the mother who bare them; but little will care the other sons of Troy, so that thou fall not beneath the hand of Achilles. Come within the walls, dear child; come to save the sons and daughters of Troy; come in pity for me, thy father, for whom, in my old age, an evil fate is in store, to see sons slain with the sword, and daughters carried into captivity, and babes dashed upon the ground. Ay, and last of all, the dogs which I have reared in my palace will devour me, lapping my blood and tearing my flesh as I lie on the threshold of my home. That a young man should fall in battle and suffer such lot as happens to the slain, this is to be borne; but that such dishonor should be done to the white hair and white beard of the old, mortal eyes can see no fouler sight than this."

Thus old Priam spake, but could not turn the heart of his son. And from the wall on the other side of the gate his mother called to him, weeping sore, and if perchance she might thus move his pity, she bared her bosom in his sight, and said, —

"Pity me, my son; think of the breast which I gave thee in the old days, and stilled thy cries. Come within the walls; wait not for this man, nor stand in battle against him. If he slay thee, nor I, nor thy wife, shall pay thee the last honors of the dead, but far away by the ships of the Greeks the dogs and vultures will devour thee."

So father and mother besought their son, but all in vain. He was still minded to abide the coming of Achilles. Just as in the mountains a great snake at its hole abides the coming of a man : fierce glare its eyes, and it coils its tail about its hole: so Hector waited for Achilles; and as he waited he thought thus within himself, —

"Woe is me if I go within the walls! Polydamas will be the first to reproach me, for he advised me to bring back the sons of Troy to the city before the night when Achilles roused himself to war. But I would not listen to him. Would that I had! it had been much better for us; but now I have destroyed the people by my folly. I fear the sons and daughters of Troy, what they may say; I fear lest some coward reproach me; 'Hector trusted in his strength, and lo! he has destroyed the people.' Better were it for me either to slay Achilles or to fall by his hand with honor here before the walls. Or, stay: shall I put down my shield, and lay aside my helmet, and lean my spear against the wall and go to meet the great Achilles, and promise that we will give back the fair Helen, and all the wealth that Paris carried off with her; ay, and render up all the wealth that there is in the city, that the Greeks may divide it among themselves, binding the sons of Troy with an oath that they keep nothing back? But this is idle talk : he will have no shame or pity, but will slay me while I stand without arms or armor before him. It is not for us to talk as a youth and a maiden talk together. It is better to meet in arms, and see whether the ruler of Olympus will give victory to him or to me."

Thus he thought in his heart; and Achilles came near, brandishing over his right shoulder the great Pelian spear, and the flash of his arms was as the flame of fire or as the rising sun. And Hector trembled when he saw him, nor dared to abide his coming. Fast he fled from the gates, and fast Achilles pursued him, as a hawk, fastest of all the birds of air, pursues a dove upon the mountains. Past the watch-tower they ran, past the wind-blown fig-tree, along the wagon-road which went about the walls, and they came to the fair-flowing fountain where from two springs rises the stream of eddying Scamander. Hot is one spring, and a steam ever goes up from it, as from a burning fire; and cold is the other, cold, even in the summer heats, as hail or snow or ice. There are fair basins of stone where the wives and fair daughters of Troy were wont to wash their garments, but that was in the old days of peace, or ever the Greeks came to the land. Past the springs they ran, one flying, the other pursuing: brave was he that fled, braver he that pursued; it was no sheep for sacrifice or shield of ox-hide for which they ran, but for the life of Hector, the tamer of horses. Thrice they ran round the city, and all the gods looked on.

And Zeus said, "This is a piteous sight that I behold. My heart is grieved for Hector — Hector, who has ever worshipped me with sacrifice, now on the heights of Ida, and now in the citadel of Troy; and now the great Achilles is pursuing him round the city of Priam. Come, ye gods, let us take counsel together. Shall we save him from death, or let him fall beneath the hand of Achilles?"

Then Athené said, "What is this that thou sayest, great sire? — to rescue a man whom fate has appointed to die? Do it, if it be thy will; but we, the other gods, approve it not."

Zeus answered her, "My heart is loath; yet I would do thee pleasure. Be it as thou wilt."

Then Athené came down in haste from the top of Olympus, and still Hector fled and Achilles pursued, just as a dog pursues a fawn upon the hills. And ever Hector made for the gates, or to get shelter beneath the towers, if haply those that stood upon them might defend him with their spears; and ever Achilles would get before him, and drive him towards the plain. So they ran, one making for the city, and the other driving him to the plain. Just as in a dream, when one seems to fly and another seems to pursue, and the one cannot escape and the other cannot overtake, so these two ran together. But as for Hector, Apollo even yet helped him, and gave him strength and nimble knees, else could he not have held out against Achilles, who was swiftest of foot among the sons of men.

Now Achilles had beckoned to the Greeks that no man should throw his spear at Hector, lest, perchance, he should be robbed of his glory. And when the two came in their running for the fourth time to the springs of Scamander, Zeus held out the great balance of doom, and in one scale he put the fate of Achilles, and in the other the fate of Hector; and lo! the scale of Hector sank down to the realms of death, and Apollo left him.

Then Athené lighted down from the air close to Achilles and said, "This, great Achilles, is our day of glory, for we shall slay Hector, mighty warrior though he be. For it is his doom to die, and not Apollo's self shall save him. But stand thou still and take breath, and I will give this man heart to meet thee in battle."

So Achilles stood, leaning upon his spear. And Athené took the shape of Deïphobus, and came near to Hector and said, —

"Achilles presses thee hard, my brother, pursuing thee

thus round the city of Priam. Come, let us make a stand and encounter him."

Then Hector answered him, "Deïphobus, I always loved thee best of all my brothers; but now I love thee yet more, for that thou alone, while all others remained within, hast ventured forth to stand by my side."

But the false Deïphobus said, "Much did father and mother and all my comrades beseech me to remain. But my heart was sore troubled for thee, and I could not stay. But let us stand and fight this man, not stinting our spears, and see whether he shall carry our spoil to the ships or we shall slay him here."

Then the two chiefs came near to each other, and Hector with the waving plume spake first and said, "Thrice, great Achilles, hast thou pursued me round the walls of Troy, and I dared not stand up against thee; but now I fear thee no more. Only let us make this covenant between us: if Zeus give me the victory, I will do no dishonor to thy body; thy arms and armor will I take, and give back thy body to the Greeks; and do thou promise to do likewise."

But Achilles scowled at him and said, "Hector, talk not of covenants to me. Men and lions make no oaths between each other, neither is there any agreement between wolves and sheep. So there shall be no covenant between me and thee. One of us two shall fall; and now is the time for thee to show thyself a warrior, for of a truth Athené will slay thee by my spear, and thou shalt pay the penalty for all my comrades whom thou hast slain."

Then he threw the mighty spear, but Hector saw it coming and avoided it, crouching on the ground, so that the mighty spear flew above his head and fixed itself in the earth. But Athené snatched it from the ground and gave it back to Achilles, Hector not perceiving.

Then Hector spake to Achilles: "Thou hast missed thy aim, great Achilles. It was no word of Zeus that thou spakest, prophesying my doom, but thou soughtest to cheat me, terrifying me by thy words. Thou shalt not drive thy steel into my back, but here into my breast, if the gods will it so. But now look out for my spear. Would it might bury itself in thy flesh. The battle would be easier for the men of Troy were thou only out of the way."

And as he spake he threw his long-shafted spear. True aim he took, for the spear struck the very middle of Achilles' shield. It struck, but pierced it not, but bounded far away, for the shield was not of mortal make. And Hector stood dismayed, for he had not another spear, and when he called to Deïphobus that he should give him another, lo! Deïphobus was gone. Then Hector knew that his end was come, and he said to himself, "Now have the gods called me to my doom. I thought that Deïphobus was near; but he is within the walls, and the help which he promised me was but a cheat with which Athené cheated me. Zeus and Apollo are with me no more; but, if I must die, let me at least die in such a deed as men of after time may hear of."

So he spake, and drew the mighty sword that hung by his side; then, as an eagle rushes through the clouds to pounce on a leveret or a lamb, rushed on the great Achilles. But he dealt never a blow; for Achilles charged to meet him, his shield before his breast, his helmet bent forward as he ran, with the long plumes streaming behind, and the gleam of his spear-point was as the gleam of the evening star, which is the fairest of all the stars in heaven. One moment he thought where he should drive it home, for the armor which Hector had won from Patroclus guarded him well; but one spot there was, where by the collar-bone the neck joins the shoulder (and nowhere is the stroke of sword or spear more deadly). There he drave in the spear, and the point stood out behind the neck, and Hector fell in the dust.

Then Achilles cried aloud, "Hector, thou thoughtest in the day when thou didst spoil Patroclus of his arms that thou wouldst be safe from vengeance, taking, forsooth, no account of me. And lo! thou art fallen before me, and now the dogs and vultures shall devour thee, but to him all the Greeks shall give due burial."

But Hector, growing faint, spake to him, "Nay, great Achilles, by thy life, and by thy knees, and by thy parents dear, I pray thee, let not the dogs of the Greeks devour me. Take rather the ransom, gold and bronze, that my father and mother shall pay thee, and let the sons and daughters of Troy give me burial rites."

But Achilles scowled at him, and cried, "Dog, seek not to entreat me! I could mince that flesh of thine and devour it raw, such grief hast thou wrought me. Surely the dogs shall devour thee, nor shall any man hinder. No ransom, though it were ten times told, should buy thee back; no, not though Priam should offer thy weight in gold."

Then Hector, who was now at the point to die, spake to him. "I know thee well, what manner of man thou art, that the heart in thy breast is iron only. Only beware lest some vengeance from the gods come upon thee in the day when Paris and Apollo shall slay thee, for all thy valor, by the Scæan gates."

So speaking, he died. But Achilles said, "Die, hound;

but my fate I meet when Zeus and the other gods decree."

Then he drew his spear out of the corpse and stripped off the arms; and all the Greeks came about the dead man, marvelling at his stature and beauty, and no man came but wounded the dead corpse. And one would say to another, "Surely this Hector is less dreadful now than in the day when he would burn our ships with fire."

Then Achilles devised a ruthless thing in his heart. He pierced the ankle-bones of Hector, and so bound the body with thongs of ox-hide to the chariot, letting the head drag behind, the head that once was so fair, and now was so disfigured in the dust. So he dragged Hector to the ships. And Priam saw him from the walls, and scarce could his sons keep him back, but that he should go forth and beg the body of his dear son from him who had slain him. And Hecuba his mother also bewailed him, but Andromaché knew not as yet of what had befallen. For she sat in her dwelling, wearing a great purple mantle broidered with flowers. And she bade her maidens make ready a bath for Hector, when he should come back from the battle, nor knew that he should never need it more. But the voice of wailing from the town came to her, and she rose up hastily in great fear, and dropped the shuttle from her hand and called to her maidens, —

"Come with me, ye maidens, that I may see what has befallen, for I heard the voice of Queen Hecuba, and I fear me much that some evil has come to the children of Priam. For it may be that Achilles has run between Hector and the city, and is pursuing him to the plain, for never will Hector abide with the army, but will fight in the front, so bold is he."

Then she hasted through the city like as she were mad.

And when she came to the wall she stood and looked; and lo! the horses of Achilles were dragging Hector to the ships. Then did darkness come on her, and she fell back fainting, and from her fair head dropped the net and the wreath and the diadem which golden Aphrodité gave her on the day when Hector of the waving plume took her from the house of Eëtion to be his wife.

CHAPTER VI.

Although Hector, that was the chief stay of Troy was dead, yet could not King Agamemnon take the city. And when it came to pass that Achilles was slain, being smitten by Paris with an arrow (but some say that Apollo slew him), then did he wellnigh despair. But the soothsayers said, "Send, O King, for Philoctetes, and thou shalt have thy desire."

Now Philoctetes had been companion to Hercules in many of his labors, and also had been with him when he died upon Mount Æta. For which cause Hercules gave him the bow and the arrows which he bare, having received them at the first from Apollo. A very mighty bow it was, shooting arrows so as none other could do, and the arrows were sure dealers of death, for they had been dipped in the blood of the great dragon of Lerna, and the wounds which they made no physician might heal. But it chanced that the Prince, being on his voyage to Troy, landed at the island of Chrysa, where there was an altar of Athené, the goddess of the place, and, desiring to show the altar to his companions, he approached it too nearly; whereupon the serpent that guarded it, lest it should be profaned, bit him in the foot. The wound was very sore and could not be healed, but tormented him day and night with grievous pains, making him groan and cry aloud. And when men were troubled with his complainings, and also with the noisome stench of his wound, the chiefs took counsel together, and it seemed good to the sons of Atreus, King Agamemnon and King Menelaüs, who were the leaders of the host, that he should be left alone on the island of Lemnos. This matter they committed to Ulysses, who did according to their bidding. Now, therefore, the king took counsel with his chiefs; and they chose Ulysses, who was crafty beyond all other men, to accomplish this matter, and with him they sent Neoptolemus, the son of Achilles, who excelled in strength, even as his father had done.

Now when these two were landed upon the island, Ulysses led the way to the place where in time past he had left Philoctetes. A cave it was in the cliff, with two mouths to it, of which the one looked to the east and the other to the west, so that in winter time a man might see the sun and be warm, but in summer the wind blew through it, bringing coolness and sleep, and a little below was a spring of fair water to drink. Then said Ulysses to Neoptolemus, "Go and spy out the place, and see whether or no the man be there."

And the Prince went up and looked into the cave, and found that it was empty, but that there were signs of one who dwelt there, a bed of leaves, and a cup of wood, very rudely fashioned, and pieces of wood for kindling fires, and also, a very piteous sight, the rags wherewith the sick man was wont to dress his wound. And when he had told what he saw, Ulysses said, "That the man dwelleth here is manifest; nor can he be far away, for how can one that is wounded travel far? Doubtless he is gone to some place whither the birds resort to slay them, or, haply, to find some herb wherewith to assuage his pain. But do thou set one who will wait for his coming, for it would fare ill with me should he find me."

And when the watch had been set Ulysses said again, "I will tell what it is needful for thee to say and do. Only thou must be bold, son of Achilles, and that not only with thy hand, but in heart also, if what I shall now unfold to thee shall seem new or strange. Hearken then: when the man shall ask thee who thou art, and whence thou comest, thou shalt answer him that thou art the son of Achilles, and that thou hast left the host of the Greeks, because they had done thee great wrong, for that, having prayed thee to come as not being able to take the great city of Troy without thee, yet they would not deliver to thee the arms of thy father Achilles, but gave them to Ulysses. And here thou mayest speak against me all kinds of evil, for such words will not trouble me, but if thou accomplish not this thing thou wilt trouble the whole host of the Greeks. For know that without this man's bow thou canst not take the city of Troy; know also that thou only canst approach him without peril, not being of the number of those who sailed with him at the first. And if it please thee not to get the bow by stealth, for this indeed thou must do — and I know thee to be one that loveth not to speak falsely or to contrive deceit — yet bethink thee that victory is sweet. Be thou bold to-day, and we will be righteous to-morrow."

Then the Prince made reply, "'Tis not in me, son of Laertes, to work by craft and guile, neither was it in my father before me. I am ready to carry off this man with a strong arm; and how, being a cripple, shall he stand against us? but deceit I will not use. And though I should be loath to fail thee in this our common enterprise, yet were this better than to prevail by fraud."

Then said Ulysses, "And I, too, in my youth would do all things by the hand and not by the tongue; but now I know that the tongue hath alone the mastery."

And the Prince replied, "But thou biddedst me speak the thing that is false."

"I bid thee prevail over Philoctetes by craft."

"But why may I not persuade him, or even constrain him by force?"

"To persuasion he will not hearken, and force thou mayest not use, for he hath arrows that deal death without escape."

"But is it not a base thing for a man to lie?"

"Surely not, if a lie save him."

"Tell me what is the gain to me if this man come to Troy."

"Without this bow and these arrows Troy falleth not. For though it is the pleasure of the Gods that thou take the city, yet canst not thou take it without these, nor indeed these without thee."

And when the Prince had mused a while, he said, "If this be so with the arms, I must needs get them."

Then Ulysses said, "Do this, and thou shalt gain a double honor."

And the Prince said, "What meanest thou by thy 'double honor'? Tell me, and I refuse no more."

"The praise of wisdom and of courage also."

"Be it so: I will do this deed, nor count it shame."

"'Tis well," said Ulysses, "and now I will despatch this watcher to the ship, whom I will send again in pilot's disguise if thou desire, and it seems needful. Also I myself will depart, and may Hermes, the god of craft, and Athené, who ever is with me, cause us to prevail."

After a while Philoctetes came up the path to the cave, very slowly, and with many groans. And when he saw the strangers (for now some of the ship's crew were with Prince Neoptolemus) he cried, "Who are ye that are come to this inhospitable land? Greeks I know you to be by your garb; but tell me more."

And when the Prince had told his name and lineage, and that he was sailing from Troy, Philoctetes cried, "Sayest thou from Troy? Yet surely thou didst not sail with us in the beginning."

"What?" cried the Prince. "Hadst thou then a share in this matter of Troy?"

And Philoctetes made reply, "Knowest thou not whom thou seest? Hast thou not heard the story of my sorrows?" And when he heard that the young man knew nothing of these things: "Surely this is sorrow upon sorrow if no report of my state hath come to the land of Greece, and I lie here alone, and my disease groweth upon me, but my enemies laugh and keep silence!" And then he told his name and fortunes, and how the Greeks had left him on the shore while he slept, and how it was the tenth year of his sojourning in the island. "For know," he said, "that it is without haven or anchorage, and no man cometh hither of his free will; and if any come unwilling, as indeed it doth sometimes chance, they speak soft words to me and give me, haply, some meat; but when I make suit to them that they carry me to my home, they will not. And this wrong the sons of Atreus and Ulysses have worked against me; for which may the gods who dwell in Olympus make them equal recompense."

"And I," said the Prince, "am no lover of these men. For when Achilles was dead——"

"How sayest thou? Is the son of Peleus dead?"

"Yea; but it was the hand of a god and not of a man that slew him."

"A mighty warrior slain by a mighty foe! But say on."

"Ulysses, and Phœnix who was my sire's foster-father, came in a ship to fetch me; and when I was come to the camp they even greeted me kindly, and sware that it was Achilles' self they saw, so like was I to my sire. And, my mourning ended, I sought the sons of Atreus and asked of them the arms of my father, but they made answer that they had given them to Ulysses; and Ulysses, chancing to be there, affirmed that they had done well, seeing that he had saved them from the enemy. And when I could prevail nothing, I sailed away in great wrath."

"'Tis even," Philoctetes made reply, "as I should have judged of them. But I marvel that the Greater Ajax endured to see such doings."

"Ah! but he was already dead."

"This is grievous news. And how fares old Nestor of Pylos?"

"But ill, for his eldest born, Antilochus, is dead."

"I could have spared any rather than these two, Ajax and Antilochus. But Patroclus, where was he when thy father died?"

"He was already slain. For 'tis ever thus that war taketh the true man and leaveth the false. But of these things I have had enough and more than enough. Henceforth my island of Scyros, though it be rocky and small, shall content me. And now, Prince Philoctetes, I go, for the wind favors us, and we must take the occasion which the gods give us."

And when Philoctetes knew that Neoptolemus was about to depart, he besought him with many prayers that he would take him also on his ship; for the voyage, he said, would not be of more than a single day. "Put me," he said, "where thou wilt, in forecastle, or hold, or stern, and set me on shore even as it may seem best to thee. Only take me from this place." And the sailors also made entreaty to the Prince that he would do so; and he, after a while, made as if he consented to their prayers.

But while Philoctetes was yet thanking him and his companions, there came two men to the cave, of whom one was a sailor in the Prince's ship, and the other a merchant. And the merchant said that he was sailing from Troy to his home, and that chancing to come to the island, and knowing that the Prince was there, he judged it well to tell him his news; 'twas briefly this, that Phœnix and the sons of Theseus had sailed, having orders from the sons of Atreus that they should bring the Prince back; and also that Ulysses and Diomed were gone on another errand, even to fetch some one of whom the rulers had need. And when the Prince would know who he might be, the merchant bade him say who it was standing near; and when he heard that it was Philoctetes, he cried, "Haste thee to thy ship, son of Achilles, for this is the very man whom the two are coming to fetch. Haply thou hast not heard what befell at Troy. There is a certain Helenus, son of King Priam, and a famous soothsayer. Him Ulysses, the man of craft, took a prisoner, and brought into the assembly of Greeks; and the man prophesied to them that they should never take the city of Troy, unless they should bring thither the Prince Philoctetes from the island whereon he dwelt. And Ulysses said, 'If I bring not the man, whether willing or unwilling, then cut off my head.'"

And when Philoctetes heard this his anger was very great, and he became yet more eager to depart. But first he must go into the cave and fetch such things as he needed, herbs with which he was wont to soothe the pains of his wounds, and all the furniture of his bow. And when he spake of the bow, the Prince asked whether it was indeed the famous bow of Hercules that he carried in his hand, and would fain, he said, touch it, if only it were lawful so to do. And Philoctetes answered, "Yes, thou shalt touch it and handle it, which, indeed, no other man hath ever done, for thou hast done a good deed to me, and it was for a good deed that I myself also received it."

But when they would have gone towards the ship, the pangs of his wound came upon Philoctetes. And then at first he cried, saying that it was well with him; but at the last he could endure no more, and cried to the Prince that he should draw his sword and smite off the foot, nor heed if he should slay him; only he would be rid of the pain. And then he bade him take the bow and keep it for him while he slept, for that sleep came ever upon him after these great pains. Only he must keep it well, especially if those two, Ulysses and Diomed, should chance to come in the meanwhile. And when the Prince had promised this, Philoctetes gave him the bow, saying, "Take it, my son, and pray to the jealous gods that it bring not sorrow to thee as it hath brought sorrow to me, and to him that was its master before me."

And after a while the sick man slept. And the Prince, with the sailors that were his companions, watched by him the while.

But when the sailors would have had the Prince depart, seeing that he had now the great bow and the arrows, for whose sake he had come, he would not, for they would be of no avail, he said, without the archer himself. And in no long space of time the sick man woke. Right glad was he to see that the strangers had not departed, for, indeed, he had scarce hoped that this might be. Therefore commending the young man much for his courage and loving kindness, he would have him help him straightway to the ship, that his pain having now ceased awhile, they might be ready to depart without delay. So they went, but the Prince was sorely troubled in his mind and cried, "Now what shall I do?" and "now am I at my wits' end, so that even words fail me." At which words, indeed, Philoctetes was grieved, thinking that it repented the Prince of his purpose, so that he said, "Doth the trouble of my disease then hinder thee from taking me in thy ship?"

Then said the Prince, "All is trouble when a man leaveth his nature to do things that are not fitting."

And Philoctetes made answer, "Nay, is not this a fitting thing, seeing of what sire thou art the son, to help a brave man in his trouble?"

"Can I endure to be so base," said the Prince, "hiding that which I should declare, and speaking the thing that is false?" And while Philoctetes still doubted whether he repented not of his purpose, he cried aloud, "I will hide the thing no longer. Thou shalt sail with me to Troy."

"What sayest thou?"

"I say that thou shalt be delivered from these pains, and shalt prevail together with me over the great city of Troy."

"What treachery is this? What hast thou done to me? Give me back the bow."

"Nay, that I cannot do, for I am under authority, and must needs obey."

And when Philoctetes heard these words, he cried with a very piteous voice, "What a marvel of wickedness thou art that hast done this thing. Art thou not ashamed to work such wrong to a suppliant? Give me my bow, for it is my life. But I speak in vain, for he goeth away and heedeth me not. Hear me then, ye waters and cliffs, and ye beasts of the field, who have been long time my wonted company, for I have none else to hearken to me. Hear what the son of Achilles hath done to me. For he sware that he would carry me to my home, and lo! he taketh me to Troy. And he gave me the right hand of fellowship, and now he robbeth me of the bow, the sacred bow of Hercules. Nay,—for I will make trial of him once more,—give back this thing to me and be thy true self. What sayest thou? Nothing? Then am I undone. O cavern of the rock wherein I have dwelt, behold how desolate I am! Never more shall I slay with my arrows bird of the air or beast of the field; but that which I hunted shall pursue me, and that on which I fed shall devour me."

And the Prince was cut to the heart when he heard these words, hating the thing which he had done, and cursing the day on which he had come from Scyros to the plains of Troy. Then turning himself to the sailors, he asked what he should do, and was even about to give back the bow, when Ulysses, who was close at hand, watching what should be done, ran forth crying that he should hold his hand.

Then said Philoctetes, "Is this Ulysses that I see? Then am I undone."

"'Tis even so: and as for what thou asketh of this youth, that he should give back the bow, he shall not do it; but rather thou shalt sail with us to Troy; and if thou art not willing, these that stand by shall take thee by force."

"Lord of fire, that rulest this land of Lemnos, hearest thou this?"

"Nay, 'tis Zeus that is master here, and Zeus hath commanded this deed."

"What lies are these? Thou makest the gods false as thyself."

"Not so. They are true and I also. But this journey thou must take."

"Methinks I am a slave, and not freeborn, that thou talkest thus."

"Thou art peer to the bravest, and with them shalt take the great city of Troy."

"Never; I had sooner cast myself down from this cliff."

Then Ulysses cried to the men that they should lay hold on him; and this they straightway did. Then Philoctetes in many words reproached him with all the wrongs that he had done; how at the first he had caused him to be left on this island, and now had stolen his arms, not with his own hands, indeed, but with craft and deceit, serving himself of a simple youth, who knew not but to do as he was bidden. And he prayed to the gods that they would avenge him on all that had done him wrong, and chiefly on this man Ulysses.

Then Ulysses made reply, "I can be all things as occasion serveth; such as thou sayest, if need be; and yet no man more pious if the time call for goodness and justice. One thing only I must needs do, and that is to prevail. Yet here I will yield to thee. Thou wilt not go; so be it. Loose him! We need thee not, having these arms of thine. Teucer is with us, an archer not one whit less skilful than thou. And now I leave thee to this Lemnos of thine. May be this bow shall bring me the honor which thou refusest."

When he had thus spoken he departed, and the Prince Neoptolemus with him. Only the Prince gave permission to the sailors that they should tarry with the sick man till it was time to make ready for the voyage.

Then Philoctetes bewailed himself, crying to his bow, "O my bow, my beloved, that they have wrested from my hands, surely, if thou knowest aught, thou grievest to see that the man who was the comrade of Hercules will never hold thee more, but that base hands will grasp thee, mixing thee with all manner of deceit." And then again he called to the birds of the air and the beasts of the field, that they should not fly from him any more, seeing that he had now no help against them, but should come and avenge themselves upon him and devour him. And still the sailors would have comforted him. Also they sought to persuade him that he should listen to the chiefs; but he would not, crying that the lightning should smite him before he would go to Troy and help them that had done him such wrong. And at the last he cried that they should give him a spear or a sword, that he might be rid of his life.

But while they thus talked together, the Prince came back like one that is in haste, with Ulysses following him, who cried, "Wherefore turnest thou back?"

"To undo what I did amiss."

"How sayest thou? When didst thou thus?"

"When I listened to thee, and used deceit to a brave man."

"What wilt thou then? (I fear me much what this fool may do.)"

"I will give back this bow and these arrows to him from whom I took them by craft."

"That shalt thou not do."

"But who shall hinder me?"

"That will I, and all the sons of the Greeks with me."

"This is idle talk for a wise man as thou art."

"Seest thou this sword whereto I lay my hand?"

"If thou talkest of swords, thou shalt see right soon that I also have a sword."

"Well — I let thee alone. To the host will I tell this matter; they shall judge thee."

"Now thou speakest well; be ever as wise; so shalt thou keep thy foot out of trouble."

Then the Prince called to Philoctetes, who, being loosed by the sailors, had hidden himself in the cave, and asked of him again whether he were willing to sail with him, or were resolved to abide in the island.

And when the man had denied that he would go, and had begun again to call down a curse on the sons of Atreus, and on Ulysses, and on the Prince himself, then the Prince bade him stay his speech, and gave him back the bow and the arrows.

And when Ulysses, seeing this deed, was very wroth, and threatened vengeance, Philoctetes put an arrow to the string, and drew the bow to the full, and would have shot at the man, but the Prince stayed his hand.

And then the Prince was urgent with him that he should cease from his anger, and should sail with him to Troy, saying that there he should be healed by the great physician, the son of Asclepius, and should also win great glory by taking the city, and that right soon; for that the soothsayer Helenus had declared that it was the will of the gods that the city of Troy should be taken that same summer.

But for all this he prevailed nothing; for Philoctetes was obstinate that he would not go to Troy, nor do any pleasure to the chiefs who had done him such wrong. But he would that the Prince should fulfil the promise which he had made, that he would carry him in his ship to his own country. And this the Prince said that he would do.

And now the two were about to depart to the ship, when lo! there appeared in the air above their heads the great Hercules. Very wonderful was he to behold, with bright raiment, and a great glory shining from his face, even as the everlasting gods beheld him with whom he dwelt in the palace of Olympus. And Hercules spake, saying,—

"Go not yet, son of Pœas, before thou hearest what I shall say to thee. For 'tis Hercules whom thou seest and hearest; and I am come from my dwelling in heaven to declare to thee the will of Zeus. Know then that even as I attained to this blessedness after much toil, so shall it be with thee. For thou shalt go to the land of Troy; and first thou shalt be healed of thy grievous sickness, and afterwards thou shalt slay Paris with thine arrows, and shalt take the city of Troy, whereof thou shalt carry the spoils to thy home, even to Pœas thy father, having received from thy fellows the foremost prize for valor. But remember that all that thou winnest in this warfare thou must take as an offering to my tomb. And to thee, son of Achilles, I say; thou canst not take the city of Troy without this man, nor he without thee. Whereof, as two lions that consort together, guard ye each other. And I will send Asclepius to heal him of his sickness; for it is the will of the gods that Troy should yet again be taken by my bow. And remember this, when ye lay waste the land, to have the gods and that which belongeth to them in reverence."

Then said Philoctetes, "O my master, whom I have long desired to hear and see, I will do as thou sayest."

And the Prince also gave his consent.

Then Philoctetes bade farewell to the island in these words : —

> "Home that hast watched with me, farewell!
> And nymphs that haunt the springs or dwell
> In seaward meadows, and the roar
> Of waves that break upon the shore;
> Where often, through the cavern's mouth,
> The drifting of the rainy South
> Hath coldly drenched me as I lay;
> And Hermes' hill, whence many a day,
> When anguish seized me, to my cry
> Hoarse-sounding echo made reply.
> O fountains of the land, and thou,
> Pool of the Wolf, I leave you now;
> Beyond all hope I leave thy strand,
> O Lemnos, sea-encircled land!
> Grant me with favoring winds to go
> Whither the mighty Fates command,
> And this dear company of friends,
> And mastering Powers who shape our ends
> To issues fairer than we know."

CHAPTER VII.

It fell out that at the last Troy was taken by a stratagem. Now the stratagem was this: The Greeks made a great Horse of wood, feigning it to be a peace-offering to the gods, that they might have a safe return to their homes.

In the belly of this there hid themselves certain of the bravest of the chiefs, as Menelaüs, and Ulysses, and Thoas the Ætolian, and Machaon, the great physician, and Pyrrhus, son of Achilles (but Achilles himself was dead, slain by Paris, Apollo helping, even as he was about to take the city), and others also, and with them Epeius himself. But the rest of the people made as if they had departed to their homes; only they went not further than Tenedos, which was an island near to the coast.

Great joy was there in Troy when it was noised abroad that the men of Greece had departed. The gates were opened, and the people went forth to see the plain and the camp. And one said to another, as they went, "Here they set the battle in array, and there were the tents of the fierce Achilles, and there lay the ships." And some stood and marvelled at the great peace-offering to Minerva, even the Horse of wood. And Thymœtes, who was one of the elders of the city, was the first who advised that it should be brought within the walls and set in the citadel. Now whether he gave this counsel out of a false heart, or because the gods would have it so, no man knows. But Capys, and others with him, said that it should be drowned in water, or burned with fire, or that men should pierce it and see whether there were aught within. And the people were divided, some crying one thing and some another. Then came forward the priest Laocoön, and a great company with him, crying, "What madness is this? Think ye that the men of Greece are indeed departed, or that there is any profit in their gifts? Surely, there are armed men in this mighty Horse; or haply they have made it that they may look down upon our walls. Touch it not, for as for these men of Greece, I fear them, even though they bring gifts in their hands."

And as he spake he cast his great spear at the Horse, so that it sounded again. But the gods would not that Troy should be saved.

Meanwhile there came certain shepherds, dragging with them one whose hands were bound behind his back. He had come forth to them, they said, of his own accord, when they were in the field. And first the young men gathered about him mocking him, but when he cried aloud, "What place is left for me, for the Greeks suffer me not to live, and the men of Troy cry for vengeance upon me?" they rather pitied him, and bade him speak, and say whence he came and what he had to tell.

Then the man spake, turning to King Priam: "I will speak the truth, whatever befall me. My name is Sinon, and I deny not that I am a Greek. Haply thou hast heard the name of Palamedes, whom the Greeks slew, but now, being dead, lament; and the cause was that, because he counselled peace, men falsely accused him of treason. Now, of this Palamedes I was a poor kinsman, and followed him to Troy. And when he was dead, through the false witness of Ulysses, I lived in great grief and trouble, nor could I hold my peace, but sware that if ever I came back to Argos I would avenge me of him that had done this deed. Then did Ulysses seek occasion against me, whispering evil things, nor rested till at the last, Calchas the soothsayer helping him — but what profit it that I should tell these things? For doubtless ye hold one Greek to be even as another. Wherefore slay me, and doubtless ye will do a pleasure to Ulysses and the sons of Atreus."

Then they bade him tell on, and he said, —

"Often would the Greeks have fled to their homes, being weary of the war, but still the stormy sea hindered them. And when this Horse that ye see had been built, most of all did the dreadful thunder roll from the one end of the heaven to the other. Then the Greeks sent one who should inquire of Apollo; and Apollo answered them thus: 'Men of Greece, even as ye appeased the winds with blood when ye came to Troy, so must ye appease them with blood now that ye would go from thence.' Then did men tremble to think on whom the doom should fall, and Ulysses, with much clamor, drew forth Calchas the soothsayer into the midst, and bade him say who it was that the gods would have as a sacrifice. Then did many forebode evil for me. Ten days did the soothsayer keep silence, saying that he would not give any man to death. But then, for in truth the two had planned the matter beforehand, he spake, appointing me to die. And to this thing they all agreed, each being glad to turn to another that which he feared for himself. But when the day was come, and all things were ready, the salted meal for the sacrifice and the garlands, lo! I burst my bonds and fled, and hid myself in the sedges of a pool, waiting till they should have set sail, if haply that might be. But never shall I see country, or father, or children again. For doubtless on these will they take vengeance for my flight. Only do thou, O king, have pity on me, who have suffered many things, not having harmed any man."

And King Priam had pity on him, and bade them loose his bonds, saying, "Whoever thou art, forget now thy country. Henceforth thou art one of us. But tell me true: why made they this huge Horse? Who contrived it? What seek they by it, — to please the gods or to further their siege?"

Then said Sinon, and as he spake he stretched his hands to the sky, "I call you to witness, ye everlasting fires of heaven, that with good right I now break my oath of fealty and reveal the secrets of my countrymen. Listen then, O king. All our hope has ever been in the help of Minerva. But, from the day when Diomed and Ulysses dared, having bloody hands, to snatch her image from her holy place in Troy, her face was turned from us. Well do I remember how the eyes of the image, well-nigh before they had set it in the camp, blazed with wrath, and how the salt sweat stood upon its limbs, aye, and how it thrice leapt from the ground, shaking shield and spear. Then Calchas told us that we must cross the seas again, and seek at home fresh omens for our war. And this, indeed, they are doing even now, and will return anon. Also the soothsayer said, 'Meanwhile ye must make the likeness of a Horse, to be a peace-offering to Minerva. And take heed that ye make it huge of bulk, so that the men of Troy may not receive it into their gates, nor bring it within their walls, and get safety for themselves thereby. For if,' he said, 'the men of Troy harm this image at all, they shall surely perish; but if they bring it into their city, then shall Asia lay siege hereafter to the city of Pelops, and our children shall suffer the doom which we would fain have brought on Troy.'"

These words wrought much on the men of Troy, and as they pondered on them, lo! the gods sent another marvel to deceive them. For while Laocoön, the priest of Neptune was slaying a bull at the altar of his god, there came two serpents across the sea from Tenedos, whose heads and necks, whereon were thick manes of hair, were high above the waves, and many scaly coils trailed behind in the waters. And when they reached the land they still sped forward. Their eyes were red as blood and blazed with fire, and their forked tongues hissed loud for rage. Then all the men of Troy grew pale with fear and fled away, but these turned not aside this way or that, seeking Laocoön where he stood. And first they wrapped themselves about his little sons, one serpent about each, and began to devour them. And when the father would have given help to his children, having a sword in his hand, they seized upon himself, and bound him fast with their folds. Twice they compassed about his body, and twice his neck, lifting their heads far above him. And all the while he strove to tear them away with his hands, his priest's garlands dripping with blood. Nor did he cease to cry horribly aloud, even as a bull bellows when after an ill stroke of the axe it flees from the altar. But when their work was done, the two glided to the citadel of Minerva, and hid themselves beneath the feet and the shield of the goddess. And men said one to another, "Lo! the priest Laocoön has been judged according to his deeds; for he cast his spear against this holy thing, and now the gods have slain him." Then all cried out together that the Horse of wood must be drawn to the citadel. Whereupon they opened the Scæan Gate, and pulled down the wall that was thereby, and put rollers under the feet of the Horse, and joined ropes thereto. So, in much joy, they drew it into the city, youths and maidens singing about it the while, and laying their hands to the ropes with great gladness. And yet there wanted not signs and tokens of evil to come. Four times it halted on the threshold of the gate, and men might have heard a clashing of arms within. Cassandra also opened her mouth, prophesying evil: but no man heeded her, for that was ever the doom upon her, not to be believed speaking truth. So the men of Troy drew the Horse into the city. And that night they kept a feast to all the gods with great joy, not knowing that the last day of the great city had come.

But when night was now fully come, and the men of Troy lay asleep, lo! from the ship of King Agamemnon there rose up a flame for a signal to the Greeks; and these straightway manned their ships, and made across the sea from Tenedos, there being a great calm, and the moon also giving them light. Sinon likewise opened a secret door that was in the great Horse, and the chiefs issued forth therefrom, and opened the gates of the city, slaying those that kept watch.

Meanwhile there came a vision to Æneas, who now, Hector being dead, was the chief hope and stay of the men of Troy. It was Hector's self that he seemed to see, but not such as he had seen him coming back rejoicing with the arms of Achilles, or setting fire to the ships, but even as he lay after that Achilles dragged him at his chariot wheels, covered with dust and blood, his feet swollen and pierced through with thongs. To him said Æneas, not knowing what he said, "Why hast thou tarried so long? Much have we suffered waiting for thee! And what grief hath marked thy face? and whence these wounds?"

But to this the spirit answered nothing, but said, groaning the while, "Fly, son of Venus, fly, and save thee from these flames. The enemy is in the walls, and Troy hath utterly perished. If any hand could have saved our city, this hand had done so. Thou art now the hope of Troy. Take then her gods, and flee with them for company, seeking the city that thou shalt one day build across the sea."

And now the alarm of battle came nearer and nearer, and Æneas, waking from sleep, climbed upon the roof, and looked on the city. As a shepherd stands, and sees a fierce flame sweeping before the south wind over the cornfields or a flood rushing down from the mountains, so he stood. And as he looked, the great palace of Deïphobus sank down in the fire, and the house of Ucalegon, that was hard by, blazed forth, till the sea by Sigeüm shone with the light. Then, scarce knowing what he sought, he girded on his armor, thinking, perchance, that he might yet win some place of vantage, or, at the least, might avenge himself on the enemy, or find honor in his death. But as he passed from out of his house there met him Panthus, the priest of Apollo that was on the citadel, who cried to him, "O Æneas, the glory is departed from Troy, and the Greeks have the mastery in the city; for armed men are coming forth from the great Horse of wood, and thousands also swarm in at the gates, which Sinon hath treacherously opened." And as he spake others came up under the light of the moon, as Hypanis, and Dymas, and young Corœbus, who had but newly come to Troy, seeking Cassandra to be his wife. To whom Æneas spake:

"If ye are minded, my brethren, to follow me to the death, come on. For how things fare this night ye see. The gods who were the stay of this city have departed from it; nor is aught remaining to which we may bring succor. Yet can we die as brave men in battle. And haply he that counts his life to be lost may yet save it." Then, even as ravening wolves hasten through the mist seeking for prey, so they went through the city, doing dreadful deeds. And for a while the men of Greece fled before them.

First of all there met them Androgeos with a great company following him, who, thinking them to be friends, said, "Haste, comrades, why are ye so late? We are spoiling this city of Troy, and ye are but newly come from the ships." But forthwith, for they answered him not as he had looked for, he knew that he had fallen among enemies. Then even as one who treads upon a snake unawares among thorns, and flies from it when it rises angrily against him with swelling neck, so Androgeos would have fled. But the men of Troy rushed on, and seeing that they knew all the place, and that great fear was upon the Greeks, slew many men. Then said Corœbus, "We have good luck in this matter, my friends. Come now, let us change our shields, and put upon us the armor of these Greeks. For whether we deal with our enemy by craft or by force, who will ask?" Then he took to himself the helmet and shield of Androgeos, and also girded the sword upon him. In like manner did the others, and thus going disguised among the Greeks slew many, so that some again fled to the ships and some were fain to climb into the Horse of wood. But lo! men came dragging by the hair from the temple of Minerva the virgin Cassandra, whom when Corœbus beheld, and how she lifted up her eyes to heaven (but as for her hands, they were bound with iron), he endured not the sight, but threw himself upon those that dragged her, the others following him. Then did a grievous mischance befall them, for the men of Troy that stood upon the roof of the temple cast spears against them, judging them to be enemies. The Greeks also, being wroth that the virgin should be taken from them, fought the more fiercely, and many who had before been put to flight in the city came against them, and prevailed, being indeed many against few. Then first of all fell Corœbus, being slain by Peneleus the Bœotian, and Rhipeus also, the most righteous of all the sons of Troy. But the gods dealt not with him after his righteousness. Hypanis also was slain and Dymas, and Panthus escaped not for all that more than other men he feared the gods and was also the priest of Apollo.

Then was Æneas severed from the rest, having with him two only, Iphitus and Pelias, Iphitus being an old man and Pelias sorely wounded by Ulysses. And these, hearing a great shouting, hastened to the palace of King Priam, where the battle was fiercer than in any place beside. For some of the Greeks were seeking to climb the walls, laying ladders thereto, whereon they stood, holding forth their shields with their left hands, and with their right grasping the roofs. And the men of Troy, on the other hand, being in the last extremity, tore down the battlements and the gilded beams wherewith the men of old had adorned the palace. Then Æneas, knowing of a secret door whereby the unhappy Andromaché in past days had been wont to enter, bringing her son Astyanax to his grandfather, climbed on to the roof, and joined himself to those that fought therefrom. Now upon this roof there was a tower, whence all Troy could be seen and the camp of the Greeks and the ships. This the men of Troy loosened from its foundations with bars of iron, and thrust it over, so that it fell upon the enemy, slaying many of them. But not the less did others press forward, casting the while stones and javelins and all that came to their hands.

Meanwhile others sought to break down the gates of the palace, Pyrrhus, son of Achilles, being foremost among them, clad in shining armor of bronze. Like to a serpent was he, which sleeps indeed during the winter, but in the spring comes forth into the light, full fed on evil herbs, and, having cast his skin and renewed his youth, lifts his head into the light of the sun and hisses with forked tongue. And with Pyrrhus were tall Periphas, and Automedon, who had been armor-bearer to his father Achilles, and following them the youth of Scyros, which was the kingdom of his grandfather Lycomedes. With a great battle-axe he hewed through the doors, breaking down also the door-posts, though they were plated with bronze, making, as it were, a great window, through which a man might see the palace within, the hall of King Priam and of the kings who had reigned aforetime in Troy. But when they that were within perceived it, there arose a great cry of women wailing aloud and clinging to the doors and kissing them. But ever Pyrrhus pressed on, fierce and strong as ever was his father Achilles, nor could aught stand against him, either the doors or they that guarded them. Then, as a river bursts its banks and overflows the plain, so did the sons of Greece rush into the palace.

But old Priam, when he saw the enemy in his hall, girded on him his armor, which now by reason of old age he had long laid aside, and took a spear in his hand, and would have gone against the adversary, only Queen Hecuba called to him from where she sat. For she and her daughters had fled to the great altar of the household gods, and sat crowded about it like unto doves that are driven by a storm. Now the altar stood in an open court that was in the midst of the palace, with a great bay-tree above it. So when she saw Priam, how he had girded himself with armor as a youth, she cried to him and said, "What hath bewitched thee, that thou girdest thyself with armor? It is not the sword that shall help us this day; no, not though my own Hector were here, but rather the gods and their altars. Come hither to us, for here thou wilt be safe, or at the least wilt die with us."

So she made the old man sit down in the midst. But lo! there came flying through the palace, Polites, his son, wounded to death by the spear of Pyrrhus, and Pyrrhus close behind him. And he, even as he came into the sight of his father and his mother, fell dead upon the ground. But when King Priam saw it he contained not himself, but cried aloud, "Now may the gods, if there be any justice in heaven, recompense thee for this wickedness, seeing that thou hast not spared to slay the son before his father's eyes. Great Achilles, whom thou falsely callest thy sire, did not thus to Priam, though he was an enemy, but reverenced right and truth, and gave the body of Hector for burial, and sent me back to my city."

And as he spake the old man cast a spear, but aimless and without force, and that pierced not even the boss of the shield. Then said the son of Achilles, "Go thou and tell my father of his unworthy son and all these evil deeds. And that thou mayest tell him, die!" And as he spake he caught in his left hand the old man's white hair, and dragged him, slipping the while in the blood of his own son, to the altar, and then, lifting his sword high for a blow, drave 't to the hilt in the old man's side. So King Priam, who had ruled mightily over many peoples and countries in the land of Asia, was slain that night, having first seen Troy burning about him, and his citadel laid even with the ground. So was his carcase cast out upon the earth, headless, and without a name.

CHAPTER VIII.

THE ADVENTURES OF ULYSSES.

When the great city of Troy was taken, all the chiefs who had fought against it set sail for their homes. But there was wrath in heaven against them, for indeed they had borne themselves haughtily and cruelly in the day of their victory. Therefore they did not all find a safe and happy return. For one was shipwrecked, and another was shamefully slain by his false wife in his palace, and others found all things at home troubled and changed, and were driven to seek new dwellings elsewhere. And some, whose wives and friends and people had been still true to them through those ten long years of absence, were driven far and wide about the world before they saw their native land again. And of all, the wise Ulysses was he who wandered farthest and suffered most.

He was well-nigh the last to sail, for he had tarried many days to do pleasure to Agamemnon, lord of all the Greeks. Twelve ships he had with him — twelve he had brought to Troy — and in each there were some fifty men, being scarce half of those that had sailed in them in the old days, so many valiant heroes slept the last sleep by Simoïs and Scamander, and in the plain on the sea-shore, slain in battle or by the shafts of Apollo.

First they sailed north-west to the Thracian coast, where the Ciconians dwelt, who had helped the men of Troy. Their city they took, and in it much plunder, slaves and oxen, and jars of fragrant wine, and might have escaped unhurt, but that they stayed to hold revel on the shore. For the Ciconians gathered their neighbors, being men of the same blood, and did battle with the invaders, and drove them to their ship. And when Ulysses numbered his men, he found that he had lost six out of each ship.

Scarce had he set out again when the wind began to blow fiercely; so, seeing a smooth sandy beach, they drave the ships ashore and dragged them out of reach of the waves, and waited till the storm should abate. And the third morning being fair, they sailed again, and journeyed prosperously till they came to the very end of the great Peloponnesian land, where Cape Malea looks out upon the southern sea. But contrary currents baffled them, so that they could not round it, and the north wind blew so strongly that they must fain drive before it. And on the tenth day they came to the land where the lotus grows — a wondrous fruit, of which whosoever eats cares not to see country or wife or children again. Now the Lotus-eaters, for so they called the people of the land, were a kindly folk, and gave of the fruit to some of the sailors, not meaning them any harm, but thinking it to be the best that they had to give. These, when they had eaten, said that they would not sail any more over the sea; which, when the wise Ulysses heard, he bade their comrades bind them and carry them, sadly complaining, to the ships.

Then, the wind having abated, they took to their oars, and rowed for many days till they came to the country where the Cyclopes dwell. Now, a mile or so from the shore there was an island, very fair and fertile, but no man dwells there or tills the soil, and in the island a harbor where a ship may be safe from all winds, and at the head of the harbor a stream falling from a rock, and whispering alders all about it. Into this the ships passed safely, and were hauled up on the beach, and the crews slept by them, waiting for the morning. And the next day they hunted the wild goats, of which there was great store on the island, and feasted right merrily on what they caught, with draughts of red wine which they had carried off from the town of the Ciconians.

But on the morrow, Ulysses, for he was ever fond of adventure, and would know of every land to which he came what manner of men they were that dwelt there, took one of his twelve ships and bade row to the land. There was a great hill sloping to the shore, and there rose up here and there a smoke from the caves where the Cyclopes dwelt apart, holding no converse with each other, for they were a rude and savage folk, but ruled each his own household, not caring for others. Now very close to the shore was one of these caves, very huge and deep, with laurels round about the mouth, and in front a fold with walls built of rough stone, and shaded by tall oaks and pines. So Ulysses chose out of the crew the twelve bravest, and bade the rest guard the ship, and went to see what manner of dwelling this was, and who abode there. He had his sword by his side, and on his shoulder a mighty skin of wine, sweet-smelling and strong, with which he might win the heart of some fierce savage, should he chance to meet with such, as indeed his prudent heart forecasted that he might.

So they entered the cave, and judged that it was the dwelling of some rich and skilful shepherd. For within there were pens for the young of the sheep and of the goats, divided all according to their age, and there were baskets full of cheeses, and full milkpails ranged along the wall. But the Cyclops himself was away in the pastures. Then the companions of Ulysses besought him that he would depart, taking with him, if he would, a store of cheeses and sundry of the lambs and of the kids. But he would not, for he wished to see, after his wont, what manner of host this strange shepherd might be. And truly he saw it to his cost!

It was evening when the Cyclops came home, a mighty giant, twenty feet in height, or more. On his shoulder he bore a vast bundle of pine logs for his fire, and threw them down outside the cave with a great crash, and drove the flocks within, and closed the entrance with a huge rock, which twenty wagons and more could not bear. Then he milked the ewes and all the she-goats, and half of the milk he curdled for cheese, and half he set ready for himself, when he should sup. Next he kindled a fire with the pine logs, and the flame lighted up all the cave, showing him Ulysses and his comrades.

"Who are ye?" cried Polyphemus, for that was the giant's name. "Are ye traders, or, haply, pirates?"

For in those days it was not counted shame to be called a pirate.

Ulysses shuddered at the dreadful voice and shape, but bore him bravely, and answered, "We are no pirates, mighty sir, but Greeks, sailing back from Troy, and subjects of the great King Agamemnon, whose fame is spread from one end of heaven to the other. And we are come to beg hospitality of thee in the name of Zeus, who rewards or punishes hosts and guests according as they be faithful the one to the other, or no."

"Nay," said the giant, "it is but idle talk to tell me of Zeus and the other gods. We Cyclopes take no account of gods, holding ourselves to be much better and stronger than they. But come, tell me where have you left your ship?"

But Ulysses saw his thought when he asked about the ship, how he was minded to break it, and take from them all hope of flight. Therefore he answered him craftily,—

"Ship have we none, for that which was ours King Poseidon brake, driving it on a jutting rock on this coast, and we whom thou seest are all that are escaped from the waves."

Polyphemus answered nothing, but without more ado caught up two of the men, as a man might catch up the whelps of a dog, and dashed them on the ground, and tore them limb from limb, and devoured them, with huge draughts of milk between, leaving not a morsel, not even the very bones But the others, when they saw the dreadful deed, could only weep and pray to Zeus for help. And when the giant had ended his foul meal, he lay down among his sheep and slept.

Then Ulysses questioned much in his heart whether he should slay the monster as he slept, for he doubted not that his good sword would pierce to the giant's heart, mighty as he was. But, being very wise, he remembered that, should he slay him, he and his comrades would yet perish miserably. For who should move away the great rock that lay against the door of the cave? So they waited till the morning. And the monster woke, and milked his flocks, and afterwards, seizing two men, devoured them for his meal. Then he went to the pastures, but put the great rock on the mouth of the cave, just as a man puts down the lid upon his quiver.

All that day the wise Ulysses was thinking what he might best do to save himself and his companions, and the end of his thinking was this: there was a mighty pole in the cave, green wood of an olive tree, big as a ship's mast, which Polyphemus purposed to use, when the smoke should have dried it, as a walking staff. Of this he cut off a fathom's length, and his comrades sharpened it and hardened it in the fire, and then hid it away. At evening the giant came back, and drove his sheep into the cave, nor left the rams outside, as he had been wont to do before, but shut them in. And having duly done his shepherd's work, he made his cruel feast as before. Then Ulysses came forward with the wine-skin in his hand, and said, —

"Drink, Cyclops, now that thou hast feasted. Drink and see what precious things we had in our ship. But no one hereafter will come to thee with such like, if thou dealest with strangers as cruelly as thou hast dealt with us."

Then the Cyclops drank, and was mightily pleased, and said, "Give me again to drink, and tell me thy name, stranger, and I will give thee a gift such as a host should give. In good truth this is a rare liquor. We, too, have vines, but they bear not wine like this, which indeed must be such as the gods drink in heaven."

Then Ulysses gave him the cup again, and he drank. Thrice he gave it to him, and thrice he drank, not knowing what it was, and how it would work within his brain.

Then Ulysses spake to him. "Thou didst ask my name, Cyclops. Lo! my name is No Man. And now that thou knowest my name, thou shouldst give me thy gift."

And he said, "My gift shall be that I will eat thee last of all thy company."

And as he spoke he fell back in a drunken sleep. Then Ulysses bade his comrades be of good courage, for the time was come when they should be delivered. And they thrust the stake of olive wood into the fire till it was ready, green as it was, to burst into flame, and they thrust it into the monster's eye; for he had but one eye, and that in the midst of his forehead, with the eyebrow below it. And Ulysses leant with all his force upon the stake, and thrust it in with might and main. And the burning wood hissed in the eye, just as the red-hot iron hisses in the water when a man seeks to temper steel for a sword.

Then the giant leapt up, and tore away the stake, and cried aloud, so that all the Cyclopes who dwelt on the mountain side heard him and came about his cave, asking him, "What aileth thee, Polyphemus, that thou makest this uproar in the peaceful night, driving away sleep? Is any one robbing thee of thy sheep, or seeking to slay thee by craft or force?"

And the giant answered, "No Man slays me by craft."

"Nay, but," they said, "if no man does thee wrong, we cannot help thee. The sickness which great Zeus may send, who can avoid? Pray to our father, Poseidon, for help."

Then they departed; and Ulysses was glad at heart for the good success of his device, when he said that he was No Man.

But the Cyclops rolled away the great stone from the door of the cave, and sat in the midst, stretching out his hands to feel whether perchance the men within the cave would seek to go out among the sheep.

Long did Ulysses think how he and his comrades should best escape. At last he lighted upon a good device, and much he thanked Zeus for that this once the giant had driven the rams with the other sheep into the cave. For, these being great and strong, he fastened his comrades under the bellies of the beasts, tying them with osier twigs, of which the giant made his bed. One ram he took, and fastened a man beneath it, and two others he set, one on either side. So he did with the six, for but six were left out of the twelve who had ventured with him from the ship. And there was one mighty ram, far larger than all the others, and to this Ulysses clung, grasping the fleece tight with both his hands. So they waited for the morning. And when the morning came, the rams rushed forth to the pasture; but the giant sat in the door and felt the back of each as it went by, nor thought to try what might be underneath. Last of all went the great ram. And the Cyclops knew him as he passed, and said, —

"How is this, thou, who art the leader of the flock? Thou art not wont thus to lag behind. Thou hast always been the first to run to the pastures and streams in the morning, and the first to come back to the fold when evening fell; and now thou art last of all. Perhaps thou art troubled about thy master's eye, which some wretch — No Man, they call him — has destroyed, having first mastered me with wine. He has not escaped, I ween. I would that thou couldst speak, and tell me where he is lurking. Of a truth I would dash out his brains upon the ground, and avenge me of this No Man."

So speaking, he let him pass out of the cave. But when they were out of reach of the giant, Ulysses loosed his hold of the ram, and then unbound his comrades. And they hastened to their ship, not forgetting to drive before them a good store of the Cyclops' fat sheep. Right glad were those that had abode by the ship to see them. Nor did they lament for those that had died, though they were fain to do so, for Ulysses forbade, fearing lest the noise of their weeping should betray them to the giant, where they were. Then they all climbed into the ship, and sitting well in order on the benches, smote the sea with their oars, laying-to right lustily, that they might the sooner get away from the accursed land. And when they had rowed a hundred yards or so, so that a man's voice could yet be heard by one who stood upon the shore, Ulysses stood up in the ship and shouted, —

"He was no coward, O Cyclops, whose comrades thou didst so foully slay in thy den. Justly art thou punished, monster, that devourest thy guests in thy dwelling. May the gods make thee suffer yet worse things than these!"

Then the Cyclops, in his wrath, broke off the top of a great hill, a mighty rock, and hurled it where he had heard the voice. Right in front of the ship's bow it fell, and a great wave rose as it sank, and washed the ship back to the shore. But Ulysses seized a long pole with both hands and pushed the ship from the land, and bade his comrades ply their oars, nodding with his head, for he was too wise to speak, lest the Cyclops should know where they were. Then they rowed with all their might and main.

And when they had gotten twice as far as before, Ulysses made as if he would speak again; but his comrades sought to hinder him, saying, "Nay, my lord, anger not the giant any more. Surely we thought before we were lost, when he threw the great rock, and washed our ship back to the shore. And if he hear thee now, he may crush our ship and us, for the man throws a mighty bolt, and throws it far."

But Ulysses would not be persuaded, but stood up and

said, "Hear, Cyclops! If any man ask who blinded thee, say that it was the warrior Ulysses, son of Laertes, dwelling in Ithaca."

And the Cyclops answered with a groan, "Of a truth, the old oracles are fulfilled, for long ago there came to this land one Telemus, a prophet, and dwelt among us even to old age. This man foretold to me that one Ulysses would rob me of my sight. But I looked for a great man and a strong, who should subdue me by force, and now a weakling has done the deed, having cheated me with wine. But come thou hither, Ulysses, and I will be a host indeed to thee. Or, at least, may Poseidon give thee such a voyage to thy home as I would wish thee to have. For know that Poseidon is my sire. May be that he may heal me of my grievous wound."

And Ulysses said, "Would to God I could send thee down to the abode of the dead, where thou wouldst be past all healing, even from Poseidon's self."

Then Cyclops lifted up his hands to Poseidon and prayed, —

"Hear me, Poseidon, if I am indeed thy son and thou my father. May this Ulysses never reach his home! or, if the Fates have ordered that he should reach it, may he come alone, all his comrades lost, and come to find sore trouble in his house!"

And as he ended he hurled another mighty rock, which almost lighted on the rudder's end, yet missed it as by a hair's breadth. So Ulysses and his comrades escaped, and came to the island of the wild goats, where they found their comrades, who indeed had waited long for them, in sore fear lest they had perished. Then Ulysses divided amongst his company all the sheep which they had taken from the Cyclops. And all, with one consent, gave him for his share the great ram which had carried him out of the cave, and he sacrificed it to Zeus. And all that day they feasted right merrily on the flesh of sheep and on sweet wine, and when the night was come, they lay down upon the shore and slept.

After sailing awhile, they came to the island of Æolus, who is the king of the winds, and who dwelt there with his children, six sons and six daughters. Right well did Æolus entertain them, feasting them royally for a whole month, while he heard from Ulysses the story of all that had been done at Troy. And when Ulysses prayed him that he would help him on his way homewards, Æolus hearkened to him, and gave him the skin of an ox in which he had bound all contrary winds, so that they should not hinder him. But he let a gentle west wind blow, that it might carry him and his comrades to their home. For nine days it blew and now they were near to Ithaca, their country, so that they saw lights burning in it, it being night-time. But now, by an ill chance, Ulysses fell asleep, being wholly wearied out, for he had held the helm for nine days, nor trusted it to any of his comrades. And while he slept his comrades, who had cast eyes of envy on the great ox-hide, said one to another, —

"Strange it is how men love and honor this Ulysses whithersoever he goes. And now he comes back from Troy with much spoil, but we with empty hands. Let us see what it is that Æolus hath given, for doubtless in this ox-hide is much silver and gold."

So they loosed the great bag of ox-hide, and lo! all the winds rushed out, and carried them far away from their country. But Ulysses, waking with the tumult, doubted much whether he should not throw himself into the sea and so die. But he endured, thinking it better to live.

Only he veiled his face and so sat, while the ships drave before the winds, till they came once more to the island of Æolus. Then Ulysses went to the palace of the king, and found him feasting with his wife and children, and sat him down on the threshold. Much did they wonder to see him, saying, "What evil power has hindered thee, that thou didst not reach thy country and home?"

Then he answered, "Blame not me, but the evil counsels of my comrades, and sleep, which mastered me to my hurt. But do ye help me again."

But they said, "Begone; we may not help him whom the gods hate; and hated of them thou surely art."

So Æolus sent him away. Then again they launched their ships and set forth, toiling wearily at the oars, and sad at heart.

Six days they rowed, nor rested at night, and on the seventh they came to Lamos, which was a city of the Læstrygons, in whose land the night is as the day, so that a man might earn double wage, if only he wanted not sleep — shepherd by day and herdsman by night. There was a fair haven with cliffs about it, and a narrow mouth with great rocks on either side. And within are no waves, but always calm.

Now Ulysses made fast his ship to the rocks, but the others entered the haven. Then he sent two men and a herald with them, and these came upon a smooth road by which waggons brought down wood from the mountain to the city. Here they met a maiden, the stalwart daughter of Antiphates, king of the land, and asked of her who was lord of that country. Whereupon she showed them her father's lofty palace. And they, entering this, saw the maiden's mother, big as a mountain, horrible to behold, who straightway called to Antiphates, her husband. The messengers, indeed, fled to the ships; but he made a great shout, and the Læstrygons came flocking about him, giants, not men. And these broke off great stones from the cliffs, each stone as much as a man could carry, and cast them at the ships, so that they were broken. And the men they speared, as if they were fishes, and devoured them. So it happened to all the ships in the haven. Ulysses only escaped, for he cut the hawser with his sword, and bade his men ply their oars, which indeed they did right willingly.

After a while they came to the island of Æaea, where Circé dwelt, who was the daughter of the Sun. Two days and nights they lay upon the shore in great trouble and sorrow. On the third, Ulysses took his spear and sword and climbed a hill that there was, for he wished to see to what manner of land they had come. And having climbed it, he saw the smoke rising from the palace of Circé, where it stood in the midst of a wood. Then he thought awhile: should he go straightway to the palace that he saw, or first return to his comrades on the shore? And this last seemed better; and it chanced that as he went he saw a great stag which was going down to the river to drink, for indeed the sun was now hot, and casting his spear at it he pierced it through. Then he fastened together the feet with green withes and a fathom's length of rope, and slinging the beast round his neck, so carried it to the ship, leaning on his spear; for indeed it was heavy to bear, nor could any man have carried it on the shoulder with one hand. And when he was come to the ship, he cast down his burden. Now the men were sitting with their faces muffled, so sad were they. But when he bade them be of good cheer, they looked up and marvelled at the great stag. And all that day they feasted on deer's flesh and sweet wine, and at night lay down to sleep on the shore. But when morning was come, Ulysses called them all together and spake, —

"I know not, friends, where we are. Only I know, having seen smoke yesterday from the hill, that there is a dwelling in this island."

It troubled the men much to hear this, for they thought of the Cyclops and of the Læstrygons; and they wailed aloud, but there was no counsel in them. Wherefore Ulysses divided them into two companies, setting Eurylochus over the one and himself over the other, and shook lots in a helmet who should go and search out the island, and the lot of Eurylochus leapt out. So he went, and comrades twenty and two with him. And in an open space in the wood they found the palace of Circé. All about were wolves and lions; yet these harmed not the men, but stood up on their hind legs, fawning upon them, as dogs fawn upon their master when he comes from his meal. And the men were afraid. And they stood in the porch and heard the voice of Circé as she sang with a lovely voice and plied the loom. Then said Polites, who was dearest of all his comrades to Ulysses, —

"Some one within plies a great loom, and sings with a loud voice. Some goddess is she, or woman. Let us make haste and call."

So they called to her, and she came out and beckoned to them that they should follow. So they went, in their folly. And she bade them sit, and mixed for them a mess, red wine, and in it barley-meal and cheese and honey, and mighty drugs withal, of which, if a man drank, he forgot all that he loved. And when they had drunk she smote them with her wand. And lo! they had of a sudden the heads and the voices and the bristles of swine, but the heart of a man was in them still. And Circé shut them in sties, and gave them mast and acorns and cornel to eat.

But Eurylochus fled back to the ship. And for a while he could not speak, so full was his heart of grief, but at the last he told the tale of what had befallen. Then Ulysses took his silver-studded sword and his bow, and bade Eurylochus guide him by the way that he had gone.

Nor would he hearken when Eurylochus would have hindered him, but said, "Stay here by the ship, eating and drinking, if it be thy will, but I must go, for necessity constrains me."

And when he had come to the house, there met him Hermes of the golden wand, in the shape of a fair youth, who said to him, —

"Art thou come to rescue thy comrades that are now swine in Circé's house? Nay, but thou shalt never go back thyself. Yet, stay; I will give thee such a drug as shall give thee power to resist all her charms. For when she shall have mixed thee a mess, and smitten thee with her wand, then do thou rush upon her with thy sword, making as if thou wouldst slay her. And when she shall pray for peace, do thou make her swear by the great oath that binds the gods that she will not harm thee."

Then Hermes showed Ulysses a certain herb, whose root was black, but the flower white as milk. "Moly," the gods call it, and very hard it is for mortal man to find. Then Ulysses went into the house, and all befell as Hermes had told him. For Circé would have changed him as she had changed his comrades. Then he rushed at her with his sword, and made her swear the great oath which binds the gods that she would not harm him.

But afterwards, when they sat at meat together, the goddess perceived that he was silent and ate not. Wherefore she said, "Why dost thou sit, Ulysses, as though thou wert dumb? Fearest thou any craft of mine? Nay, but that may not be, for have I not sworn the great oath that binds the gods?"

And Ulysses said, "Nay, but who could think of meat and drink when such things had befallen his companions?"

Then Circé led the way, holding her wand in her hand, and opened the doors of the sties, and drove out the swine that had been men. Then she rubbed on each another mighty drug, and the bristles fell from their bodies and they became men, only younger and fairer than before. And when they saw Ulysses they clung to him and wept for joy, and Circé herself was moved with pity.

Then said she, "Go, Ulysses, to thy ship, and put away all the goods and tackling in the caves that are on the shore, but come again hither thyself, and bring thy comrades with thee."

Then Ulysses went. Right glad were they who had stayed to see him, glad as are the calves who have been penned in the fold-yard when their mothers come back in the evening. And when he told them what had been, and would have them follow him, they were all willing, save only Eurylochus, who said, —

"O ye fools, whither are we going? To the dwelling of Circé, who will change us all into swine, or wolves, or lions, and keep us in prison, even as the Cyclops did! For was it not this same foolhardy Ulysses that lost our comrades there?"

Then was Ulysses very wroth, and would have slain Eurylochus, though near of kin to him. But his comrades hindered him, saying, "Let him abide here and keep the ship, if he will. But we will go with thee to the dwelling of Circé."

Then Ulysses forbore. Nor did Eurylochus stay behind, but followed with the rest. So they went to the dwelling of Circé, who feasted them royally, so that they remained with her for a whole year, well content.

But when the year was out they said to Ulysses, "It were well to remember thy country, if it is indeed the will of the gods that thou shouldst return thither."

Then Ulysses besought Circé that she would send him on his way homewards, as indeed she had promised to do. And she answered, —

"I would not have you abide in my house unwillingly. Yet must thou first go another journey, even to the dwellings of the dead, there to speak with the seer Tiresias."

But Ulysses was sore troubled to hear such things, and wept aloud, saying, "Who shall guide us in this journey? — for never yet did ship make such a voyage as this."

Then said Circé, "Seek no guide; only raise the mast of thy ship and spread the white sails, and sit in peace. So shall the north wind bear thee to the place on the ocean shore where are the groves of Persephoné, tall poplars and willows. There must thou beach thy ship. And after that thou must go alone."

Then she told him all that he must do if he would hold converse with the dead seer Tiresias, and hear what should befall him. So the next morning he roused his companions, telling them that they should now return. But it chanced that one of them, Elpenor by name, was sleeping on the roof, for the coolness, being heavy with wine. And when he heard the stir of his comrades, he rose up, nor thought of the ladder, but fell from the roof and brake his neck. And the rest being assembled, Ulysses told them how they must take another journey first, even to the dwellings of the dead. This they were much troubled to hear, yet they made ready the ship and departed.

So they came to the place of which Circé had told them. And when all things had been rightly done, Ulysses saw spirits of the dead. First of all came Elpenor, and he marvelled much to see him, saying, —

"How camest thou hither? — on foot or in the ship?"

Then he answered, telling how he had died; and he said, "Now, as thou wilt go back, I know, to the island of Circé, suffer me not to remain unburied, but make above me a mound of earth, for men in aftertimes to see, and put upon it my oar, with which I was wont to row while I yet lived."

These things Ulysses promised that he would do. Afterwards came the spirit of Tiresias, holding a sceptre of gold in his hand. And when Ulysses asked him of his return, he said, —

"Thy return shall be difficult, because of the anger of Poseidon, whose son thou madest blind. Yet, when thou comest to the island of the Three Capes, where feed the oxen of the Sun, if thou leave these unhurt, thou and thy comrades shall return to Ithaca. But otherwise they shall perish, and thou shalt return, after long time, in a ship not thine own, and shalt find in thy palace, devouring thy goods, men of violence, suitors of thy wife. These shalt thou slay, openly or by craft. Nor yet shalt thou rest, but shalt go to a land where men know not the sea, nor eat their meat with salt; and thou shalt carry thy oar on thy shoulder. And this shall be a sign to thee, when another wayfarer, meeting thee, shall ask whether it be a winnowing fan that thou bearest on thy shoulder; then shalt thou fix thy oar in the earth, and make a sacrifice to Poseidon, and so return. So shalt thou die at last in peace."

Then Tiresias departed. After this he saw his mother,

and asked how it fared with his home in Ithaca, and she told him all. And many others he saw, wives and daughters of the heroes of old time. Also there came King Agamemnon, who told him how Ægisthus, with Clytemnestra, his wicked wife, had slain him in his own palace, being newly returned from Troy. Fain would the King have heard how it fared with Orestes, his son, but of this Ulysses could tell him nothing. Then came the spirit of Achilles, and him Ulysses comforted, telling him how bravely and wisely his son Neoptolemus had borne himself in Troy.

Also he saw the spirit of Ajax, son of Telamon; but Ajax spake not to him, having great wrath in his heart, because of the arms of Achilles. For the two, Ajax and Ulysses, had contended for them, Achilles being dead, before the assembly of the Greeks, and the Greeks had given them to Ulysses, whereupon Ajax, being very wroth, had laid hands upon himself.

And having seen many other things, Ulysses went back to his ship, and returned with his companions to the island of Circé. And being arrived there, first they buried Elpenor, making a mound over him, and setting up on it his oar, and afterwards Circé made them a feast. But while the others slept she told to Ulysses all that should befall him, saying,—

"First thou wilt come to the island of the Sirens, who sing so sweetly, that whosoever hears them straightway forgets wife and child and home. In a meadow they sit, singing sweetly, but about them are bones of men. Do thou, then, close with wax the ears of thy companions, and make them bind thee to the mast, so that thou mayest hear the song and yet take no hurt. And do thou bid them, when thou shalt pray to be loosed, not to hearken, but rather to bind thee the more. And this peril being past, there lie others in thy path, of which thou must take thy choice. For either thou must pass between the rocks which the gods call the Wanderers—and these close upon all that passes between them, even the very doves in their flight, nor has any ship escaped them, save only the ship *Argo*, which Heré loved—or thou must go through the strait, where there is a rock on either hand. In the one rock dwells Scylla, in a cave so high above the sea that an archer could not reach it with his arrow. A horrible monster is she. Twelve unshapely feet she hath, and six long necks, and on each a head with three rows of teeth. In the cave she lies, but her heads are without, fishing for sea-dogs and dolphins, or even a great whale, if such should chance to go by. Think not to escape her, Ulysses, for, of a truth, with each head will she take one of thy companions. But the other rock is lower and more flat, with a wild fig-tree on the top. There Charybdis thrice a day draws in the dark water, and thrice a day sends it forth. Be not thou near when she draws it in; not even Poseidon's self could save thee. Choose rather to pass near to Scylla, for it is better to lose six of thy companions than that all should perish."

Then said Ulysses, "Can I not fight with this Scylla, and so save my companions?"

But Circé answered, "Nay, for she is not of mortal race. And if thou linger to arm thyself, thou wilt but lose six others of thy companions. Pass them with all the speed that may be, and call on Crataïs, who is the mother of Scylla, that she may keep her from coming the second time. Then wilt thou come to the island of the Three Capes, where feed the oxen of the Sun. Beware that thy companions harm them not."

The next day they departed. Then Ulysses told his companions of the Sirens, and how they should deal with him. And after a while, the following wind that had blown ceased, and there was a great calm; so they took down the sails and laid them in the ship, and put forth the oars to row. Then Ulysses made great cakes of wax, kneading them (for the sun was now hot), and put into the ears of his companions. And they bound him to the mast and so rowed on. Then the Sirens sang, —

> "Hither, Ulysses, great Achaian name,
> Turn thy swift keel, and listen to our lay;
> Since never pilgrim near these regions came,
> In black ship on the azure fields astray,
> But heard our sweet voice ere he sailed away,
> And in his joy passed on with ampler mind.
> We know what labors were in ancient day
> Wrought in wide Troia, as the gods assigned;
> We know from land to land all toils of all mankind." [1]

Then Ulysses prayed that they would loose him, nodding his head, for their ears were stopped; but they plied their oars, and Eurylochus and Perimedes put new bonds upon him.

After this they saw a smoke and surf, and heard a mighty roar, and their oars dropped out of their hands for fear; but Ulysses bade them be of good heart, for that by his counsel they had escaped other dangers in past time. And the rowers he bade row as hard as they might. But to the helmsman he said, "Steer the ship outside the smoke and the surf, and steer close to the cliffs, lest the ship shoot off unawares and lose us." But of Scylla he said nothing, fearing lest they should lose heart and cease rowing altogether. Then he armed himself, and stood in the prow waiting till Scylla should appear.

[1] Worsley.

But on the other side Charybdis was sucking in the water with a horrible noise, and with eddies so deep that a man might see the sand at the bottom. But while they looked trembling at this, Scylla caught six of the men from the ship, and Ulysses heard them call him by his name as the monster carried them away. And never, he said in after days, did he see with his eyes so piteous a sight.

But after this they came to the land where fed the oxen of the Sun. And Ulysses said, "Let us pass by this island, for there shall we find the greatest evil that we have yet suffered." But they would not hearken; only they said that the next day they would sail again.

Then spake Ulysses, "Ye constrain me, being many to one. Yet promise me this, that ye will not take any of the sheep or oxen, for if ye do great trouble will come to us."

So they promised. But for a whole month the south wind blew and ceased not. And their store of meat and drink being spent, they caught fishes and birds, as they could, being sore pinched with hunger. And at the last it chanced that Ulysses, being weary, fell asleep. And while he slept, his companions, Eurylochus persuading them, took of the oxen of the Sun, and slew them, for they said that their need was great, and that when they came to their own land they would build a temple to the Sun to make amends. But the Sun was very wroth with them. And a great and dreadful thing happened, for the hides crept, and the meat on the spits bellowed.

Six days they feasted on the oxen, and on the seventh they set sail. But when they were now out of sight of land, Zeus brought up a great storm over the sea, and a mighty west wind blew, breaking both the forestay and the backstay of the mast, so that it fell. And after this a thunderbolt struck the ship, and all the men that were in it fell overboard and died. But Ulysses lashed the keel to the mast with the backstay, and on these he sat, borne by the winds across the sea.

All night was he borne along, and in the morning he came to Charybdis. And it chanced that Charybdis was then sucking in the water; but Ulysses, springing up, clung to a wild fig-tree that grew from the rock, but could find no rest for his feet, nor yet could climb into the tree. All day long he clung, waiting till the raft should come forth again; and at evening, at the time when a judge rises from his seat after judging many causes, the raft came forth. Then he loosed his hands and fell, so that he sat astride upon the raft.

After this he was borne for nine days upon the sea, till he came to the island Ogygia, where dwelt the goddess Calypso.

CHAPTER IX.

FOR seven years Ulysses tarried in the island of Calypso. And in the eighth year Zeus sent Hermes to the goddess, to bid her let Ulysses go. So Hermes donned his golden sandals, and took his wand in his hand, and came to the island of Ogygia, and to the cave where Calypso dwelt. A fair place it was. In the cave was burning a fire of sweet-smelling wood, and Calypso sat at her loom and sang with a lovely voice. And round about the cave was a grove of alders and poplars and cypresses, wherein many birds, falcons and owls and sea-crows, were wont to roost; and all about the mouth of the cave was a vine with purple clusters of grapes; and there were four fountains which streamed four ways through meadows of parsley and violet. But Ulysses was not there, for he sat, as was his wont, on the sea-shore, weeping and groaning because he might not see wife and home and country.

And Calypso spied Hermes, and bade him come within, and gave him meat and drink, ambrosia and nectar, which are the food of the gods. And when he had ended his meal, she asked him of his errand. So he told her that he was come, at the bidding of Zeus, in the matter of Ulysses, for that it was the pleasure of the gods that he should return to his native country, and that she should not hinder him any more. It vexed Calypso much to hear this, for she would fain have kept Ulysses with her always, and she said, —

"Ye gods are always jealous when a goddess loves a mortal man. And as for Ulysses, did not I save him when Zeus had smitten his ship with a thunderbolt, and all his comrades had perished? And now let him go, — if it pleases Zeus. Only I cannot send him, for I have neither ship nor rowers. Yet will I willingly teach him how he may safely return."

And Hermes said, "Do this thing speedily, lest Zeus be wroth with thee."

So he departed. And Calypso went seeking Ulysses, and found him on the shore of the sea, looking out over the waters, as was his wont, and weeping, for he was weary of his life, so much did he desire to see Ithaca again. She stood by him and said, —

"Weary not for thy native country, nor waste thyself with tears. If thou wilt go, I will speed thee on thy way. Take therefore thine axe and cut thee beams, and join them together, and make a deck upon them, and I will give thee bread and water and wine, and clothe thee also, so that thou mayest return safe to thy native country, for the gods will have it so."

"Nay," said Ulysses, "what is this that thou sayest? Shall I pass in a raft over the dreadful sea, over which even ships go not without harm? I will not go against thy will; but thou must swear the great oath of the gods that thou plannest no evil against me."

Then Calypso smiled and said, "These are strange words. By the Styx I swear that I plan no harm against thee, but only such good as I would ask myself, did I need it; for indeed my heart is not of iron, but rather full of compassion."

Then they two went to the cave and sat down to meat, and she set before him food, such as mortal men eat, but she herself ate ambrosia and drank nectar, as the gods are wont. And afterwards she said, —

"Why art thou so eager for thy home? Surely if thou knewest all the trouble that awaits thee, thou wouldst not go, but wouldst rather dwell with me. And though thou desirest all the day long to see thy wife, surely I am not less fair than she."

"Be not angry," Ulysses made reply. "The wise Penelopé cannot indeed be compared to thee, for she is a mortal woman and thou art a goddess. Yet is my home dear to me, and I would fain see it again."

The next day Calypso gave him an axe with a handle of olive wood, and an adze, and took him to the end of the island, where there were great trees, long ago sapless and dry, alder and poplar and pine. Of these he felled twenty, and lopped them, and worked them by the line. Then the goddess brought him a gimlet, and he made holes in the logs and joined them with pegs. And he made decks and side-planking also; also a mast and a yard, and a rudder wherewith to turn the raft. And he fenced it about with a bulwark of osier against the waves. The sails, indeed, Calypso wove, and Ulysses fitted them with braces and halyards and sheets. And afterwards, with ropes, he moored the raft to the shore.

On the fourth day all was finished, and on the fifth day he departed. And Calypso gave him goodly garments, and a skin of wine, and a skin of water, and a rich provender in a wallet of leather. She sent also a fair wind blowing behind, and Ulysses set his sails and proceeded joyfully on his way; nor did he sleep, but watched the sun and the stars, still steering, as indeed Calypso had bidden, to the left. So he sailed for seventeen days, and on the eighteenth he saw the hills of Phæacia and the land, which had the shape of a shield.

But Poseidon spied him as he sailed, and was wroth to see him so near to the end of his troubles. Wherefore he sent all the winds of heaven down upon him. Sore troubled was Ulysses, and said to himself, "It was truth that Calypso spake when she said how that I should suffer many troubles returning to my home. Would that I had died that day when many a spear was cast by the men of Troy over the dead Achilles. Then would the Greeks have buried me; but now shall I perish miserably."

And as he spake a great wave struck the raft and tossed him far away, so that he dropped the rudder from his hand. Nor for a long time could he rise, so deep was he sunk, and so heavy was the goodly clothing which Calypso had given him. Yet at the last he rose, and spat the salt water out of his mouth, and, so brave was he, sprang at the raft and caught it and sat thereon, and was borne hither and thither by the waves. But Ino saw him and pitied him—a woman she had been, and was now a goddess of the sea—and came and sat upon the waves, saying,—

"Luckless mortal, why doth Poseidon hate thee so? He shall not slay thee, though he fain would do it. Put off these garments and swim to the land of Phæacia, putting this veil under thy breast. And when thou art come to the land, loose it from thee, and cast it into the sea; but when thou castest it, look away."

But Ulysses doubted what this might be, and thought that he would yet stay on the raft while the timbers held together, for that the land was far away. But as he thought, yet another great wave struck it, and scattered the timbers. And he sat upon one of them, as a man sits upon a horse; and then he stripped off the garments which Calypso had given him, and so, leaping into the sea, made to swim to the land.

And Poseidon saw him, and said, "Get to the shore if thou canst, but even so thou art not come to the end of thy troubles."

So for two days and two nights he swam, Athené helping him, for otherwise he had perished. But on the third day there was a calm, and he saw the land from the top of a great wave, for the waves were yet high, close at hand. Dear as a father to his son, rising up from grievous sickness, so dear was the land to Ulysses. But when he came near he heard the waves breaking along the shore, for there was no harbor there, but only cliffs and rugged rocks. And while he doubted what he should do, a great wave bore him to the shore. Then would he have perished, all his bones being broken; but Athené put it in his heart to lay hold of a great rock till the wave had spent itself. And even then had he died, for the ebb caught him and bore him far out to sea; but he bethought him that he would swim along, if haply he might see some landing-place. And at last he came to the mouth of a river, where there were no rocks. Then at last he won his way to the land. His knees were bent under him, and his hands dropped at his side, and the salt water ran out of his mouth and nostrils. Breathless was he, and speechless; but when he came to himself, he loosed the veil from under his breast and cast it into the sea.

Then he lay down on the rushes by the bank of the river and kissed the earth, thinking within himself, " What now shall I do? for if I sleep here by the river, I fear that the dew and the frost may slay me; for indeed, in the morning-time the wind from the river blows cold. And if I go up to the wood, to lay me down to sleep in the thicket, I fear that some evil beast may devour me."

But it seemed better to go to the wood. So he went. Now this was close to the river, and he found two bushes, of wild olive one, and of fruitful olive the other. So thickly grown together were they, that the winds blew not through them, nor did the sun pierce them, nor yet the rain. Thereunder crept Ulysses, and found great store of leaves, shelter enough for two or three, even in a great storm. Then, even as a man who dwells apart from others cherishes his fire, hiding it under the ashes, so Ulysses cherished his life under the leaves. And Athené sent down upon his eyelids deep sleep, that might ease him of his toil.

CHAPTER X.

NAUSICAA AND ALCINOÜS.

Now the king of Phæacia was Alcinoüs, and he had five sons and one daughter, Nausicaa. To her, where she slept with her two maidens by her, Athené went, taking the shape of her friend, the daughter of Dymas, and said, —

"Why hath thy mother so idle a daughter, Nausicaa? Lo! thy garments lie unwashed, and thy wedding must be near, seeing that many nobles in the land are suitors to thee. Ask then thy father that he give thee the wagon with the mules, for the laundries are far from the city, and I will go with thee."

And when the morning was come, Nausicaa awoke, marvelling at the dream, and went seeking her parents. Her mother she found busy with her maidens at the loom, and her father she met as he was going to the council with the chiefs of the land. Then she said, "Give me, father, the wagon with the mules, that I may take the garments to the river to wash them. Thou shouldest always have clean robes when thou goest to the council; and there are my five brothers also, who love to have newly-washed garments at the dance."

But of her own marriage she said nothing. And her father, knowing her thoughts, said, "It is well. The men shall harness the wagon for thee."

So they put the clothing into the wagon. And her mother put also food and wine, and olive oil also, wherewith she and her maidens might anoint themselves after the bath. So they climbed into the wagon and went to the river. And then they washed the clothing, and spread it out to dry on the rocks by the sea. And after that they had bathed and anointed themselves, they sat down to eat and drink by the river side; and after the meal they played at ball, singing as they played, and Nausicaa, fair as Artemis when she hunts on Taygetus or Erymanthus wild goats and stags, led the song. But when they had nearly ended their play, the princess, throwing the ball to one of her maidens, cast it so wide that it fell into the river. Whereupon they all cried aloud, and Ulysses awoke. And he said to himself, "What is this land to which I have come? Are they that dwell therein fierce or kind to strangers? Just now I seemed to hear the voice of nymphs, or am I near the dwellings of men?"

Then he twisted leaves about his loins, and rose up and went towards the maidens, who indeed were frighted to see him (for he was wild of aspect), and fled hither and thither. But Nausicaa stood and fled not. Then Ulysses thought within himself, should he go near and clasp her knees, or, lest haply this should anger her, should he stand and speak? And this he did, saying,—

"I am thy suppliant, O queen. Whether thou art a goddess, I know not. But if thou art a mortal, happy thy father and mother, and happy thy brothers, and happiest of all he who shall win thee in marriage. Never have I seen man or woman so fair. Thou art like a young palm-tree that but lately I saw in Delos, springing by the temple of the god. But as for me, I have been cast on this shore, having come from the island Ogygia. Pity me, then, and lead me to the city, and give me something, a wrapper of this linen, maybe, to put about me. So may the gods give thee all blessings!"

And Nausicaa made answer, "Thou seemest, stranger, to be neither evil nor foolish; and as for thy plight, the gods give good fortune or bad, as they will. Thou shalt not lack clothing or food, or anything that a suppliant should have. And I will take thee to the city. Know also that this land is Phæacia, and that I am daughter to Alcinoüs, who is king thereof."

Then she called to her maidens, "What mean ye, to flee when ye see a man? No enemy comes hither to harm us, for we are dear to the gods, and we also live in an island of the sea, so that men may not approach to work us wrong; but if one cometh here overborne by trouble, it is well to succor him. Give this man, therefore, food and drink, and wash him in the river, where there is shelter from the wind."

So they brought him down to the river, and gave him a tunic and a cloak to clothe himself withal, and also oil-olive in a flask of gold. Then, at his bidding, they departed a little space, and he washed the salt from his skin and out of his hair, and anointed himself, and put on the clothing. And Athené made him taller and fairer to see, and caused the hair to be thick on his head, in color as a hyacinth. Then he sat down on the sea-shore, right beautiful to behold, and the maiden said,—

"Not without some bidding of the gods comes this man to our land. Before, indeed, I deemed him uncomely, but now he seems like to the gods. I should be well content to have such a man for a husband, and maybe he might will to abide in this land. But give him, ye maidens, food and drink."

So they gave him, and he ate ravenously, having fasted long. Then Nausicaa bade yoke the mules, and said to Ulysses,—

"Follow thou with the maidens, and I will lead the way in the wagon. For I would not that the people should speak lightly of me. And I doubt not that were thou with me, some one of the baser sort would say, 'Who is this stranger, tall and fair, that cometh with Nausicaa? Will he be her husband? Perchance it is some god who has come down at her prayer, or a man from far away; for of us men of Phæacia she thinks scorn.' It would be shame that such words should be spoken. And indeed it is ill-done of a maiden who, father and mother unknowing, companies with men. Do thou, then, follow behind, and when we are come to the city, tarry in a poplar grove that thou shalt see ('tis the grove of Athené) till I shall have come to my father's house. Then follow; and for the house, that any one, even a child can show thee, for the other Phæacians dwell not in such. And when thou art come within the doors, pass quickly through the hall to where my mother sits. Close to the hearth is her seat, and my father's hard by, where he sits with the wine-cup in his hand, as a god. Pass him by, and lay hold of her knees, and pray her that she give thee safe return to thy country."

It was evening when they came to the city. And Nausicaa drove the wagon to the palace. Then her brothers came out to her, and loosed the mules and carried in the clothing. Then she went to her chamber, where Eurymedusa, who was her nurse, lighted a fire and prepared a meal. Meanwhile Ulysses came from the grove, and, lest any one should see him, Athené spread a mist about him; and when he had now reached the city, she took the shape of a young maiden carrying a pitcher, and met him.

Then Ulysses asked her, "My child, canst thou tell me where dwells Alcinoüs? for I am a stranger in this place."

And she answered, "I will show thee, for indeed he dwells nigh to my own father. But be thou silent, for we Phæacians love not strangers over much." Then she led him to the palace. A wondrous place it was, with walls of brass and doors of gold, hanging on posts of silver; and on either side of the door were dogs of gold and silver, the work of Hephæstus, and against the wall, all along from the threshold to the inner chamber, were set seats, on which sat the chiefs of the Phæacians, feasting; and youths wrought in gold stood holding torches in their hands, to give light in the darkness. Fifty women were in the house grinding corn and weaving robes, for the women of the land are no less skilled to weave than are the men to sail the sea. And round about the house were gardens beautiful exceedingly, with orchards of fig and apple and pear and pomegranate and olive. Drought hurts them not, nor frost, and harvest comes after harvest without ceasing. Also there was a vineyard; and some of the grapes were parching in the sun, and some were being gathered, and some again were but just turning red. And there were beds of all manner of flowers; and in the midst of all were two fountains which never failed.

These things Ulysses regarded for a space, and then passed into the hall. And there the chiefs of Phæacia were drinking their last cup to Hermes. Quickly he passed through them, and put his hands on the knees of Areté, and said, — and as he spake the mist cleared from about him, and all that were in the hall beheld him, —

"I am a suppliant to thee, and to thy husband, and to thy guests. The gods bless thee and them, and grant you to live in peace, and that your children should come peacefully after you. Only do you send me home to my native country."

And he sat down in the ashes of the hearth. Then for a space all were silent; but at the last spake Echeneüs, who was the oldest man in the land, —

"King Alcinoüs, this ill becomes you that this man should sit in the ashes of the hearth. Raise him and bid him sit upon a seat, and let us pour out to Father Zeus, who is the friend of suppliants, and let the keeper of the house give him meat and drink."

And Alcinoüs did so, bidding his eldest born, Laodamas, rise from his seat. And an attendant poured water on his hands, and the keeper of the house gave him meat and drink. Then, when all had poured out to Father Zeus, King Alcinoüs said that they would take counsel on the morrow about sending this stranger to his home. And they answered that it should be so, and went each to his home. Only Ulysses was left in the hall, and Alcinoüs and Areté with him. And Areté saw his cloak and tunic, that she and her maidens had made them, and said, —

"Whence art thou, stranger? and who gave thee these garments?"

So Ulysses told her how he had come from the island of Calypso, and what he had suffered, and how Nausicaa had found him on the shore, and had guided him to the city.

But Alcinoüs blamed the maiden that she had not herself brought him to the house. "For thou wast her suppliant," he said.

"Nay," said Ulysses; "she would have brought me, but I would not, fearing thy wrath." For he would not have the maiden blamed.

Then said Alcinoüs, "I am not one to be angered for such cause. Gladly would I have such a one as thou art to be my son-in-law, and I would give him house and wealth. But no one would I stay against his will. And as for sending thee to thy home, that is easy; for thou shalt sleep, and they shall take thee meanwhile."

And after this they slept. And the next day the King called the chiefs to an assembly, and told them of his purpose, that he would send this stranger to his home, for that it was their wont to show such kindness to such as needed it. And he bade fifty and two of the younger men make ready a ship, and that the elders should come to his house, and bring Demodocus, the minstrel, with them, for that he was minded to make a great feast for this stranger before he departed. So the youths made ready the ship. And afterwards there were gathered together a great multitude, so that the palace was filled from the one end to the other. And Alcinoüs slew for them twelve sheep and eight swine and two oxen. And when they had feasted to the full, the minstrel sang to them of how Achilles and Ulysses had striven together with fierce words at a feast, and how King Agamemnon was glad, seeing that so the prophecy of Apollo was fulfilled, saying that when valor and counsel should fall out, the end of Troy should come. But when Ulysses heard the song, he wept, holding his mantle before his face.

This Alcinoüs perceived, and said to the chiefs, "Now that we have feasted and delighted ourselves with song, let us go forth, that this stranger may see that we are skilful in boxing and wrestling and running."

So they went forth, a herald leading Demodocus by the hand, for the minstrel was blind. Then stood up many Phæacian youths, and the fairest and strongest of them all was Laodamas, eldest son to the King, and after him Euryalus. And next they ran a race, and Clytoneus was the swiftest. And among the wrestlers Euryalus was the best; and of the boxers, Laodamas. And in throwing the quoit Elatrius excelled; and in leaping at the bar, Amphialus.

Then Laodamas, Euryalus urging him, said to Ulysses, "Father, wilt thou not try thy skill in some game, and put away the trouble from thy heart?"

But Ulysses answered, "Why askest thou this? I think of my troubles rather than of sport, and sit among you, caring only that I may see again my home."

Then said Euryalus, "And in very truth, stranger, thou hast not the look of a wrestler or boxer. Rather would one judge thee to be some trader, who sails over the sea for gain."

"Nay," answered Ulysses, "this is ill said. So true is it that the gods give not all gifts to all men, beauty to one and sweet speech to another. Fair of form art thou, no god could better thee; but thou speakest idle words. I am not unskilled in these things, but stood among the first in the old days; but since have I suffered much in battle and shipwreck. Yet will I make trial of my strength, for thy words have angered me."

Whereupon he took a quoit, heavier far than such as the Phæacians were wont to throw, and sent it with a whirl. It hurtled through the air, so that the brave Phæacians crouched to the ground in fear, and fell far beyond all the rest.

Then said Ulysses, "Come now, I will contend in wrestling or boxing, or even in the race, with any man in Phæacia, save Laodamas only, for he is my friend. I can shoot with the bow, and only Philoctetes could surpass me; and I can cast a spear as far as other men can shoot an arrow. But as for the race, it may be that some one might outrun me, for I have suffered much on the sea."

But they all were silent, till the King stood up and said, "Thou hast spoken well. But we men of Phæacia are not mighty to wrestle or to box; only we are swift of foot, and skilful to sail upon the sea. And we love feasts, and dances, and the harp, and gay clothing, and the bath. In these things no man may surpass us."

Then the King bade Demodocus the minstrel sing again. And when he had done so, the King's two sons, Alius and Laodamas, danced together; and afterwards they played with the ball, throwing it into the air, cloud high, and catching it right skilfully.

And afterwards the king said, "Let us each give this stranger a mantle and a tunic and a talent of gold, and let Euryalus make his peace with words and with a gift."

And they all (now there were twelve princes, and Alcinoüs the thirteenth) said that it should be so; also Euryalus gave Ulysses a sword with a hilt of silver and a scabbard of ivory. And after this Ulysses went to the bath, and then they all sat down to the feast. But as he went to the hall, Nausicaa, fair as a goddess, met him and said, —

"Hail, stranger; thou wilt remember me in thy native country, for thou owest me thanks for thy life."

And he answered, "Every day in my native country will I remember thee, for indeed, fair maiden, thou didst save my life."

And when they were set down to the feast, Ulysses sent a portion of the chine, which the King had caused to be set before him, to the minstrel Demodocus, with a message that he should sing to them of the Horse of wood which Epeius made, Athené helping him, and how Ulysses brought it into Troy, full of men of war who should destroy the city.

Then the minstrel sang how that some of the Greeks sailed away, having set fire to their tents, and some hid themselves in the horse with Ulysses, and how the men of Troy sat around, taking counsel what they should do with it, and some judged that they should rip it open, and some that they should throw it from the hill-top, and others again that they should leave it to be a peace-offering to the gods; and how the Greeks issued forth from their lurking-place and spoiled the city, and how Ulysses and Menelaüs went to the house of Deïphobus.

So he sang, and Ulysses wept to hear the tale. And when Alcinoüs perceived that he wept, he bade Demodocus cease from his song, for that some that were there liked it not. And to Ulysses he said that he should tell them who was his father and his mother, and from what land he came, and what was his name. All these things Ulysses told them, and all that he had done and suffered, down to the time when the Princess Nausicaa found him on the river shore. And when he had ended, King Alcinoüs bade that the princes should give Ulysses yet other gifts; and after that they went each man to his house to sleep.

The next day King Alcinoüs put all the gifts into the ship. And when the evening was come, Ulysses bade farewell to the King and to the Queen, and departed.

CHAPTER XI.

ULYSSES AND THE SWINEHERD.

Now Ulysses slept while the ship was sailing to Ithaca. And when it was come to the shore he yet slept. Wherefore the men lifted him out, and put him on the shore with all his goods that the princes of the Phæacians had given him, and so left him. After a while he awoke, and knew not the land, for there was a great mist about him, Athené having contrived that it should be so, for good ends, as will be seen. Very wroth was he with the men of Phæacia, thinking that they had cheated him; nor did it comfort him when he counted his goods to find that of these he had lost nothing.

But as he walked by the sea, lamenting his fate, Athené met him, having the shape of a young shepherd, fair to look upon, such as are the sons of kings; and Ulysses, when he saw him, was glad, and asked him how men called the country wherein he was.

And the false shepherd said, "Thou art foolish, or, may be, hast come from very far, not to know this country. Many men know it, both in the east and in the west. Rocky it is, not fit for horses, nor is it very broad; but it is fertile land, and full of wine; nor does it want for rain, and a good pasture it is for oxen and goats; and men call it Ithaca. Even in Troy, which is very far, they say, from this land of Greece, men have heard of Ithaca."

This Ulysses was right glad to hear. Yet he was not minded to say who he was, but rather to feign a tale.

So he said, "Yes, of a truth, I heard of this Ithaca in Crete, from which I am newly come with all this wealth, leaving also as much behind for my children. For I slew Orsilochus, son of Idomeneus the king, because he would have taken from me my spoil. Wherefore I slew him, lying in wait for him by the way. Then made I covenant with certain Phœnicians that they should take me to Pylos or to Elis; which thing indeed they were minded to do, only the wind drave them hither, and while I slept they put me upon the shore, and my possessions with me, and departed to Sidon."

This pleased Athené much, and she changed her shape, becoming like a woman, tall and fair, and said to Ulysses, —

"Right cunning would he be who could cheat thee. Even now in thy native country ceasest thou not from cunning words and deceits! But let these things be; for thou, I trow, art the wisest of mortal men, and I excel among the gods in council. For I am Athené, daughter of Zeus, who am ever wont to stand by thee and help thee. And now we will hide these possessions of thine; and thou must be silent, nor tell to any one who thou art, and endure many things, so that thou mayest come to thine own again."

But still Ulysses doubted, and would have the goddess tell him whether of a truth he had come back to his native land. And she, commending his prudence, scattered the mist that was about him.

Then Ulysses knew the land, and kissed the ground, and prayed to the Nymphs that they would be favorable to him. And after this, Athené guiding him, he hid away his possessions in a cave, and put a great stone on the mouth. Then the two took counsel together.

And Athené said, "Think, man of many devices, how thou wilt lay hands on these men, suitors of thy wife, who for three years have sat in thy house devouring thy substance. And she hath answered them craftily, making many promises, but still waiting for thy coming."

Then Ulysses said, "Truly I had perished, even as Agamemnon perished, but for thee. But do thou help me, as of old in Troy, for with thee at my side I would fight with three hundred men."

Then said Athené, "Lo! I will cause that no man shall know thee, for I will wither the fair flesh on thy limbs, and take the bright hair from thy head, and make thine eyes dull. And the suitors shall take no account of thee, neither shall thy wife nor thy son know thee. But go to the swineherd Eumæus, where he dwells by the fountain of Arethusa, for he is faithful to thee and to thy house. And I will hasten to Sparta, to the house of Menelaüs, to fetch Telemachus, for he went thither, seeking news of thee."

Then Athené changed him into the shape of a beggar man. She caused his skin to wither, and his hair to fall off, and his eyes to grow dim, and put on him filthy rags, with a great stag's hide about his shoulders, and in his hand a staff, and a wallet on his shoulder fastened by a rope.

Then she departed, and Ulysses went to the house of Eumæus, the swineherd. A great courtyard there was, and twelve sties for the sows, and four watchdogs, big as wild beasts, for such did the swineherd breed. He himself was shaping sandals, and of his men three were with the swine in the fields, and one was driving a fat beast to the city, to be meat for the suitors. But when Ulysses came near, the dogs ran upon him, and he dropped his staff and sat down, and yet would have suffered harm, even on his own threshold; but the swineherd ran forth and drave away the dogs, and brought the old man in, and gave him a seat of brushwood, with a great goat-skin over it.

And Ulysses said, "Zeus and the other gods requite thee for this kindness."

Then the two talked of matters in Ithaca, and Eumæus told how the suitors of the Queen were devouring the substance of Ulysses. Then the false beggar asked him of the King, saying that perchance, having travelled far, he might know such an one.

But Eumæus said, "Nay, old man, thus do all wayfarers talk, yet we hear no truth from them. Not a vagabond fellow comes to this land but our Queen must see him, and ask him many things, weeping the while. And thou, I doubt not, for a cloak or a tunic, would tell a wondrous tale. But Ulysses, I know, is dead, and either the fowls of the air devour him or the fishes of the sea."

And when the false beggar would have comforted him, saying he knew of a truth that Ulysses would yet return, he hearkened not. Moreover he prophesied evil for Telemachus also, who had gone to seek news of his father, but would surely be slain by the suitors, who were even now lying in wait for him as he should return. And after this he asked the stranger who he was and whence he had come. Then Ulysses answered him craftily,—

"I am a Cretan, the son of one Castor, by a slave woman. Now my father, while he lived, did by me as by his other sons. But when he died they divided his goods, and gave me but a small portion, and took my dwelling from me. Yet I won a rich wife for myself, for I was brave and of good repute. No man would sooner go to battle or to ambush than I, and I loved ships and spears and arrows, which some men hate, I trow. Nine times did I lead my followers in ships against strangers, and the tenth time I went with King Idomeneus to Troy. And when the city of Priam had perished, I went back to my native country, and there for the space of one month I tarried with my wife, and afterwards I sailed with nine ships to Egypt. On the fifth day, — for the gods gave us a prosperous voyage, — we came to the river of Egypt. There did my comrades work much wrong to the people of the land, spoiling their fields, and leading into captivity their wives and children; nor would they hearken to me when I would have stayed them. Then the Egyptians gathered an army, and came upon them, and slew some and took others. And I, throwing down helmet and spear and shield, hasted to the king of the land where he sat in his chariot, and prayed that he would have mercy on me, which thing he did. And with him I dwelt for seven years, gathering much wealth. But in the eighth year there came a trader of Phœnicia, who beguiled me, that I went with him to his country. And there I tarried for a year; and afterwards he carried me in his ship to Libya, meaning to sell me as a slave; but Zeus brake the ship, so that I only was left alive. Nine days did I float, keeping hold of the mast, and on the tenth a wave cast me on the land of Thresprotia, where King Pheidon kindly entreated me, giving me food and raiment. There did I hear tell of Ulysses; yea, and saw the riches which he had gathered together, which King Pheidon was keeping till he himself should come back from Dodona, from the oracle of Zeus. Thence I sailed in a ship for Dulichium, purposing to go to King Acastus, but the sailors were minded to sell me for a slave. Therefore they left me bound in the ship, but themselves took their supper on the shore. But in the meanwhile I brake my bonds, the gods helping me, and leaping into the sea, swam to the land, and hid myself in a wood that was near."

All this tale did Ulysses tell; but Eumæus doubted whether these things were so, thinking rather that the beggar-man said these things to please him. After this they talked much; and when the swineherd's men were returned, they all feasted together. And the night being cold, and there being much rain, Ulysses was minded to see whether one would lend him a cloak; wherefore he told this tale:—

"Once upon a time there was laid an ambush near to the city of Troy. And Menelaüs and Ulysses and I were the leaders of it. In the reeds we sat, and the night was cold, and the snow lay upon our shields. Now all the others had cloaks, but I had left mine behind at the ships. So when the night was three parts spent I spake to Ulysses, 'Here am I without a cloak; soon, methinks, shall I perish with the cold.' Soon did he bethink him of a remedy, for he was ever ready with counsel. Therefore to me he said, 'Hush, lest some one hear thee,' and to the others, 'I have been warned in a dream. We are very far from the ships and in peril. Wherefore let some one run to the ships to King Agamemnon, that he send more men to help.' Then Thoas, son of Andræmon, rose up and ran, casting off his cloak, and this I took, and slept warmly therein. Were I this night such as then I was, I should not lack such kindness even now."

Then said Eumæus, "This is well spoken, old man. Thou shalt have a cloak to cover thee. But in the morning thou must put on thy own rags again. Yet perchance, when the son of Ulysses shall come, he will give thee new garments."

After this they slept, but Eumæus tarried without, keeping watch over the swine.

It came to pass the next morning that Telemachus, that

was son of King Ulysses, came to the dwelling of Eumæus, for he was newly returned from Sparta, whither he had gone if haply he might hear some tidings of his father.

And Ulysses heard the steps of a man, and, as the dogs barked not, said to Eumæus, "Lo! there comes some comrade or friend, for the dogs bark not."

And as he spake, Telemachus stood in the doorway, and the swineherd let fall from his hand the bowl in which he was mixing wine, and ran to him and kissed his head and his eyes and his hands. As a father kisses his only son coming back to him from a far country after ten years, so did the swineherd kiss Telemachus. And when Telemachus came in, the false beggar, though indeed he was his father, rose, and would have given place to him; but Telemachus suffered him not. And when they had eaten and drunk, Telemachus asked of the swineherd who this stranger might be.

Then the swineherd told him as he had heard, and afterwards said, "I hand him to thee; he is thy suppliant; do as thou wilt."

But Telemachus answered, "Nay, Eumæus. For am I master in my house? Do not the suitors devour it? And does not my mother doubt whether she will abide with me, remembering the great Ulysses, who was her husband, or will follow some one of those who are suitors to her? I will give this stranger, indeed, food and clothing and a sword, and will send him whithersoever he will, but I would not that he should go among the suitors, so haughty are they and violent."

Then said Ulysses, "But why dost thou bear with these men? Do the people hate thee, that thou canst not avenge thyself on them? and hast thou not kinsmen to help thee? As for me, I would rather die than see such shameful things done in house of mine."

And Telemachus answered, "My people hate me not; but as for kinsmen, I have none, for Acrisius had but one son, Laertes, and he again but one, Ulysses, and Ulysses had none other but me. Therefore do these men spoil my substance without let, and, it may be, will take my life also. These things, however, the gods will order. But do thou, Eumæus, go to Penelopé, and tell her that I am returned, but let no man know thereof, for there are that counsel evil against me; but I will stay here meanwhile."

So Eumæus departed. But when he had gone Athené came, like a woman tall and fair; but Telemachus saw her not, for it is not given to all to see the immortal gods; but Ulysses saw her, and the dogs saw her, and whimpered for fear. She signed to Ulysses, and he went forth, and she said, —

"Hide not the matter from thy son, but plan with him how ye may slay the suitors, and lo! I am with you."

Then she made his garments white and fair, and his body lusty and strong, and his face swarthy, and his cheeks full, and his beard black. And when he was returned to the house, Telemachus marvelled to see him, and said, —

"Thou art not what thou wast. Surely thou art some god from heaven."

But Ulysses made reply, "No god am I, only thy father, whom thou hast so desired to see."

And when Telemachus yet doubted, Ulysses told him how that Athené had so changed him. Then Telemachus threw his arms about him, weeping, and both wept together for a while. And afterwards Telemachus asked him of his coming back. And Ulysses, when he had told him of this, asked him how many were the suitors, and whether they two could fight with them alone.

Then said Telemachus, "Thou art, I know, a great warrior, my father, and a wise, but this thing we cannot do; for these men are not ten, no, nor twice ten, but from Dulichium come fifty and two, and from Samos four and twenty, and from Zacynthus twenty, and from Ithaca twelve; and they have Medon the herald, and a minstrel also, and attendants."

Then said Ulysses, "Go thou home in the morning and mingle with the suitors, and I will come as an old beggar; and if they entreat me shamefully, endure to see it, yea, if they drag me to the door. Only, if thou wilt, speak to them prudent words; but they will not heed thee, for indeed their doom is near. Heed this also: when I give thee the token, take all the arms from the dwelling and hide them in thy chamber. And when they shall ask thee why thou doest thus, say that thou takest them out of the smoke, for that they are not such as Ulysses left behind him when he went to Troy, but that the smoke has soiled them. Say, also, that haply they might stir up strife sitting at their cups, and that it is not well that arms should be at hand, for that the very steel draws on a man to fight. But keep two swords and two spears and two shields, — these shall be for thee and me. Only let no one know of my coming back — not Laertes, nor the swineherd, no, nor Penelopé herself."

But after a while the swineherd came back from the city, having carried his tidings to the Queen. And this she also had heard from the sailors of the ships. Also the ship of the suitors which they had sent to lie in wait for the young man was returned. And the suitors were in great wrath and fear, because their purpose had failed, and also because Penelopé the queen knew what they had been minded to do, and hated them because of it.

CHAPTER XII.

ULYSSES IN HIS HOME.

THE next day Telemachus went to the city. But before he went he said to Eumæus that he should bring the beggar-man to the city, for that it was better to beg in the city than in the country. And the false beggar also said that he wished this. And Telemachus, when he was arrived, went to the palace and greeted the nurse Eury-clea and his mother Penelopé, who was right glad to see him, but to whom he told nought of what had happened. And after this he went to Piræus, and bade him keep the gifts which King Menelaüs had given him till he should be in peace in his own house; and if things should fall out otherwise, that he should keep them for himself. And then he went to fetch the seer Theoclymenus, that he might bring him to the palace. And the seer, when he was come thither, prophesied good concerning Ulysses, how that he would certainly return and take vengeance for all the wrong that had been done to him.

Now in the meanwhile Eumæus and the false beggar were coming to the city. And when they were now near to it, by the fountain which Ithacus and his brethren had made, where was also an altar of the Nymphs, Melanthius the goatherd met them, and spake evil to Eumæus, rebuking him that he brought this beggar to the city. And he came near and smote Ulysses with his foot on the thigh, but moved him not from the path. And Ulysses thought a while, should he smite him with his club and slay him, or dash him on the ground. But it seemed to him better to endure.

But Eumæus lifted up his hands and said, "Oh, now may the Nymphs of the fountain fulfil this hope, that Ulysses may come back to his home, and tear from thee this finery of thine, wherein thou comest to the city, leaving thy flock for evil shepherds to devour!"

So they went on to the palace. And at the door of the court there lay the dog Argus, whom in the old days Ulysses had reared with his own hand. But ere the dog grew to his full, Ulysses had sailed to Troy. And, while he was strong, men used him in the chase, hunting wild goats and roe-deer and hares. But now he lay on a dunghill, and the lice swarmed upon him. Well he knew his master, and, for that he could not come near to him, wagged his tail and drooped his ears.

And Ulysses, when he saw him, wiped away a tear, and said, "Surely this is strange, Eumæus, that such a dog, being of so fine a breed, should lie here upon a dunghill."

And Eumæus made reply, "He belongeth to a master who died far away. For indeed, when Ulysses had him of old, he was the strongest and swiftest of dogs; but now my dear lord has perished far away, and the careless women tend him not. For when the master is away the slaves are careless of their duty. Surely a man, when he is made a slave, loses half the virtue of a man."

And as he spake, the dog Argus died. Twenty years had he waited, and saw his master at the last.

After this the two entered the hall. And Telemachus, when he saw them, took from the basket bread and meat, as much as his hands could hold, and bade carry them to the beggar, and also to tell him that he might go round among the suitors, asking alms. So he went, stretching out his hand, as though he were wont to beg; and some gave, having compassion upon him and marvelling at him, and some asked who he was. But, of all, Antinoüs was the most shameless. For when Ulysses came to him and told him how he had had much riches and power in former days, and how he had gone to Egypt, and had been sold a slave into Cyprus, Antinoüs mocked him, saying, —

"Get thee from my table, or thou shalt find a worse Egypt and a harder Cyprus than before."

Then Ulysses said, "Surely thy soul is evil though thy body is fair; for though thou sittest at another man's feast, yet wilt thou give me nothing."

But Antinoüs, in great wrath, took the stool on which he sat and cast it at him, smiting his right shoulder. But Ulysses stirred not, but stood as a rock. But in his heart he thought on revenge. So he went and sat down at the door. And being there, he said, —

"Hear me, suitors of the Queen! There is no wrath if a man be smitten fighting for that which is his own, but Antinoüs has smitten me because that I am poor. May the curse of the hungry light on him therefor, ere he come to his marriage day."

Also the other suitors blamed him that he had dealt so cruelly with this stranger. Also the Queen was wroth when she heard it, as she sat in the upper chamber with her maidens about her.

But as the day passed on there came a beggar from the city, huge of bulk, mighty to eat and drink, but his strength was not according to his size. Arnæus was his name, but the young men called him Irus, because he was their messenger, after Iris, the messenger of Zeus. He spake to Ulysses, —

"Give place, old man, lest I drag thee forth; the young

men even now would have it so, but I think it shame to strike such an one as thee."

Then said Ulysses, "There is room for thee and for me; get what thou canst, for I do not grudge thee aught, but beware lest thou anger me, lest I harm thee, old though I am."

But Irus would not hear words of peace, but still challenged him to fight.

And when Antinoüs saw this he was glad, and said, "This is the goodliest sport that I have seen in this house. These two beggars would fight; let us haste and match them."

And the saying pleased them; and Antinoüs spake again: "Hear me, ye suitors of the Queen! We have put aside these paunches of the goats for our supper. Let us agree then that whosoever of these two shall prevail, shall have choice of these, that which pleaseth him best, and shall hereafter eat with us, and that no one else shall sit in his place."

Then said Ulysses, "It is hard for an old man to fight with a young. Yet will I do it. Only do ye swear to me that no one shall strike me a foul blow while I fight with this man."

Then Telemachus said that this should be so, and they all consented to his words. And after this Ulysses girded himself for the fight. And all that were there saw his thighs, how great and strong they were, and his shoulders, how broad, and his arms, how mighty. And they said one to another, "There will be little of Irus left, so stalwart seems this beggar-man." But as for Irus himself, he would have slunk out of sight, but they that were set to gird him compelled him to come forth.

Then said the Prince Antinoüs, "How is this, thou

braggart, that thou fearest this old man, all woe-begone as he is? Harken thou to this. If this man prevails against thee, thou shalt be cast into a ship and taken to the land of King Echetus, who will cut off thy ears and thy nose for his dogs to eat."

So the two came together. And Ulysses thought whether he should strike the fellow and slay him out of hand, or fell him to the ground. And this last seemed the better of the two. So when Irus had dealt his blow, he smote him on the jaw, and brake in the bone, so that he fell howling on the ground, and the blood poured amain from his mouth.

Then all the suitors laughed aloud. But Ulysses dragged him out of the hall, and propped him by the wall of the courtyard, putting a staff in his hand, and saying, "Sit there, and keep dogs and swine from the door, but dare not hereafter to lord it over men, lest some worse thing befall thee."

Then Antinoüs gave him a great paunch, and Amphinomus gave two loaves, and pledged him in a cup, saying, "Good luck to thee, father, hereafter, though now thou seemest to have evil fortune."

And Ulysses made reply, "O Amphinomus, thou hast much wisdom, methinks, and thy father, I know, is wise. Take heed, therefore. There is nought feebler upon earth than man. For in the days of his prosperity he thinketh nothing of trouble, but when the gods send evil to him, there is no help in him. I also trusted once in myself and my kinsmen, and now — behold me what I am! Let no man, therefore, do violence and wrong, for Zeus shall requite such deeds at the last. And now these suitors of the Queen are working evil to him who is absent. Yet will he return some day and slay his enemies. Fly thou, therefore, while yet there is time, nor meet him when he comes."

So he spake, with kindly thought.

But his doom was on Amphinomus that he should die.

And that evening, the suitors having departed to their own dwellings, Ulysses and Telemachus took the arms from the hall, as they had also planned to do. And while they did so Telemachus said, "See, my father, this marvellous brightness that is on the pillars and the ceiling. Surely some god is with us."

And Ulysses made reply, "I know it: be silent. And now go to thy chamber and sleep, and leave me here, for I have somewhat to say to thy mother and her maidens."

And when the Queen and her maidens came into the hall (for it was their work to cleanse it and make it ready for the morrow), Penelopé asked him of his family and his country. And at first he made as though he would not answer, fearing, he said, lest he should trouble her with the story of that which he had suffered. But afterwards, for she urged him, telling him what she herself had suffered, her husband being lost and her suitors troubling her without ceasing, he feigned a tale that should satisfy her. For he told her how that he was a man of Crete, a brother of King Idomeneus, and how he had given hospitality to Ulysses, what time he was sailing to Troy with the sons of Atreus.

And when the queen, seeking to know whether he spake the truth, asked him of Ulysses what manner of man he was, and with what clothing he was clothed, he answered her rightly, saying, "I remember me that he had a mantle, twofold, woollen, of sea-purple, clasped with a brooch of gold, whereon was a dog that held a fawn by the throat; marvellously wrought they were, so hard held the one, so strove the other to be free. Also he had a tunic, white and smooth, which the women much admired to see. But whether some one had given him these things I know not, for indeed many gave him gifts, and I also, even a sword and a tunic. Also he had a herald with him, one Eurybates, older than him, dark-skinned, round in the shoulders, with curly hair."

And Penelopé, knowing these things to be true, wept aloud, crying that she should see her husband no more. But the false beggar comforted her, saying that Ulysses was in the land of the Thresprotians, having much wealth with him, only that he had lost his ships and his comrades, yet nevertheless would speedily return.

Then Penelopé bade her servants make ready a bed for the stranger of soft mats and blankets, and also that one of them should bathe him. But the mats and blankets he would not have, saying that he would sleep as before; and for the bathing, he would only that some old woman, wise and prudent, should do this. Wherefore the queen bade Euryclea, the keeper of the house, do this thing for him, for that he had been the comrade of her lord, and indeed was marvellously like to him in feet and hands.

And this the old woman was right willing to do, for love for her master, "for never," she said, "of all strangers that had come to the land, had come one so like to him." But when she had prepared the bath for his feet, Ulysses sat by the fire, but as far in the shadow as he might, lest the old woman should see a great scar that was upon his leg, and know him thereby.

Now the scar had chanced in this wise. He had come to see his grandfather Autolycus, who was the most cunning of men, claiming certain gifts which he had promised to him in the old days when, being then newly born, he was set on his grandfather's knees in the halls of Laertes, and his grandfather had given him this name. And on the day of his coming there was a great feast, and on the day after a hunting on Mount Parnassus. In this hunting, therefore, Ulysses came in the heart of a wood upon a place where lay a great wild boar; and the beast, being stirred by the noise, rose up, and Ulysses charged him with his spear; but before he could slay the beast, it ripped a great wound just above the knee. And afterwards Ulysses slew it, and the young men bound up the wound, singing a charm to stanch the blood.

By this scar, then, the old nurse knew that it was Ulysses himself, and said, "O Ulysses, O my child, to think that I knew thee not!"

And she looked towards the Queen, as meaning to tell the thing to her. But Ulysses laid his hand on her throat, "Mother, wouldst thou kill me? I am returned after twenty years; and none must know till I shall be ready to take vengeance."

And the old woman held her peace. And after this Penelopé talked with him again, telling him her dreams, how she had seen a flock of geese in her palace, and how that an eagle had slain them; and when she mourned for the geese, lo! a voice that said, "These geese are thy suitors, and the eagle thy husband."

And Ulysses said that the dream was well. And then she said that on the morrow she must make her choice, for that she had promised to bring forth the great bow that was Ulysses', and whosoever should draw it most easily, and shoot an arrow best at a mark, he should be her husband.

And Ulysses made answer to her, "It is well, lady. Put not off this trial of the bow, for before one of them shall draw the string the great Ulysses shall come and duly shoot at the mark that shall be set."

After this Penelopé slept, but Ulysses watched

CHAPTER XIII.

THE TRIAL OF THE BOW.

THE next day many things cheered Ulysses for that which he had to do; for first Athené had told him that she would stand at his side, and next he heard the thunder of Zeus in a clear sky, and last it chanced that a woman who sat at the mill grinding corn, being sore weary of her task, and hating the suitors, said, "Grant, Father Zeus, that this be the last meal which these men shall eat in the house of Ulysses!"

And after a while the suitors came and sat down, as was their wont, to the feast. And the servants bare to Ulysses, as Telemachus had bidden, a full share with the others. And when Ctesippus, a prince of Samos, saw this (he was a man heedless of right and of the gods), he said, "Is it well that this fellow should fare even as we? Look now at the gift that I shall give him." Whereupon he took a bullock's foot out of a basket wherein it lay, and cast it at Ulysses.

But he moved his head to the left and shunned it, and it flew on, marking the wall. And Telemachus cried in great wrath,—

"It is well for thee, Ctesippus, that thou didst not strike this stranger. For surely, hadst thou done this thing, my spear had pierced thee through, and thy father had made good cheer, not for thy marriage, but for thy burial."

Then said Agelaüs, "This is well said. Telemachus should not be wronged, no, nor this stranger. But, on the other hand, he must bid his mother choose out of the suitors whom she will, and marry him, nor waste our time any more."

And Telemachus said, "It is well. She shall marry whom she will. But from my house I will never send her against her will."

And the suitors laughed; but their laughter was not of mirth, and the flesh which they ate dripped with blood, and their eyes were full of tears. And the eyes of the seer Theoclymenus were opened, and he cried, —

"What ails you, miserable ones? For your heads and your faces and your knees are covered with darkness, and the voice of groaning comes from you, and your cheeks are wet with tears. Also the walls and the pillars are sprinkled with blood, and the porch and the hall are full of shadows that move towards hell, and the sun has perished from the heaven, and an evil mist is over all."

But they laughed to hear him; and Eurymachus said, "This stranger is mad; let us send him out of doors into the market-place, for it seems that here it is dark."

Also they scoffed at Telemachus, but he heeded them not, but sat waiting till his father should give the sign.

After this Penelopé went to fetch the great bow of Ulysses which Iphitus had given to him. From the peg on which it hung she took it with its sheath, and sitting down, she laid it on her knees and wept over it, and after this rose up and went to where the suitors sat feasting in the hall. The bow she brought, and also the quiver full of arrows, and standing by the pillar of the dome, spake thus, —

"Ye suitors who devour this house, making pretence that ye wish to wed me, lo! here is a proof of your skill. Here is the bow of the great Ulysses. Whoso shall bend it easiest in his hands, and shoot an arrow most easily through the helve-holes of the twelve axes that Telemachus shall set up, him will I follow, leaving this house, which I shall remember only in my dreams."

Then she bade Eumæus bear the bow and the arrows to the suitors. And the good swineherd wept to see his master's bow, and Philætius, the herdsman of the kine, wept also, for he was a good man, and loved the house of Ulysses.

Then Telemachus planted in due order the axes wherein were the helve-holes, and was minded himself to draw the bow; and indeed would have done the thing, but Ulysses signed to him that he should not. Wherefore he said, "Methinks I am too weak and young; ye that are elder should try the first."

Then first Leiodes, the priest, who alone among the suitors hated their evil ways, made trial of the bow. But he moved it not, but wearied his hands with it, for they were tender, and unwont to toil. And he said, "I cannot bend this bow; let some other try; but it shall be grief and pain to many this day, I trow."

And Antinoüs was wroth to hear such words, and bade Melanthius bring forth from the stores a roll of fat, that they might anoint the string and soften it withal. So they softened the string with fat, but not for that the more could they bend it, for they tried all of them in vain, till only Antinoüs and Eurymachus were left, who indeed were the bravest and the strongest of them all.

Now the swineherd and the herdsman of the kine had gone forth out of the yard, and Ulysses came behind them and said, "What would ye do if Ulysses were to come back to his home? Would ye fight for him, or for the suitors?"

And both said they would fight for him.

And Ulysses said, "It is even I who am come back in the twentieth year, and ye, I know, are glad at heart that I am come; nor know I of any one besides. And if ye will help me as brave men to-day, wives shall ye have, and possessions and houses near to mine own. And ye shall be brothers and comrades to Telemachus. And for a sign, behold this scar, which the wild boar made when I hunted with Autolycus."

Then they wept for joy and kissed Ulysses, and he also kissed them. And he said to Eumæus that he should bring the bow to him when the suitors had tried their fortune therewith; also that he should bid the women keep within doors, nor stir out if they should hear the noise of battle. And Philætius he bade lock the doors of the hall, and fasten them with a rope.

After this he came back to the hall, and Eurymachus had the bow in his hands, and sought to warm it at the fire. Then he essayed to draw it, but could not. And he groaned aloud, saying, "Woe is me! not for loss of this marriage only, for there are other women to be wooed in Greece, but that we are so much weaker than the great Ulysses. This is indeed shame to tell."

Then said Antinoüs, "Not so; to-day is a holy day of the God of Archers; therefore we could not draw the bow. But to-morrow will we try once more, after due sacrifice to Apollo."

And this saying pleased them all; but Ulysses said, "Let me try this bow, for I would fain know whether I have such strength as I had in former days."

At this all the suitors were wroth, and chiefly Antinoüs,

but Penelopé said that it should be so, and promised the man great gifts if he could draw this bow.

But Telemachus spake thus, "Mother, the bow is mine to give or to refuse. And no man shall say me nay, if I will that this stranger make trial of it. But do thou go to thy chamber with thy maidens, and let men take thought for these things."

And this he said, for that he would have her depart from the hall forthwith, knowing what should happen therein. But she marvelled to hear him speak with such authority, and answered not, but departed. And when Eumæus would have carried the bow to Ulysses, the suitors spake roughly to him, but Telemachus constrained him to go. Therefore he took the bow and gave it to his master. Then went he to Euryclea, and bade her shut the door of the women's chambers and keep them within, whatsoever they might hear. Also Philætius shut the doors of the hall, and fastened them with a rope.

Then Ulysses handled the great bow, trying it, whether it had taken any hurt; but the suitors thought scorn of him. Then when he had found it to be without flaw, just as a minstrel fastens a string upon his harp, and strains it to the pitch, so he strung the bow without toil; and holding the string in his right hand, he tried its tone, and the tone was sweet as the voice of a swallow. Then he took an arrow from the quiver, and laid the notch upon the string and drew it, sitting as he was, and the arrow passed through every ring, and stood in the wall beyond. Then he said to Telemachus, —

"There is yet a feast to be held before the sun go down."

And he nodded the sign to Telemachus. And forthwith the young man stood by him, armed with spear and helmet and shield.

CHAPTER XIV.

THE SLAYING OF THE SUITORS.

Then spake he among the suitors, "This labor has been accomplished. Let me try at yet another mark."

And he aimed his arrow at Antinoüs. But the man was just raising a cup to his lips, thinking not of death, for who had thought that any man, though mightiest of mortals, would venture on such a deed, being one among many? Right through the neck passed the arrow-head, and the blood gushed from his nostrils, and he dropped the cup and spurned the table from him.

And all the suitors, when they saw him fall, leapt from their seats; but when they looked, there was neither spear nor shield upon the wall. And they knew not whether it was by chance or of set purpose that the stranger had smitten him. But Ulysses then declared who he was, saying,—

"Dogs, ye thought that I should never come back. Therefore have ye devoured my house, and made suit to my wife while I yet lived, and feared not the gods nor regarded men. Therefore a sudden destruction is come upon you all."

Then, when all the others trembled for fear, Eurymachus said, "If thou be indeed Ulysses of Ithaca, thou hast said well. Foul wrong has been done to thee in the house and in the field. But lo! he who was the mover of it all lies here, even Antinoüs. Nor was it so much this marriage that he sought, as to be king of this land, having destroyed thy house. But we will pay thee back for all that we have devoured, even twenty times as much."

But Ulysses said, "Speak not of paying back. My hands shall not cease from slaying till I have taken vengeance on you all."

Then said Eurymachus to his comrades, "This man will not stay his hands. He will smite us all with his arrows where he stands. But let us win the door, and raise a cry in the city; soon then will this archer have shot his last."

And he rushed on, with his two-edged knife in his hand. But as he rushed, Ulysses smote him on the breast with an arrow, and he fell forwards. And when Amphinomus came on, Telemachus slew him with his spear, but drew not the spear from the body, lest some one should smite him unawares.

Then he ran to his father and said, "Shall I fetch arms for us and our helpers?"

"Yea," said he, "and tarry not, lest my arrows be spent."

So he fetched from the armory four shields and four helmets and eight spears. And he and the servants, Eumæus and Philætius, armed themselves. Also Ulysses, when his arrows were spent, donned helmet and shield, and took a mighty spear in each hand. But Melanthius, the goatherd, crept up to the armory and brought down therefrom twelve helmets and shields, and spears as many. And when Ulysses saw that the suitors were arming themselves, he feared greatly, and said to his son, —

"There is treachery here. It is one of the women, or, it may be, Melanthius, the goatherd."

And Telemachus said, "This fault is mine, my father, for I left the door of the chamber unfastened."

And soon Eumæus spied Melanthius stealing up to the chamber again, and followed him, and Philætius with him. There they caught him, even as he took a helmet in one hand and a shield in the other, and bound his feet and hands, and fastened him aloft by a rope to the beams of the ceiling.

Then these two went back to the hall, and there also came Athené, having the shape of Mentor. Still, for she would yet further try the courage of Ulysses and his son, she helped them not as yet, but changing her shape, sat on the roof-beam like unto a swallow.

And then cried Agelaüs, "Friends, Mentor is gone, and helps them not. Let us not cast our spears at random, but let six come on together, if perchance we may prevail against them."

Then they cast their spears, but Athené turned them aside, one to the pillar and another to the door and another to the wall. But Ulysses and Telemachus and the two herdsmen slew each his man; and yet again they did so, and again. Only Amphimedon wounded Telemachus, and Ctesippus grazed the shoulder of Eumæus. But Telemachus struck down Amphimedon, and the herdsman of the kine slew Ctesippus, saying, "Take this, for the ox foot which thou gavest to our guest." And all the while Athené waved her flaming ægis-shield from above, and the suitors fell as birds are scattered and torn by eagles.

Then Leiodes, the priest, made supplication to Ulysses, saying, "I never wrought evil in this house, and would have kept others from it, but they would not. Nought have I done save serve at the altar; wherefore slay me not."

And Ulysses made reply, "That thou hast served at the altar of these men is enough, and also that thou wouldest wed my wife."

So he slew him; but Phemius, the minstrel, he spared, for he had sung among the suitors in the hall of compulsion, and not of good will; and also Medon, the herald, bidding them go into the yard without. There they sat, holding by the altar and looking fearfully every way, for yet they feared that they should die.

So the slaughtering of the suitors was ended; and now Ulysses bade cleanse the hall, and wash the benches and the tables with water, and purify them with sulphur. And when this was done, that Euryclea, the nurse, should go to Penelopé and tell her that her husband was indeed returned. So Euryclea went to her chamber and found the Queen newly woke from slumber, and told her that her husband was returned, and how that he had slain the suitors, and how that she had known him by the scar where the wild boar had wounded him.

And yet the Queen doubted, and said, "Let me go down and see my son, and these men that are slain, and the man who slew them."

So she went, and sat in the twilight by the other wall, and Ulysses sat by a pillar, with his eyes cast down, waiting till his wife should speak to him. But she was sore perplexed; for now she seemed to know him, and now she knew him not, being in such evil case, for he had not suffered that the women should put new robes upon him.

And Telemachus said, "Mother, evil mother, sittest thou apart from my father, and speakest not to him? Surely thy heart is harder than a stone."

But Ulysses said, "Let be Telemachus. Thy mother will know that which is true in good time. But now let us hide this slaughter for a while, lest the friends of these men seek vengeance against us. Wherefore let there be music and dancing in the hall, so that men shall say, 'This is the wedding of the Queen, and there is joy in the palace,' and know not of the truth."

So the minstrel played and the women danced. And meanwhile Ulysses went to the bath, and clothed himself in bright apparel, and came back to the hall, and Athené made him fair and young to see. Then he sat him down as before, over against his wife, and said, —

"Surely, O lady, the gods have made thee harder of heart than all women besides. Would other wife have kept away from her husband, coming back now after twenty years?"

And when she doubted yet, he spake again, "Hear thou this, Penelopé, and know that it is I myself, and not another. Dost thou remember how I built up the bed in our chamber? In the court there grew an olive tree, stout as a pillar, and round it I built a chamber of stone, and spanned the chamber with a roof; and I hung also a door, and then I cut off the leaves of the olive, and planed the trunk, to be smooth and round; and the bed I inlaid with ivory and silver and gold, and stretched upon it an ox-hide that was ornamented with silver."

Then Penelopé knew him, that he was her husband indeed, and ran to him, and threw her arms about him, and kissed him, saying, "Pardon me, my lord, if I was slow to know thee; for ever I feared, so many wiles have men, that some one should deceive me, saying that he was my husband. But now I know this, that thou art he and not another."

And they wept over each other and kissed each other. So did Ulysses come back to his home after twenty years.

THE ADVENTURES OF ÆNEAS.

CHAPTER I.

WHEN the fair city of Troy was taken and destroyed there appeared to Æneas, who alone was left of all the great chiefs that had fought against the Greeks, his mother Venus. And she spake to him, saying,—

"See now, for I will take away the mist that covers thine eyes; see how Neptune with his trident is overthrowing the walls and rooting up the city from its foundations; and how Juno stands with spear and shield in the Scæan Gate, and calls fresh hosts from the ships; and how Pallas sits on the height with the storm-cloud about her and her Gorgon shield; and how Father Jupiter himself stirs up the enemy against Troy. Fly, therefore, my son. I will not leave thee till thou shalt reach thy father's house." And as she spake she vanished in the darkness.

Then did Æneas see dreadful forms and gods who were the enemies of Troy, and before his eyes the whole city seemed to sink down into the fire. Even as a mountain oak upon the hills on which the woodmen ply their axes bows its head while all its boughs shake about it, till at last, as blow comes after blow, with a mighty groan it falls crashing down from the height, even so the city seemed to fall. Then did Æneas pass on his way, the goddess leading him, and the flames gave place to him, and the javelins harmed him not.

But when he was come to his house he bethought him first of the old man his father; but when he would have carried him to the hills, Anchises would not, being loath to live in some strange country when Troy had perished. "Nay," said he, "fly ye who are strong and in the flower of your days. But as for me, if the gods had willed that I should live, they had saved this dwelling for me. Enough is it, yea, and more than enough, that once I have seen this city taken, and lived. Bid me, then, farewell as though I were dead. Death will I find for myself. And truly I have long lingered here a useless stock and hated of the gods since Jupiter smote me with the blast of his thunder."

Nor could the old man be moved from his purpose, though his son and his son's wife, and even the child Ascanius, besought him with many tears that he should not make yet heavier the doom that was upon them. Then was Æneas minded to go back to the battle and die. For what hope was left? "Thoughtest thou, my father," he cried, "that I should flee and leave thee behind? What evil word is this that has fallen from thy lips? If the gods will have it that nought of Troy should be left, and thou be minded that thou and thine should perish with the city, be it so. The way is easy; soon will Pyrrhus be here; Pyrrhus, red with Priam's blood; Pyrrhus, who slays the son before the face of the father, and the father at the altar. Was it for this, kind Mother Venus, that thou broughtest me safe through fire and sword, to see the enemy in my home, and my father and my wife and my son lying slaughtered together? Comrades, give me my arms, and take me back to the battle. At the least I will die avenged."

But as he girded on his arms and would have departed from the house, his wife Creüsa caught his feet upon the threshold, staying him, and held out the little Ascanius, saying, "If thou goest to thy death, take wife and child with thee; but if thou hopest aught from arms, guard first the house where thou hast father and wife and child."

And lo! as she spake there befell a mighty marvel, for before the face of father and mother there was seen to shine a light on the head of the boy Ascanius, and to play upon his waving hair and glitter on his temples. And when they feared to see this thing, and would have stifled the flame or quenched it with water, the old man Anchises in great joy raised his eyes to heaven, and cried aloud, "O Father Jupiter, if prayer move thee at all, give thine aid and make this omen sure." And even as he spake the thunder rolled on his left hand, and a star shot through the skies, leaving a long trail of light behind, and passed over the house-tops till it was hidden in the woods of Ida. Then the old man lifted himself up and did obeisance to the star, and said, "I delay no more: whithersoever ye lead I will follow. Gods of my country, save my house and my grandson. This omen is of you. And now, my son, I refuse not to go."

Then said Æneas, and as he spake the fire came nearer, and the light was clearer to see, and the heat more fierce, "Climb, dear father, on my shoulders; I will bear thee, nor grow weary with the weight. We will be saved or perish together. The little Ascanius shall go with me, and my wife follow behind, not over near. And ye, servants of my house, harken to me; ye mind how that to one who passes out of the city there is a tomb and a temple of Ceres in a lonely place, and an ancient cypress-tree hard by. There will we gather by divers ways. And do thou, my father, take the holy images in thy hands, for as for me, who have but newly come from battle, I may not touch them till I have washed me in the running stream."

And as he spake he put a cloak of lion's skin upon his shoulders, and the old man sat thereon. Ascanius also laid hold of his hand, and Creüsa followed behind. So he went in much dread and trembling. For indeed before sword and spear of the enemy he had not feared, but now he feared for them that were with him. But when he was come nigh unto the gates, and the journey was well-nigh finished, there befell a grievous mischance, for there was heard a sound as of many feet through the darkness; and the old man cried to him, "Fly, my son, fly; they are coming. I see the flashing of shields and swords." But as Æneas hasted to go, Creüsa his wife was severed from him. But whether she wandered from the way or sat down in weariness, no man may say. Only he saw her no more, nor knew her to be lost till, all his company being met at the temple of Ceres, she only was found wanting. Very grievous did the thing seem to him, nor did he cease to cry out in his wrath against gods and men. Also he bade his comrades have a care of his father and his son, and of the household gods, and girded him again with arms, and so passed into the city. And first he went to the wall and to the gate by which he had come forth, and then to his house, if haply she had returned thither. But there indeed the men of Greece were come, and the fire had well-nigh mastered it. And after that he went to the citadel and to the palace of King Priam. And lo! in the porch of Juno's temple, Phœnix and Ulysses were keeping guard over the spoil, even the treasure of the temples, tables of the gods, and solid cups of gold, and raiment, and a long array of them that had been taken captive, children and women. But not the less did he seek his wife through all the streets of the city, yea, and called her aloud by name. But lo! as he called, the image of her whom he sought seemed to stand before him, only greater than she had been while she was yet alive. And the spirit spake, saying, "Why art thou vainly troubled? These things have not befallen us against the pleasure of the gods. The ruler of Olympus willeth not that Creüsa should bear thee company in thy journey. For thou hast a long journey to take, and many seas to cross, till thou come to the Hesperian shore, where Lydian Tiber flows softly through a good land and a fertile. There shalt thou have great prosperity, and take to thyself a wife of royal race. Weep not then for Creüsa, whom thou lovest, nor think that I shall be carried away to be a bond-slave to some Grecian woman. Such fate befits not a daughter of Dardanus and daughter-in-law of Venus. The mighty Mother of the gods keepeth me in this land to serve her. And now, farewell, and love the young Ascanius, even thy son and mine."

So spake the spirit, and, when Æneas wept and would have spoken, vanished out of his sight. Thrice he would have cast his arms about her neck, and thrice the image mocked him, being thin as air and fleeting as a dream. Then, the night being now spent, he sought his comrades, and found with much joy and wonder that a great company of men and women were gathered together, and were willing, all of them, to follow him whithersoever he went. And now the morning star rose over Mount Ida, and Æneas, seeing that the Greeks held the city, and that there was no longer any hope of succor, went his way to the mountains, taking with him his father.

Now for what remained of that year (for it was the time of summer when Troy was taken), Æneas, and they that were gathered to him, builded themselves ships for the voyage, dwelling the while under Mount Ida; and when the summer was well-nigh come again the work was finished, and the old man Anchises commanded that they should tarry no longer. Whereupon they sailed, taking also their gods with them.

There was a certain land of Thrace, which the god Mars loved beyond all other lands, whereof in time past the fierce Lycurgus, who would have slain Bacchus, was king. Here, therefore, for the men of the land were friendly, or, at the least, had been before evil days came upon Troy, Æneas builded him a city, and called it after his own name. But, after awhile, as he did sacrifice on a certain day to his mother, even Venus, that he might have a blessing on his work, slaying also a white bull to Jupiter, there befell a certain horrible thing. For hard by the place where he did sacrifice there was a little hill, with much cornel and myrtle upon it, whereto Æneas coming would have plucked wands having leaves upon them, that he might cover therewith the altars. But lo! when he plucked a wand there dropped drops of blood therefrom. Whereupon great fear came on him, and wonder also. And when seeking to know the cause of the thing he plucked other wands also, there dropped blood even as before. Then, having prayed to the nymphs of the land and to Father Mars that they would turn all evil from him, he essayed the third time with all his might, setting his knee against the ground, to pluck forth a wand. Whereupon there issued from the hill a lamentable voice, saying, "Æneas, why doest thou me such cruel hurt, nor leavest me in peace in my grave? For indeed I am no stranger to thee, nor strange is this blood which thou seest. Fly, for the land is cruel, and the shore greedy of gain. I am Polydorus. Here I was pierced through with spears, which have grown into these wands that thou seest."

But Æneas when he heard the voice was sore dismayed, and he remembered him how King Priam, thinking that it might fare ill with him and the great city of Troy, had sent his son, Polydorus, by stealth, and much gold with him, to Polymestor, who was king of Thrace, and how the king, when Troy had now perished, slew the boy, and took the gold to himself. For of a truth the love of gold is the root of all evil. And Æneas told the thing to his father and to the chiefs; and the sentence of all was that they should depart from the evil land. But first they made a great funeral for Polydorus, making a high mound of earth, and building thereon an altar to the dead. This also they bound about with garlands of sad-colored wool and cypress, and the women of Troy stood about it with their hair loosened, as is the use of them that mourn. They offered also bowls of warm milk and blood, and laid the spirit in the tomb, bidding him farewell three times with a loud voice.

After this, when the time for voyaging was come, and the south wind blew softly, they launched the ships and set sail. And first they came to the island of Delos, which, having been used to wander over the sea, the Lord of the Silver Bow made fast, binding it to Myconos and Gyaros, and found there quiet anchorage. And when they landed to worship, there met them Anius, who was priest and king of the place, having a crown of bay-leaves about his head, who knew Anchises for a friend in time past, and used to them much hospitality. Then did they pray to the god saying, "Give us, we beseech thee, a home where we may dwell, and a name upon the earth, and a city that shall abide, even a second Troy for them that have escaped from the hands of Achilles and the Greeks. And do thou answer us, and incline our hearts that we may know."

But when Æneas had ended these words, straightway the place was shaken, even the gates of the temple and the bay-trees that were hard by. And when they were all fallen to the ground there came a voice, saying, "Son of Dardanus, the land that first bare you shall receive you again. Seek, then, your ancient mother. Then shall the children of Æneas bear rule over all lands, yea, and their children's children to many generations." Which when they had heard, they greatly rejoiced, and would fain know what was the city whither Phœbus would have them go, that they might cease from their wanderings. Then Anchises, pondering in his heart the things which he had learnt from the men of old time, spake thus: "There lieth in mid-ocean a certain island of Crete, wherein is a mountain, Ida. There was the first beginning of our nation. Thence came Teucer, our first father, to the land of Troy. Let us go, then, whither the gods would send us, first doing sacrifice to the Winds; and, indeed, if but Jupiter help us, 'tis but a three days' journey for our ships."

So they offered sacrifice, a bull to Neptune and a bull to the beautiful Apollo, and a black sheep to the Storm and a white sheep to the West Wind. There came also a rumor that Idomeneus the Cretan had fled from his father's kingdom, and that the land was ready for him who should take it. Whereupon the men of Troy set sail with a good heart, and passing among the islands that are called Cyclades, the wind blowing favorably behind them, so came to Crete. There they builded a city, and called its name Pergamea, after Pergama, which was the citadel of Troy. And for a while they tilled the soil; also they married and were given in marriage, as purposing to abide in the land. But there came a wasting sickness on the men, and a blight also on the trees and harvests, filling the year with death. The fields likewise were parched with drought, and the staff of bread was broken. Then the old Anchises bade them go yet again to the oracle at Delos, and inquire of the god what end there should be of these troubles, whence they should seek for help, and whither they should go.

But as Æneas slept there appeared to him the household gods, which he had carried out of the burning of Troy, very clear to see in the light of the moon, which shone through the window of his chamber. And they spake unto him, saying, "Apollo bids us tell thee here that which he will tell thee if thou goest to Delos. We who have followed thee over many seas, even we will bring thy children's children to great honor, and make their city ruler over many nations. Faint not, therefore, at thy long wandering. Thou must seek yet another home. For it was not in Crete that Apollo bade thee dwell. There is a land which the Greeks call Hesperia; an ancient land, whose inhabitants are mighty men of valor; a land of vineyards and wheat. There is our proper home, and thence came Dardanus our father. Do thou, therefore, tell these things to the old man Anchises. Seek ye for the land of Hesperia, which men also call Italy; but as for Crete, Jupiter willeth not that ye should dwell there."

And for a while Æneas lay in great fear, with a cold sweat upon him, so clear was the vision of those whom he saw, nor in anywise like unto a dream. Then he rose up from his bed, and after prayer and sacrifice told the thing to Anchises. And the old man saw that he had been deceived in this matter, and he said, "O my son, now do I remember how Cassandra was wont to prophesy these things to me, and would speak of Hesperia and of the land of Italy. But, indeed, no man thought in those days that the men of Troy should voyage to Hesperia, nor did any take account of the words of Cassandra. But now let us heed the oracle of Apollo, and depart."

So the men of Troy made their ships ready and departed. And after a while, when they could no more see the land, there fell a great storm upon them, with a strong wind and great rolling waves, and much lightning also. Thus were they driven out of their course, and for three days and nights saw neither the sun nor the stars. But on the fourth day they came to a land where they saw hills, and smoke rising therefrom. Then did the men ply their oars amain, and soon came to the shore. Now this place they found to be one of certain islands which men name the Strophades. And upon these islands dwell creatures which are called Harpies, very evil indeed, having the countenances of women and wings like unto the wings of birds, and long claws. Also their faces are pale as with much hunger. Now when the men of Troy were come to this land, they saw many herds of oxen and flocks of goats thereon, nor any one to watch them. Of these they slew such as they needed, and, not forgetting to give due share to the gods, made a great feast upon the shore. But lo! even while they made merry, there came a great rushing of wings, and the Harpies came upon them, making great havoc of the meat and fouling all things most horribly. And when they had departed, the men of Troy sought another place where they might do sacrifice and eat their meat in peace. But when the Harpies had come thither also and done in the same fashion, Æneas commanded that the men should draw their swords and do battle with the beasts. Therefore, the Harpies coming yet again, Misenus with his trumpet gave the sound for battle. But lo! they fought as those that beat the air, seeing that neither sword nor spear availed to wound the beasts. Then again these departed, one only remaining, by name, Celæno, who, sitting on a rock, spake after this fashion: "Do ye purpose, sons of Laomedon, to fight for these cattle that ye have wrongfully taken, or to drive the Harpies from their kingdom and inheritance? Hear, therefore, my words, which indeed the almighty Father told to Phœbus, and Phœbus told to me. Ye journey to Italy, and to Italy shall ye come. Only ye shall not build a city, and wall it about with walls, till dreadful hunger shall cause you to eat the very tables whereon ye sup."

So saying, she departed. But when great fear was fallen upon all, Anchises lifted up his hands to heaven and prayed to the gods that they would keep that evil from them.

Then they set sail, and, the south wind blowing, passed by Zacynthus and Dulichium, and also Ithaca, which they cursed as they passed, because it was the land of the hateful Ulysses, and so came to Actium, where they landed. There also they did sacrifice to the gods, and had games of wrestling and others, rejoicing that they had passed safely through so many cities of their enemies. And there they wintered, and Æneas fixed on the doors of the temple of Apollo a shield of bronze which he had won in battle from the valiant Abas, writing thereon these words, "ÆNEAS DEDICATES THESE ARMS WON FROM THE VICTORIOUS GREEKS."

But when the spring was come they set sail, and, leaving behind them the land of Phæacia, came to Buthrotum that is in Epirus. There indeed they heard a marvellous thing, even that Helenus, the son of Priam, was king in these parts, in the room of Pyrrhus, the son of Achilles, having also to wife Andromaché, who was the widow of Hector. And when Æneas, wishing to know whether these things were so, journeyed towards the city, lo! in a grove hard by, by a river which also was called Simoïs, there stood this same Andromaché, and made offerings to the spirit of Hector not without many tears. And at the first when she saw Æneas, and that he wore such arms as the men of Troy were used to wear, she swooned with fear, but after a while spake thus: "Is this indeed a real thing that I see? Art thou alive? or, if thou art dead, tell me, where is my Hector?" So she cried and wept aloud. And Æneas answered her: "Yes, lady, this is flesh and blood, and not a spirit, that thou seest. But as for thee, what fortune has befallen thee? Art thou still wedded to Pyrrhus?"

And she, casting down her eyes, made answer, "O daughter of Priam, happy beyond thy sisters in that thou wast slain at the tomb of Achilles, nor wast taken to be a prey of the conqueror! But as for me I was borne across the sea, to be slave to the haughty son of Achilles. And when he took to wife Hermione, who was the daughter of Helen, he gave me to Helenus, as a slave is given to a slave. But Pyrrhus, after awhile, Orestes slew, taking him unawares, even by the altar of his father. And when he was dead, part of his kingdom came to Helenus, who hath called the land Chaonia, after Chaon of Troy, and hath also builded a citadel, a new Pergama, upon the hills. But tell me, was it some storm that drave thee hither, or chance, or, lastly, some sending of the gods? And is Ascanius yet alive — the boy whom I remember? Doth he yet think of his mother that is dead? And is he stout and of a good courage, as befits the son of Æneas and sister's son to Hector?"

And while she spake there came Helenus from the city with a great company, and bade welcome to his friends with much joy. And Æneas saw how that all things were ordered and named even as they had been at Troy, only the things at Troy had been great, and these were very small. And afterwards King Helenus made a feast to them in his house, and they drank together and were merry.

But after certain days were passed, Æneas, seeing that the wind favored them, spake to Helenus, knowing him also to be a prophet of the gods: "Tell me now, seeing that thou art wise in all manner of divination and prophecy, how it will fare with us. For indeed all things have seemed to favor us, and we go not on this journey against the will of the gods, yet did the Harpy Celæno prophesy evil things, that we should endure great extremity of hunger. Say, then, of what things I should most beware, and how I shall best prosper."

Then Helenus, after due sacrifice, led Æneas to the temple of Phœbus. And when they were come thither, and the god had breathed into the seer, even into Helenus, the spirit of prophecy, he spake, saying, "Son of Venus, that thou takest thy journey across the sea with favor of the gods is manifest. Hearken, therefore, and I will inform thee of certain things, though indeed they be few out of many, by which thou mayest more safely cross unknown seas and get thee to thy haven in Italy. Much indeed the Fates suffer me not to know, and much Juno forbids me to speak. Know then, first of all, that Italy, which thou ignorantly thinkest to be close at hand, is yet far away across many seas. And let this be a sign to thee that thou art indeed come to the place where thou wouldst be. When thou shalt see a white sow and thirty pigs at her teats, then hast thou found the place of thy city that shall be. And as to the devouring of thy tables for famine, heed it not: Apollo will help thee at need. But seek not to find a dwelling-place on this shore of Italy which is near at hand, seeing that it is inhabited by the accursed sons of Greece. And when thou hast passed it by, and art come to the land of Sicily, and shalt see the strait of Pelorus open before thee, do thou keep to thy left hand and avoid the way that is on thy right. For here in days past was the land rent asunder, so that the waters of the sea flow between cities and fields that of old time were joined together. And on the right hand is Scylla, and on the left Charybdis the whirlpool. But Scylla dwelleth in her cave, a monster dreadful to behold; for to the middle she is a fair woman, but a beast of the sea below, even the belly of a dolphin, with heads as of a wolf. Wherefore it will be better for thee to fetch a compass round the whole land of Sicily than to come nigh these things, or to see them with thine eyes. Do thou also remember this, at all places and times, before all other gods to worship Juno, that thou mayest persuade her, and so make thy way safely to Italy. And when thou art come thither, seek the Sibyl that dwelleth at Cumæ, the mad prophetess that writeth the sayings of Fate upon the leaves of a tree. For these indeed at first abide in their places, but, the gate being opened, the wind blows them hither and thither. And when they are scattered she careth not to join them again, so that they who would inquire of her depart without an answer. Refuse not to tarry awhile, that thou mayest take counsel of her, though all things seem to prosper thy journey, and thy comrades chide thy delay. For she shall tell thee all that shall befall thee in Italy, — what wars thou shalt wage, and what perils thou must endure, and what avoid. So much, and no more, is it lawful for me to utter. Do thou depart, and magnify our country of Troy even to the heaven."

And when the seer had ended these sayings, he commanded his people that they should carry to the ships gifts: gold, and carvings of ivory, and much silver, and caldrons that had been wrought at Dodona; also a coat of chain mail, and a helmet with a fair plume, which Pyrrhus had worn. Also he gave gifts to the old man Anchises Horses, too, he gave, and guides for the journey, and tackling for the ships, and arms for the whole company. Then did he bid farewell to the old Anchises. Andromaché also came, bringing broidered robes, and for Ascanius a Phrygian cloak, and many like things, which she gave him, saying, "Take these works of my hands, that they may witness to thee of the abiding love of her that was once Hector's wife. For in truth thou art the very image of my Astyanax, so like are thy eyes and face and hands. And indeed he would now be of an age with thee." Then Æneas also said farewell, weeping the while. "Be ye happy, whose wanderings are over and rest already won; ye have no seas to cross, nor fields of Italy, still flying as we advance, to seek. Rather ye have the likeness of Troy before your eyes. And be sure that if ever I come to this land of Italy which I seek, there shall be friendship between you and me, and between your children and my children, forever."

Then they set sail, and at eventide drew their ships to the land and slept on the beach. But at midnight Palinurus, the pilot, rising from his bed, took note of the winds and of the stars, even of Arcturus, and the Greater Bear and the Less, and Orion with his belt of gold. Seeing therefore that all things boded fair weather to come, he blew loud the signal that they should depart; which they did forthwith. And when the morning was now growing red in the east, behold a land with hills dimly seen and shores lying low in the sea. And, first of all, the old man Anchises cried, "Lo! there is Italy," and after him all the company. Then took Anchises a mighty cup, and filled it with wine, and, standing on the stern, said, "Gods of sea and land, and ye that have power of the air, give us an easy journey, and send such winds as may favor us." And even as he spake the wind blew more strongly behind. Also the harbor mouth grew wider to behold, and on the hills was seen a temple of Minerva. And lo! upon the shore four horses white as snow, which the old man seeing, said, "Thou speakest of war, land of the stranger; for the horse signifieth war, yet doth he also use himself to run in the chariot, and to bear the bit in company; therefore also will we hope for peace." Then did they sacrifice to Minerva, and to Juno also, which rites the seer Helenus had chiefly commanded. And this being done they trimmed their sails and departed from the shore, fearing lest some enemy, the Greeks being in that place, should set upon them. So did they pass by Tarentum, which Hercules builded, also the hills of Caulon, and Scylacium, where many ships are broken. And from Scylacium they beheld Ætna, and heard a great roaring of the sea, and saw also the waves rising up to heaven. Then said Anchises, "Lo! this is that Charybdis whereof the seer Helenus spake to us. Ply your oars, my comrades, and let us fly therefrom." So they strove amain in rowing, and Palinurus also steered to the left, all the other ships following him. And many times the waves lifted them to the heaven, and many times caused them to go down to the deep. But at the last, at setting of the sun, they came to the land of the Cyclops.

There, indeed, they lay in a harbor, well sheltered from all winds that blow, but all the night Ætna thundered dreadfully, sending forth a cloud with smoke of pitch, and ashes fiery hot, and also balls of fire, and rocks withal that had been melted with heat. For indeed men say that the giant Enceladus lieth under this mountain, being scorched with the lightning of Jupiter, and that from him cometh forth this flame; also that when, being weary, he turneth from one side to the other, the whole land of the Three Capes is shaken. All that night they lay in much fear, nor knew what the cause of this uproar might be, for indeed the sky was cloudy, nor could the moon be seen.

And when it was morning, lo! there came forth from the woods a stranger, very miserable to behold, in filthy garments fastened with thorns, and with beard unshaven, who stretched out to them his hands as one who prayed. And the men of Troy knew him to be a Greek. But he, seeing them, and knowing of what country they were, stood awhile in great fear, but afterwards ran very swiftly towards them, and used to them many prayers, weeping also the while. "I pray you, men of Troy, by the stars and by the gods, and by this air which we breathe, to take me away from this land, whithersoever ye will. And indeed I ask not whither. That I am a Greek, I confess, and also that I bare arms against Troy. Wherefore drown me, if ye will, in the sea. Only let me die, if die I must, by the hands of men."

And he clung to their knees. Then Æneas bade him tell who he was, and how he came to be in this plight. And the man made answer, "I am a man of Ithaca, and a comrade of the unhappy Ulysses. My name is Achæ-menides, and my father was Adamastus. And when my comrades fled from this accursed shore, they left me in the Cyclops' cave. 'Hideous is he to see, and savage, and of exceeding great stature, and he feeds on the flesh of men. I myself saw with these eyes how he lay and caught two of my companions and brake them on the stone; aye, and I saw their limbs quiver between his teeth. Yet did he not do such things unpunished, for Ulysses endured not to behold these deeds, and when the giant lay asleep, being overcome with wine, we, after prayer made to the gods, and lots cast what each should do, bored out his eye, for one eye he had, huge as a round shield of Argos, or as the circle of the sun, and so did we avenge our comrades' death. Do ye then fly with all the speed ye may. For know that as this shepherd Polyphemus — a shepherd he is by trade — so are a hundred other Cyclopés, huge and savage as he, who dwell on these shores and wander over the hills. And now for three months have I dwelt in these woods, eating berries and cornels and herbs of the field. And when I saw your ships, I hastened to meet them. Do ye with me, therefore, as ye will, so that I flee from this accursed race."

And even while he spake the men of Troy saw the shepherd Polyphemus among his flocks, and that he made as if he would come to the shore. Horrible to behold was he, huge and shapeless and blind. And when he came to the sea, he washed the blood from the wound, grinding his teeth the while; and though he went far into the sea, yet did not the waves touch his middle. And the men of Troy, having taken the suppliant on board, fled with all their might; and he hearing their rowing would have reached to them, but could not. Therefore did he shout aloud, and the Cyclopés hearing him, hasted to the shore. Then did the men of Troy behold them, a horrid company, tall as a grove of oaks or cypresses. Nor knew they in their fear what they should do, seeing that on the one hand was the land of the Cyclopés, and on the other Scylla and Charybdis, of which the seer Helenus had bidden them beware. But while they doubted, there blew a north wind from Pelorus, wherewith they sailed onwards, and Achæmenides with them. So they came to Ortygia, whither, as men say, the river Alpheüs floweth under the sea from the land of Pelops, and so mingleth with Arethusa; and afterwards they passed the promontory of Pachynus, Camarina also, and Gela, and other cities likewise, till they came to Lilybæum, and so at last to Drepanum. There the old man Anchises died, and was buried

CHAPTER II.

NOT many days after Æneas and his companions set sail. But scarce were they out of sight of the land of Sicily when Juno espied them. Very wroth was she that they should be now drawing near to the end of their journey, and she said to herself, "Shall I be balked of my purpose nor be able to keep these men of Troy from Italy? Minerva, indeed, because one man sinned, even Ajax Oïleus, burned the fleet of the Greeks, and drowned the men in the sea. For the ships she smote with the thunderbolts of Jupiter; and as for Ajax, him she caught up with a whirlwind, and dashed him upon the rocks, piercing him through. Only I, though I be both sister and wife to Jupiter, avail nothing against this people. And who that heareth this in after time shall pay me due honor and sacrifice?"

Then she went, thinking these things in her heart, to the land of Æolia, where King Æolus keepeth the winds under bolt and bar. Mightily do they roar within the mountain, but their King restraineth them and keepeth them in bounds, being indeed set to do this very thing, lest they should carry both the heavens and the earth before them in their great fury. To him said Juno, "O Æolus, whom Jupiter hath made king of the winds, a nation which I hate is sailing over the Tuscan sea. Loose now thy storms against them, and drown their ships in the sea. And hearken what I will do for thee. Twelve maidens I have that wait on me continually, who are passing fair, and the fairest of all, even Deïopea, I will give thee to wife."

To whom answered King Æolus, "It is for thee, O Queen, to order what thou wilt, it being of thy gift that I hold this sovereignty and eat at the table of the gods."

So saying he drave in with his spear the folding-doors of the prison of the winds, and these straightway in a great host rushed forth, even all the winds together, and rolled great waves upon the shore. And straightway there arose a great shouting of men and straining of cables; nor could the sky nor the light of the day be seen any more, but a darkness as of night came down upon the sea, and there were thunders and lightnings over the whole heavens.

Then did Æneas grow cold with fear; and stretching out his hands to heaven, he cried, "Happy they who fell under the walls of Troy, before their fathers' eyes! Would to the gods that thou hadst slain me, Diomed, bravest of the Greeks, even as Hector fell by the spear of Achilles, or tall Sarpedon, or all the brave warriors whose dead bodies Simoïs rolled down to the sea!"

But as he spake a blast of wind struck his sails from before, and his ship was turned broad-side to the waves. Three others also were tossed upon the rocks which men call the "Altars," and three into the quicksands of the Syrtis. And another, in which sailed the men of Lycia, with Orontes, their chief, was struck upon the stern by a great sea and sunk. And when Æneas looked, lo! there were some swimming in the waves, and broken planks also, and arms and treasures of Troy. Others also were shattered by the waves, and those of Ilioneüs and Achates, and of Abas and the old man Alethes.

But King Neptune was aware of the tumult where he sat at the bottom of the sea, and raising his head above the waves, looked forth and saw how the ships were scattered abroad and the men of Troy were in sore peril. Also he knew his sister's wrath and her craft. Then he called to him the winds and said, "What is this, ye winds, that ye trouble heaven and earth without leave of me? Now will I — but I must first bid the waves be still, only be sure that ye shall not thus escape hereafter. Begone, and tell your King that the dominion over the sea belongeth unto me, and bid him keep him to his rocks."

Then he bade the waves be still; also he scattered the clouds and brought back the sun. And Cymothea and Triton, gods of the sea, drew the ships from the rocks, Neptune also lifting them with his trident. Likewise he opened the quicksands, and delivered the ships that were therein. And this being done he crossed the sea in his chariot, and the waves beholding him sank to rest, even as it befalls when there is sedition in the city, and the people are wroth, and men throw stones and firebrands, till lo! of a sudden there cometh forth a reverend sire, a good man and true, and all men are silent and hearken to him, and the uproar is stayed. So was the sea stilled, beholding its King.

Then Æneas and his companions, being sore wearied with the storm, made for the nearest shore, even Africa, where they found a haven running far into the land, into which the waves come not till their force be spent. On either side thereof are cliffs very high, and shining woods over them. Also at the harbor's head is a cave and a spring of sweet water within, a dwelling-place of the Nymphs. Hither came Æneas, with seven ships. Right glad were the men of Troy to stand upon the dry land again. Then Achates struck a spark out of flint, and they lighted a fire with leaves and the like ; also they took of the wheat which had been in the ships, and made ready to parch and to bruise it, that they might eat. Meanwhile Æneas had climbed the cliff, if haply he might see some of his companions' ships. These indeed he saw not, but he espied three great stags upon the shore and a herd following them. Wherefore, taking the arrows and the bow which Achates bare with him, he let fly, slaying the leaders and others also, till he had gotten seven, one for each ship. Then made he his way to the landing-place, and divided the prey. Also he made distribution of the wine which Acestes, their host in Sicily, had given them as they were about to depart, and spake comfortable words to them, saying, "O my friends, be ye sure that there will be an end to these troubles ; and indeed ye have suffered worse things before. Be ye of good cheer therefore. Haply ye shall one day have pleasure in thinking of these things. For be sure that the gods have prepared a dwelling-place for us in Italy, where we shall build a new Troy, in great peace and happiness. Wherefore endure unto the day of prosperity."

Then they made ready the feast, and roasted of the meat upon spits, and boiled other in water. Also they drank of the wine and were comforted. And after supper they talked much of them that were absent, doubting whether they were alive or dead.

All these things did Jupiter behold; and even as he beheld them there came to him Venus, having a sad countenance and her shining eyes dim with tears, and spake: "O great Father, that rulest all things, what have Æneas and the men of Troy sinned against thee, that the whole world is shut against them? Didst not thou promise that they should rule over land and sea? Why, then, art thou turned back from thy purpose? With this I was wont to comfort myself for the evil fate of Troy, but lo! this same fate follows them still, nor is there any end to their troubles. And yet it was granted to Antenor, himself also a man of Troy, that he should escape from the Greeks, and coming to the Liburnian land, where Timavus flows with much noise into the sea, build a city and find rest for himself. But we, who are thy children, are kept far from the land which thou hast sworn to give us."

Then her father kissed her once and again, and answered smiling, "Fear not, my daughter, the fate of thy children changeth not. Thou shalt see this city for which thou lookest, and shalt receive thy son, the great-hearted Æneas, into the heavens. Hearken, therefore, and I will tell thee things to come. Æneas shall war with the nations of Italy, and shall subdue them, and build a city, and rule therein for three years. And after the space of thirty years shall the boy Ascanius, who shall hereafter be called Iülus also, change the place of his throne from Lavinium unto Alba; and for three hundred years shall there be kings in Alba of the kindred of Hector. Then shall a priestess bear to Mars twin sons, whom a she-wolf shall suckle; of whom the one, even Romulus, shall build a city, dedicating it to Mars, and call it Rome, after his own name. To which city have I given empire without bound or end. And Juno also shall repent her of her wrath, and join counsel with me, cherishing the men of Rome, so that they shall bear rule even over Argos and Mycenæ."

And when he had said this, he sent down his messenger, even Mercury, to turn the heart of Dido and her people, where they dwelt in the city of Carthage, which they had builded, so that they should deal kindly with the strangers.

Now it came to pass on the next day that Æneas, having first hidden his ships in a bay that was well covered with trees, went forth to spy out the new land whither he was come, and Achates only went with him. And Æneas had in each hand a broad-pointed spear. And as he went there met him in the middle of the wood his mother, but habited as a Spartan virgin, for she had hung a bow from her shoulders after the fashion of a huntress, and her hair was loose, and her tunic short to the knees, and her garments gathered in a knot upon her breast. Then first the false huntress spake, "If perchance ye have seen one of my sisters wandering hereabouts, make known to me the place. She is girded with a quiver, and is clothed with the skin of a spotted lynx, or, may be, she hunts a wild boar with horn and hound."

To whom Æneas, "I have not seen nor heard sister of thine, O virgin — for what shall I call thee? for, of a surety, neither is thy look as of a mortal woman, nor yet thy voice. A goddess certainly thou art, sister of Phœbus, or, haply, one of the nymphs. But whosoever thou art, look favorably upon us and help us. Tell us in what land we be, for the winds have driven us hither, and we know not aught of place or people."

And Venus said, "Nay, stranger, I am not such as ye think. We virgins of Tyre are wont to carry a quiver and to wear a buskin of purple. For indeed it is a Tyrian city that is hard by, though the land be Lybia. And of this city Dido is Queen, having come hither from Tyre, flying from the wrong-doing of her brother. And indeed the story of the thing is long, but I will recount the chief matter thereof to thee. The husband of this Dido was one Sichæus, richest among all the men of Phœnicia, and greatly beloved of his wife, whom he married from a virgin. Now the brother of this Sichæus was Pygmalion, the King of the country, and he exceeded all men in wickedness. And when there arose a quarrel between them, the King, being exceedingly mad after gold, took him unaware, even as he did sacrifice at the altar, and slew him. And the King hid the matter many days from Dido, and cheated her with false hopes. But at the last there came to her in her dreams the likeness of the dead man, baring his wounds and showing the wickedness which had been done. Also he bade her make haste and fly from that land, and, that she might do this the more easily, told her of great treasure, gold and silver, that was hidden in the earth. And Dido, being much moved by these things, made ready for flight; also she sought for companions, and there came together to her all as many as hated the King or feared him. Then did they seize ships that chanced to be ready, and laded them with gold, even the treasure of King Pygmalion, and so fled across the sea. And in all this was a woman the leader. Then came they to this place, where thou seest the walls and citadel of Carthage, and bought so much land as they could cover with a bull's hide. And now do ye answer me this, Whence come ye, and whither do ye go?"

Then answered Æneas, "Should I tell the whole story of our wanderings, and thou have leisure to hear, evening would come ere I could make an end. We are men of Troy, who, having journeyed over many seas, have now been driven by storms to this shore of Lybia. And as for me, men call me the Prince Æneas. The land I seek is Italy, and my race is from Jupiter himself. With twenty ships did I set sail, going in the way whereon the gods sent me. And of these scarce seven are left. And now, seeing that Europe and Asia endure me not, I wander over the desert places of Africa."

But Venus suffered him not to speak more, but said, "Whoever thou art, stranger, that art come to this Tyrian city, thou art surely beloved by the gods. And now go, show thyself to the Queen. And as for thy ships and thy companions, I tell that they are safe in the haven, if I have not learnt augury in vain. See those twenty swans, how joyously they fly! And now there cometh an eagle swooping down from the sky, putting them to confusion; but now again they move in due order, and some are settling on the earth and some preparing to settle. Even so doth it fare with thy ships, for either are they already in the haven or enter thereinto with sails full set."

And as she spake she turned away, and there shone a rosy light from her neck; also there came from her hair a sweet savor as of ambrosia, and her garments grew unto her feet; and Æneas perceived that she was his mother, and cried aloud,—

"O my mother, why dost thou mock me so often with false shows, nor sufferest me to join my hand unto thy hand, and to speak with thee face to face?"

And he went towards the walls of the city. But Venus covered him and his companions with a mist, that no man might see them, or hinder them, or inquire of their business, and then departed to Paphos, where was her temple and also many altars of incense. Then the men hastened on their way, and mounting a hill which hung over the city, marvelled to behold it, for indeed it was very great and noble, with mighty gates and streets, and a multitude that walked therein. For some built the walls and the citadel, rolling great stones with their hands, and others marked out places for houses. Also they chose those that should give judgment and bear rule in the city. Some, too, digged out harbors, and others laid the foundations of a theatre, and cut out great pillars of stone. Like to bees they were, when, the summer being newly come, the young swarms go forth, or when they labor filling the cells with honey, and some receive the burdens of those that return from the fields, and others keep off the drones from the hive. Even so labored the men of Tyre. And when Æneas beheld them he cried, "Happy ye, who even now have a city to dwell in!" And being yet hidden by the mist, he went in at the gate and mingled with the men, being seen of none.

Now in the midst of the city was a wood, very thick with trees, and here the men of Carthage, first coming to the land from their voyage, had digged out of the ground that which Juno had said should be a sign to them, even a horse's head! for that, finding this, their city would be mighty in war, and full of riches. Here, then, Dido was building a temple to Juno, very splendid, with threshold of bronze, and many steps thereunto; of bronze also were the door-posts and the gates. And here befell a thing which gave much comfort and courage to Æneas; for as he stood and regarded the place, waiting also for the Queen, he saw set forth in order upon the walls the battles that had been fought at Troy, the sons of Atreus also, and King Priam, and fierce Achilles. Then said he, not without tears, "Is there any land, O Achates, that is not filled with our sorrows? Seest thou Priam? Yet withal there is a reward for virtue here also, and tears and pity for the troubles of men. Fear not, therefore. Surely the fame of these things shall profit us."

Then he looked, satisfying his soul with the paintings on the walls. For there was the city of Troy. In this part of the field the Greeks fled and the youth of Troy pursued them, and in that the men of Troy fled, and Achilles followed hard upon them in his chariot. Also he saw the white tents of Rhesus, King of Thrace, whom the fierce Diomed slew in his sleep, when he was newly come to Troy, and drave his horses to the camp before they ate of the grass of the fields of Troy or drank the waters of Xanthus. There also Troïlus was pictured, ill-matched in battle with the great Achilles. His horses bare him along; but he lay on his back in the chariot, yet holding the reins, and his neck and head were dragged upon the earth, and the spear-point made a trail in the dust. And in another place the women of Troy went suppliant-wise to the temple of Minerva, bearing a great and beautiful robe, sad and beating their breasts, and with hair unbound; but the goddess regarded them not. Also Achilles dragged the body of Hector three times round the walls of Troy, and was selling it for gold. And Æneas groaned when he saw the man whom he loved, and the old man Priam reaching out helpless hands. Also he knew himself, fighting in the midst of the Grecian chiefs; black Memnon also he knew, and the hosts of the East; and Penthesilea leading the army of the Amazons with shields shaped as the moon. Fierce she was to see, with one breast bared for battle, and a golden girdle beneath it, a damsel daring to fight with men.

But while Æneas marvelled to see these things, lo! there came, with a great throng of youths behind her, Dido, most beautiful of women, fair as Diana, when, on the banks of Eurotas or on the hills of Cynthus, she leads the dance with a thousand nymphs of the mountains about her. On her shoulder she bears a quiver, and overtops them all, and her mother, even Latona, silently rejoices to behold her. So fair and seemly to see was Dido as she bare herself right nobly in the midst, being busy in the work of her kingdom. Then she sat herself down on a lofty throne in the gate of the temple, with many armed men about her. And she did justice between man and man; also she divided the work of the city, sharing it equally or parting it by lot.

Then of a sudden Æneas heard a great clamor, and saw a company of men come quickly to the place, among whom were Antheus and Sergestus and Cloanthus, and others of the men of Troy that had been parted from him in the storm. Right glad was he to behold them, yet was not without fear; and though he would fain have come forth and caught them by the hand, yet did he tarry, waiting to hear how the men had fared, where they had left their ships, and wherefore they were come.

Then Ilioneus, leave being now given that he should speak, thus began: "O Queen, whom Jupiter permits to build a new city in these lands, we men of Troy, whom the winds have carried over many seas, pray thee that thou save our ships from fire, and spare a people that serveth the gods. For, indeed, we are not come to waste the dwellings of this land, or to carry off the spoils to our ships. For, of a truth, they who have suffered so much think not of such deeds. There is a land which the Greeks call Hesperia, but the people themselves Italy, after the name of their chief; an ancient land, mighty in arms and fertile of corn. Hither were we journeying, when a storm arising scattered our ships, and only these few that thou seest escaped to the land. And can there be nation so savage that it receiveth not shipwrecked men on its shore, but beareth arms against them, and forbiddeth them to land? Nay, but if ye care not for men, yet regard the gods, who forget neither them that do righteously nor them that transgress. We had a king, Æneas, than whom there lived not a man more dutiful to gods and men and greater in war. If indeed he be yet alive, then we fear not at all. For of a truth it will not repent thee to have helped us. And if not, other friends have we, as Acestes of Sicily. Grant us, therefore, to shelter our ships from the wind: also to fit them with fresh timber from the woods, and to make ready oars for rowing, so that, finding again our King and our companions, we may gain the land of Italy. But if he be dead, and Ascanius his son lost also, then there is a dwelling ready for us in the land of Sicily, with Acestes, who is our friend."

Then Dido, her eyes bent on the ground, thus spake, "Fear not, men of Troy. If we have seemed to deal harshly with you, pardon us, seeing that, being newly settled in this land, we must keep watch and ward over our coasts. But as for the men of Troy, and their deeds in arms, who knows them not? Think not that we in Carthage are so dull of heart, or dwell so remote from man that we are ignorant of these things. Whether, therefore, ye will journey to Italy, or rather return to Sicily and

King Acestes, know that I will give you all help, and protect you; or, if ye will, settle in this land of ours. Yours is this city which I am building. I will make no difference between man of Troy and man of Tyre. Would that your King also were here! Surely I will send those that shall seek him in all parts of Libya, lest haply he should be gone astray in any forest or strange city of the land."

And when Æneas and Achates heard these things, they were glad, and would have come forth from the cloud, and Achates said, "What thinkest thou? Lo, thy comrades are safe, saving him whom we saw with our own eyes drowned in the waves; and all other things are according as thy mother said."

And even as he spake the cloud parted from about them, and Æneas stood forth, very bright to behold, with face and breast as of a god, for his mother had given to him hair beautiful to see, and cast about him the purple light of youth, even as a workman sets ivory in some fair ornament, or compasseth about silver or marble of Paros with gold. Then spake he to the Queen, "Lo! I am he whom ye seek, even Æneas of Troy, scarcely saved from the waters of the sea. And as for thee, O Queen, seeing that thou only hast been found to pity the unspeakable sorrows of Troy, and biddest us, though we be but poor exiles and lacking all things, to share thy city and thy home, may the gods do so to thee as thou deservest. And, of a truth, so long as the rivers run to the seas, and the shadows fall on the hollows of the hills, so long will thy name and thy glory survive, whatever be the land to which the gods shall bring me." Then gave he his right hand to Ilioneus, and his left hand to Sergestus, and greeted him with great joy.

And Dido, hearing these things, was silent for a while,

but at last she spake: "What ill fortune brings thee into perils so great? what power drave thee to these savage shores? Well do I mind me how in days gone by there came to Sidon one Teucer, who, having been banished from his country, sought help from Belus that he might find a kingdom for himself. And it chanced that in those days Belus, my father, had newly conquered the land of Cyprus. From that day did I know the tale of Troy, and thy name also, and the chiefs of Greece. Also I remember that Teucer spake honorably of the men of Troy, saying that he was himself sprung of the old Teucrian stock. Come ye, therefore, to my palace. I too have wandered far, even as you, and so have come to this land, and having suffered much, have learnt to succor them that suffer."

So saying she led Æneas into her palace; also she sent to his companions in the ships great store of provisions, even twenty oxen, and a hundred bristly swine, and a hundred ewe sheep with their lambs. But in the palace a great feast was set forth, couches covered with broidered purple, and silver vessels without end, and cups of gold, whereon were embossed the mighty deeds of the men of old time.

And in the mean time Æneas sent Achates in haste to the ships, that he might fetch Ascanius to the feast. Also he bade that the boy should bring with him gifts of such things as they had saved from the ruins of Troy, a mantle stiff with broidery of gold and a veil broidered with yellow acanthus, which the fair Helen had taken with her, flying from her home; but Leda, her mother, had given them to Helen; a sceptre likewise which Ilione, first-born of the daughters of Priam, had carried, and a necklace of pearls, and a double crown of jewels and gold.

But Venus was troubled in heart, fearing evil to her son should the men of Tyre be treacherous, after their wont, and Juno remembered her wrath. Wherefore, taking counsel with herself, she called to the winged boy, even Love, that was her son, and spake, " My son, who art all my power and strength, who laughest at the thunders of Jupiter, thou knowest how Juno, being exceedingly wroth against thy brother Æneas, causeth him to wander out of the way over all lands. This day Dido hath him in her palace, and speaketh him fair; but I fear me much how these things may end. Wherefore hear thou that which I purpose. Thy brother hath even now sent for the boy Ascanius, that he may come to the palace, bringing with him gifts of such things as they saved from the ruins of Troy. Him will I cause to fall into a deep sleep, and hide in Cythera or Idalium, and do thou for one night take upon thee his likeness. And when Queen Dido at the feast shall hold thee in her lap, and kiss and embrace thee, do thou breathe by stealth thy fire into her heart."

Then did Love as his mother bade him, and put off his wings, and took upon him the shape of Ascanius, but on the boy Venus caused there to fall a deep sleep, and carried him to the woods of Idalium, and lapped him in sweet-smelling flowers. And in his stead Love carried the gifts to the Queen. And when he was come they sat down to the feast, the Queen being in the midst under a canopy. Æneas also and the men of Troy lay on coverlets of purple, to whom serving-men brought water and bread in baskets and napkins; and within fifty handmaids were ready to replenish the store of victual and to fan the fire; and a hundred others, with pages as many, loaded the tables with dishes and drinking-cups. Many men of Tyre also were bidden to the feast. Much they marvelled at the gifts of Æneas, and much at the false Ascanius. Dido also could not satisfy herself with looking on him, nor knew what trouble he was preparing for her in the time to come. And he, having first embraced the father who was not his father, and clung about his neck, addressed himself to Queen Dido, and she ever followed him with her eyes, and sometimes would hold him on her lap. And still he worked upon her that she should forget the dead Sichæus and conceive a new love in her heart.

But when they first paused from the feast, lo! men set great bowls upon the table and filled them to the brim with wine. Then did the Queen call for a great vessel of gold, with many jewels upon it, from which Belus, and all the kings from Belus, had drunk, and called for wine, and having filled it, she cried, "O Jupiter, whom they call the god of hosts and guests, cause that this be a day of joy for the men of Troy and for them of Tyre, and that our children remember it forever. Also, Bacchus, giver of joy, be present, and kindly Juno." And when she had touched the wine with her lips, she handed the great cup to Prince Bitias, who drank thereout a mighty draught, and the other princes after him. Then the minstrel Iopas, whom Atlas himself had taught, sang to the harp, of the moon, how she goes on her way, and of the sun, how his light is darkened. He sang also of men, and of the beasts of the field, whence they come; and of the stars, Arcturus, and the Greater Bear and the Less, and the Hyades; and of the winter sun, why he hastens to dip himself in the ocean; and of the winter nights, why they tarry so long. The Queen also talked much of the story of Troy, of Priam, and of Hector, asking many things, as of the arms of Memnon, and of the horses of Diomed, and of Achilles, how great he was. And at last she said to Æneas, "Tell us now thy story, how Troy was taken, and thy wanderings over land and sea." And Æneas made answer, "Nay, O Queen, but thou biddest me renew a sorrow unspeakable. Yet, if thou art minded to hear these things, hearken." And he told her all that had befallen him, even to the day when his father Anchises died.

Much was Queen Dido moved by the story, and much did she marvel at him that told it, and scarce could sleep for thinking of him. And the next day she spake to Anna, her sister, "O my sister, I have been troubled this night with ill dreams, and my heart is disquieted within me. What a man is this stranger that hath come to our shores! How noble of mien! How bold in war! Sure I am that he is of the sons of the gods. What fortunes have been his! Of what wars he told us! Surely were I not steadfastly purposed that I would not yoke me again in marriage, this were the man to whom I might yield. Only he—for I will tell thee the truth, my sister—only he, since the day when Sichæus died by his brother's hand, hath moved my heart. But may the earth swallow me up, or the almighty Father strike me with lightning, ere I stoop to such baseness. The husband of my youth hath carried with him my love, and he shall keep it in his grave."

So she spake, with many tears. And her sister made answer, "Why wilt thou waste thy youth in sorrow, without child or husband? Thinkest thou that there is care or remembrance of such things in the grave? No suitors indeed have pleased thee here or in Tyre, but wilt thou also contend with a love that is after thine own heart? Think too of the nations among whom thou dwellest, how fierce they are, and of thy brother at Tyre, what he threatens against thee. Surely it was by the will of the gods, and of Juno chiefly, that the ships of Troy came hither. And this city which thou buildest, to what greatness will it grow if only thou wilt make for thyself such alliance! How great will be the glory of Carthage if the strength of Troy be joined unto her! Only do thou pray to the gods and offer sacrifices; and, for the present, seeing that the time of sailing is now past, make excuse that these strangers tarry with thee awhile."

Thus did Anna comfort her sister and encourage her. And first the two offered sacrifice to the gods, chiefly to Juno, who careth for the bond of marriage. Also, examining the entrails of slain beasts, they sought to learn the things that should happen thereafter. And ever Dido would company with Æneas, leading him about the walls of the city which she builded. And often she would begin to speak and stay in the midst of her words. And when even was come, she would hear again and again at the banquet the tale of Troy, and while others slept would watch, and while he was far away would seem to see him and to hear him. Ascanius, too, she would embrace for love of his father, if so she might cheat her own heart. But the work of the city was stayed meanwhile; nor did the towers rise in their places, nor the youth practise themselves in arms.

Then Juno, seeing how it fared with the Queen, spake to Venus, "Are ye satisfied with your victory, thou and thy son, that ye have vanquished the two of you one woman? Well I knew that thou fearedst lest this Carthage should harm thy favorite. But why should there be war between us? Thou hast what thou seekedst. Let us make alliance. Let Dido obey a Phrygian husband, and bring the men of Tyre as her dowry."

But Venus knew that she spake with ill intent, to the

end that the men of Troy should not reign in the land of Italy. Nevertheless she dissembled with her tongue, and spake, " Who would not rather have peace with thee than war? Only I doubt whether this thing shall be to the pleasure of Jupiter. This thou must learn, seeing that thou art his wife, and where thou leadest I will follow."

So the two, taking counsel together, ordered things in this wise. The next day a great hunting was prepared. For as soon as ever the sun was risen upon the earth, the youth of the city assembled, with nets and hunting-spears, and dogs that ran by scent. And the princes of Carthage waited for the Queen at the palace door, where her horse stood champing the bit, with trappings of purple and gold. And after a while she came forth with many following her. And she had upon her a Sidonian mantle, with a border wrought with divers colors; of gold was her quiver, and of gold the knot of her hair, and of gold the clasp to her mantle. Æneas likewise came forth, beautiful as is Apollo when he leaveth Lydia and the stream of Xanthus, coming to Delos, and hath about his hair a wreath of bay-leaves and a circlet of gold. So fair was Æneas to see. And when the hunters came to the hills, they found great store of goats and stags, which they chased. And of all the company Ascanius was the foremost, thinking scorn of such hunting, and wishing that a wild boar or a lion out of the hills should come forth to be his prey.

And now befell a great storm, with much thunder and hail, from which the hunters sought shelter. But Æneas and the Queen, being left of all their company, came together to the same cave. And there they plighted their troth one to another. Nor did the Queen after that make secret of her love, but called Æneas her husband. Straightway went Rumor and told these things through the cities of

Libya. Now Rumor, men say, is the youngest daughter of Earth, a marvellous creature, moving very swiftly with feet and wings, and having many feathers upon her, and under every feather an eye and a tongue and a mouth and an ear. In the night she flieth between heaven and earth, and sleepeth not; and in the day she sitteth on some housetop or lofty tower, or spreadeth fear over mighty cities; and she loveth that which is false even as she loveth that which is true. So now she went telling through Libya how Æneas of Troy was come, and Dido was wedded to him, and how they lived careless and at ease, and thinking not of the work to which they were called.

And first of all she went to Prince Iarbas, who himself had sought Dido in marriage. And Iarbas was very wroth when he heard it, and, coming to the temple of Jupiter, spread his grief before the god, how that he had given a place on his coasts to this Dido, and would have taken her to wife, but that she had married a stranger from Phrygia, another Paris, whose dress and adornments were of a woman rather than of a man.

And Jupiter saw that this was so, and he said to Mercury, who was his messenger, "Go, speak to Æneas these words: 'Thus saith the King of gods and men. Is this what thy mother promised of thee, twice saving thee from the spear of the Greeks? Art thou he that shall rule Italy and its mighty men of war, and spread thy dominion to the ends of the world? If thou thyself forgettest these things, dost thou grudge to thy son the citadels of Rome? What dost thou here? Why lookest thou not to Italy? Depart and tarry not.'"

Then Mercury fitted the winged sandals to his feet, and took the wand with which he driveth the spirits of the dead, and came right soon to Mount Atlas, which standeth bearing the heaven on his head, and having always clouds about his top, and snow upon his shoulders, and a beard that is stiff with ice. There Mercury stood awhile; then, as a bird which seeks its prey in the sea, shot headlong down, and came to Æneas where he stood, with a yellow jasper in his sword-hilt, and a cloak of purple shot with gold about his shoulders, and spake: " Buildest thou Carthage, forgetting thine own work? The almighty Father saith to thee, 'What meanest thou? Why tarriest thou here? If thou carest not for thyself, yet think of thy son, and that the Fates have given to him Italy and Rome.'"

And Æneas saw him no more. And he stood stricken with fear and doubt. Fain would he obey the voice, and go as the gods commanded. But how should he tell this purpose to the Queen? But at the last it seemed good to him to call certain of the chiefs, as Mnestheus, and Sergestus, and Antheus, and bid them make ready the ships in silence, and gather together the people, but dissemble the cause, and he himself would watch a fitting time to speak and unfold the matter to the Queen.

Yet was not Dido deceived, for love is keen of sight. Rumor also told her that they made ready the ships for sailing. Then, flying through the city, even as one on whom has come the frenzy of Bacchus flies by night over Mount Cithæron, she came upon Æneas, and spake: "Thoughtest thou to hide thy crime, and to depart in silence from this land? Carest thou not for her whom thou leavest to die? And hast thou no fear of winter storms that vex the sea? By all that I have done for thee and given thee, if there be yet any place for repentance, repent thee of this purpose. For thy sake I suffer the wrath of the princes of Libya and of my own people; and if thou leavest me, for what should I live? — till my brother overthrow my city, or Iarbas carry me away captive? If I had but a little Æneas to play in my halls I should not seem so altogether desolate."

But Æneas, fearing the words of Jupiter, stood with eyes that relented not. At the last he spake: "I deny not, O Queen, the benefits that thou hast done unto me, nor ever, while I live, shall I forget Dido. I sought not to fly by stealth; yet did I never promise that I would abide in this place. Could I have chosen according to my will, I had built again the city of Troy where it stood; but the gods command that I should seek Italy. Thou hast thy Carthage: why dost thou grudge Italy to us? Nor may I tarry. Night after night have I seen my father Anchises warning me in dreams. Also even now the messenger of Jupiter came to me — with these ears I heard him — and bade me depart."

Then, in great wrath, with eyes askance, did Dido break forth upon him: "Surely no goddess was thy mother, nor art thou come of the race of Dardanus. The rocks of Caucasus brought thee forth, and an Hyrcanian tigress gave thee suck. For why should I dissemble? Was he moved at all my tears? Did he pity my love? Nay, the very gods are against me. This man I took to myself when he was shipwrecked and ready to perish. I brought back his ships, his companions from destruction. And now forsooth comes the messenger of Jupiter with dreadful commands from the gods. As for thee, I keep thee not. Go, seek thy Italy across the seas: only, if there is any vengeance in heaven, thou wilt pay the penalty for this wrong, being wrecked on some rock in their midst. Then wilt thou call on Dido in vain. Aye, and wherever thou shalt go I will haunt thee, and rejoice in the dwellings below to hear thy doom."

Then she turned, and hasted to go into the house. But her spirit left her, so that her maidens bear her to her chamber and laid her on her bed.

Then Æneas, though he was much troubled in his heart, and would fain have comforted the Queen, was obedient to the heavenly word, and departed to his ships. And the men of Troy busied themselves in making them ready for the voyage. Even as the ants spoil a great heap of corn and store it in their dwellings against winter, moving in a black line across the field, and some carry the great grains, and some chide those that linger, even so did the Trojans swarm along the ways and labor at the work.

But when Dido saw it, she called to Anna, her sister, and said, " Seest thou how they hasten the work along the shore? Even now the sails are ready for the winds, and the sailors have wreathed the ships with garlands, as if for departure. Go thou — the deceiver always trusted thee, and thou knowest how best to move him — go and entreat him. I harmed not him nor his people; let him then grant me this only. Let him wait for a fairer time for his journey. I ask not that he give up his purpose; only that he grant me a short breathing space, till I may learn how to bear this sorrow."

And Anna hearkened to her sister, and took the message to Æneas, yet profited nothing, for the gods shut his ears that he should not hear. Even as an oak stands firm when the north wind would root it up from the earth — its leaves are scattered all around, yet doth it remain firm, for its roots go down to the regions below, even as far as its branches reach to heaven — so stood Æneas firm, and, though he wept many tears, changed not his purpose.

Then did Dido grow weary of her life. For when she did sacrifice, the pure water would grow black and the wine be changed into blood. Also from the shrine of her husband, which was in the midst of her palace, was heard a voice calling her, and the owl cried aloud from the house-top. And in her dreams the cruel Æneas seemed to drive her before him; or she seemed to be going a long way with none to bear her company, and be seeking her own people in a land that was desert. Therefore, hiding the thing that was in her heart, she spake to her sister, saying, "I have found a way, my sister, that shall bring him back to me or set me free from him. Near the shore of the Great Sea, where the Æthiopians dwell, is a priestess, who guards the temple of the daughters of Hesperus, being wont to feed the dragons that kept the apples of gold. She is able by her charms to loose the heart from care or to bind it, and to stay rivers also, and to turn the courses of the stars, and to call up the spirits of the dead. Do thou, therefore — for this is what the priestess commands — build a pile in the open court, and put thereon the sword which he left hanging in our chamber, and the garments he wore, and the couch on which he lay, even all that was his, so that they may perish together."

And when these things were done — for Anna knew not of her purpose — and also an image of Æneas was laid upon the pile, the priestess, with her hair unbound, called upon all the gods that dwell below, sprinkling thereon water that was drawn, she said, from the lake of Avernus, and scattering evil herbs that had been cut at the full moon with a sickle of bronze. Dido also, with one foot bare and her garments loosened, threw meal upon the fire, and called upon the gods, if haply there be any, that look upon those that love and suffer wrong.

In the meantime Æneas lay asleep in the hind part of his ship, when there appeared to him in a dream the god

Mercury, even as he had seen him when he brought the commandment of Jupiter. And Mercury spake, saying, "Son of Venus, canst thou sleep? seest thou not what perils surround thee, nor hearest how the favorable west wind calls? The Queen purposes evil against thee. If thou lingerest till the morning come thou wilt see the shore covered with them that wish thee harm. Fly, then, and tarry not; for a woman is ever of many minds."

Then did Æneas in great fear start from his sleep, and call his companions, saying, "Wake, and sit on the benches, and loose the sails. 'Tis a god thus bids us fly." And even as he spake he cut the cable with his sword. And all hasted to follow him, and sped over the sea.

And now it was morning, and Queen Dido, from her watch-tower, saw the ships upon the sea. Then she smote upon her breast and tore her hair, and cried, "Shall this stranger mock us thus? Hasten to follow him. Bring down the ships from the docks, make ready sword and fire. And this was the man who bare upon his shoulders his aged father! Why did I not tear him to pieces, and slay his companions with the sword, and serve up the young Ascanius at his meal? And if I had perished, what then? for I die to-day. O Sun, that regardest all the earth, and Juno, that carest for marriage bonds, and Hecate, Queen of the dead, and ye Furies that take vengeance on evildoers, hear me. If it be ordered that he reach this land, yet grant that he suffer many things from his enemies, and be driven from his city, and beg for help from strangers, and see his people cruelly slain with the sword; and, when he shall have made peace on ill conditions, that he enjoy not long his kingdom, but die before his day, and lie unburied on the plain. And ye, men of Tyre, hate his children and his people for ever. Let there be no love or peace between you. And may some avenger arise from my grave who shall persecute the race of Dardanus with fire and sword. So shall there be war for ever between him and me."

Then she spake to old Barcé, who had been nurse to her husband Sichæus. "Bid my sister bathe herself in water, and bring with her beasts for sacrifice. And do thou also put a garland about thy head, for I am minded to finish this sacrifice which I have begun, and to burn the image of the man of Troy."

And when the old woman made haste to do her bidding, Queen Dido ran to the court where the pile was made for the burning, and mounted on the pile, and drew the sword of Æneas from the scabbard. Then did she throw herself upon the bed, and cry, "Now do I yield up my life. I have finished my course. I have built a mighty city. I have avenged my husband on him that slew him. Happy had I been, yea too happy! had the ships of Troy never come to this land." Then she kissed the bed and cried, "Shall I die unavenged? Nevertheless let me die. The man of Troy shall see this fire from the sea whereon he journeys, and carry with him an augury of death."

And when her maidens looked, lo! she had fallen upon the sword, and the blood was upon her hands. And a great cry went up through the palace, exceeding loud and bitter, even as if the enemy had taken Carthage or ancient Tyre, and the fire were mounting over the dwellings of men and of gods. And Anna her sister heard it, and rushing through the midst called her by her name, "O my sister, was this thy purpose? Were the pile and the sword and the fire for this? Why wouldst thou not suffer that I should die with thee? For surely, my sister, thou hast slain thyself, and me, and thy people, and thy city. But give me water, ye maidens, that I may wash her wounds, and if there be any breath left in her, we may yet stay it."

Then she climbed on to the pile, and caught her sister in her arms, and sought to staunch the blood with her garments. Three times did Dido strive to raise her eyes; three times did her spirit leave her. Three times she would have raised herself upon her elbow; three times she fell back upon the bed, looking with wandering eyes for the light, and groaning that she yet beheld it.

Then Juno, looking down from heaven, saw that her pain was long, and pitied her, and sent down Iris, her messenger, that she might loose the soul that struggled to be free. For, seeing that she died not by nature, nor yet by the hand of man, but before her time and of her own madness, Queen Proserpine had not shred the ringlet from her head which she shreds from them that die. Wherefore Iris, flying down with dewy wings from heaven, with a thousand colors about her from the light of the sun, stood above her head and said, " I will give thee to death, even as I am bidden, and loose thee from thy body." Then she shred the lock, and Queen Dido gave up the ghost.

CHAPTER III.

FROM Carthage Æneas journeyed to Sicily, for the wind hindered him from coming to Italy as he would fain have done. And in Sicily he held great games in honor of his father Anchises. And when these were finished he departed to Italy, leaving behind him all that were weak and faint-hearted.

The place whereunto he came was nigh unto Cumæ, which was the dwelling-place of the Sibyl. And the men turned the forepart of the ships to the sea, and made them fast with anchors. Then they leapt forth upon the shore, and kindled a fire; and some cut wood in the forest, or fetched water from the stream. But Æneas went up to the great cave of the Sibyl, where, by the inspiration of Apollo, she foretelleth things to come.

Now the temple was a marvellous place to look upon. For Dædalus, when he fled from Minos, King of Crete, flying through the air upon wings, came northwards to the land of Cumæ, and tarried there. Also he dedicated his wings in the temple. On the doors thereof was set forth, graven in stone, the death of Androgeos, and the men of Attica choosing by lot seven of their children who should be given as a ransom yearly; and, rising from the sea upon the other side, the land of Crete. Likewise the Labyrinth was there and its winding ways; but Icarus they saw not, for when his father would have wrought the manner of his death in gold his hands failed him: twice he strove and twice they failed. And when Æneas would have looked further, the priestess said, "Linger not with these things, but slay forthwith seven bullocks from the herd, and seven sheep duly chosen out of the flock." And when they came to the cave—now there are a hundred doors, and a voice cometh forth from each—the Sibyl cried, "It is time. Lo! the god, the god!" And even as she spake her look was changed and the color of her face; also her hair was loosened, and her breast panted, and she waxed greater than is the stature of a man. Then she cried, "Delayest thou to pray, Æneas of Troy? delayest thou? for the doors open not but to prayer." Nor said she more. Then Æneas prayed, saying, "O Phœbus, who didst always pity the sorrows of Troy, and didst guide the arrow of Paris that it slew the great Achilles, I have followed thy bidding, journeying over many lands, and now I lay hold on this shore of Italy, which ever seemed to fly before me. Grant thou that our ill fortune follow us no more. And all ye gods and goddesses who loved not Troy, be merciful to us. And thou, O Prophetess, give, if it may be, such answer as I would hear. So will I and my people honor thee for ever. And write it not, I pray thee, upon leaves, lest the winds carry them away, but speak with thy voice."

And for awhile the prophetess strove against the spirit; but at the last it mastered her, and the doors flew open, and she spake, saying, "The perils of the sea thou hast escaped, but there await thee yet worse perils upon the land. The men of Troy shall come to the kingdom of Lavinium. Fear not for that; yet will they fain not have come. I see battles, and the Tiber foaming with blood, and a new Xanthus and Simoïs, and another Achilles, himself also goddess-born. Juno also shall be ever against thee. And thou shalt be a suppliant to many cities. And the cause of all these woes shall be again a woman. Only yield not thou, but go ever more boldly when occasion shall serve. Little thinkest thou that thy first succor shall be from a city of the Greeks."

And when she had ended these words, Æneas made answer: "O Lady, no toil or peril shall take me unawares; for I have thought over all things in my heart. But one thing I ask of thee. Here is the door of the dwellings of the dead. Fain would I pass thereby, that I may visit my father. I carried him on my shoulders out of the fires of Troy, and with me he endured many things by land and sea, more than befitted his old age. Likewise he bade me ask this boon of thee. Do thou therefore pity both father and son, for thou hast the power, if only thou wilt. Did not Orpheus bring back his wife from the dead, having his harp only? Also Pollux goeth many times this same path, redeeming his brother from death. And why should I tell of Theseus and Hercules? And I also am of the lineage of Jupiter."

Then the Sibyl spake, saying, "Son of Anchises, it is easy to go down to hell. The door is open day and night. But to return, and struggle to the upper air, that is the labor. Few only have done it, and these of the lineage of the gods and dear to Jupiter. Yet if thou wilt attempt it, hearken unto me. There lieth hid in the forest a bough of gold which is sacred to the Queen of hell. Nor may any man go on this journey till he have plucked it, for the Queen will have it as a gift for herself. And when the bough is plucked, there ever groweth another; and if it be the pleasure of the gods that thou go, it will yield to thy hand. But know that one of thy companions lieth dead upon the shore. First must thou bury him, and after offer due sacrifice, even black sheep. So shalt thou approach the dwellings of the dead."

Then Æneas departed from the cave, and Achates went with him, and much they wondered who it might be that was dead. And when they came to the shore, lo! Misenus lay there, than whom no man was more skilful to call men to battle with the voice of the trumpet. Hector's companion he had been in old time, and then followed Æneas. And now, blowing his trumpet on the shore, he had challenged the gods of the sea to compare with him; wherefore a Triton caught him and plunged him into the sea, so that he died. Then did Æneas and his companions prepare for the burial, cutting ilex and oak and mountain-ash from the wood. But when Æneas beheld the forest, how vast it was, he said, "Now may the gods grant that in this great forest the bough of gold discover itself." And as he spake, lo! two doves flew before his face, and settled on the grass, and he knew them to be the birds of his mother, and cried, saying, "Guide me now to the bough of gold, and thou, my mother, help me as before." Then the birds flew so that he could still see them with his eyes, and he followed after them. But when they came to the mouth of Avernus, they sat both of them on a tree. And lo! the bough of gold glittered among the branches and rustled in the wind. Right gladly did Æneas break it off, and carry it to the dwelling of the Sibyl.

In the meantime the men of Troy made a great burial for Misenus on the shore, building a pile of wood, and washing and anointing the body. Also they laid the body on a bier, and on it the garments which he had worn being yet alive. Then others, with faces turned away, held a torch to the wood, whereon also were burned incense and offerings of oil. And when the burning was ended they quenched the ashes with wine. And Corynæus gathered the bones into an urn of bronze, and purified the people, sprinkling them with water with a bough of an olive-tree. Then Æneas made a great mound, and put thereon the trumpet of the man and his bow; and the mountain is called Misenus, after him, to this day.

But when the burial was ended he did as the Sibyl had commanded. A great cavern there is, from which cometh so evil a stench that no bird may fly across. There they brought four black oxen, and the priestess poured wine upon their heads and cut hairs from between the horns. And when they had burned these they slew the oxen, holding dishes for the blood. And Æneas offered a black lamb to the Furies and a barren heifer to the Queen of hell, smiting them with his sword. Then they burned the entrails with fire, pouring oil upon them. Then did the ground give a hollow sound beneath them, and the dogs howled, for the goddess was at hand. And the priestess cried, "Go ye who may not take part in this matter. And thou, Æneas, draw thy sword from its sheath and follow. Now hast thou need of all thy strength and courage." Then she plunged into the cave, and Æneas went with her.

So they went together through the land of shadows, like unto men who walk through a wood in a doubtful light, when the moon indeed hath risen, but there are clouds over the sky. And first they came to where, in front of the gates of hell, dwell Sorrow and Remorse, and pale Disease and Fear, and Hunger that tempteth men to sin, and Want, and Death, and Toil, and Slumber, that is Death's kinsman, and deadly War; also they saw the chamber of the Furies, and Discord, whose hair is of snakes that drip with blood. And in this region there is an ancient elm, in the boughs whereof dwell all manner of dreams, and shapes of evil monsters, as many as have been, such as were the Centaurs, half man half horse, and Briareus with the hundred hands, and others also. These Æneas, when he saw them, sought to slay, rushing upon them with the sword, but his guide warned him that they were shadows only.

After this they came to the river of hell, whereon plies the Boatman Charon. A long white beard hath he and unkempt; and his eyes are fixed in a fiery stare, and a scarf is knotted upon his shoulder, as is a pilot's wont. An old man he seemeth to be, but hale and ruddy. Now there was ever rushing to the bank a great crowd, wives and mothers, and valiant men of war, boys, and girls dead before they were given in marriage, and young men laid on the funeral pile before their parents' eyes. Thick they were as the leaves that fall to the earth at the first frost of autumn, or as the swallows, when they gather themselves together, making ready to fly across the sea to the lands of the sun. And of these Charon would take some into his boat; but others he would forbid, and drive from the shore. This when Æneas saw, he marvelled, and said, "O Lady, what meaneth this concourse at the river? What seek these souls? Why be some driven from the bank and some ferried across?"

And the Sibyl made answer: "This river that thou seest is the Styx, by which the gods in heaven swear, and fear to break their oath. Those whom thou seest to be driven from the bank are such as have lacked burial, but those who are ferried across have been buried duly; for none pass this stream till their bodies have been laid in the grave, otherwise they wander for a hundred years, and so at last may cross over."

Much did Æneas pity their ill fortune, and the more when he beheld Orontes and his Lycians, whom the sea had swallowed up alive before his eyes. Here likewise there met him his pilot Palinurus, to whom, when he knew him, for indeed he scarce could see him in the darkness, he said, "What god took thee from us and drowned thee in the sea? Surely, in this one matter, Apollo hath deceived me, saying that thou shouldst escape the sea and come to the land of Italy."

Then answered Palinurus, "Not so, great Æneas. For indeed to the land of Italy I came. Three nights the south wind carried me over the sea, and on the fourth day I saw the land of Italy from the top of a wave. And when I swam to the shore, and was now clinging to the rocks, my garments being heavy with water, the savage people came upon me, and took me for a prey, and slew me. And now the winds and waves bear me about as they will. Wherefore I pray thee, by thy father, and Iülus, the hope of thy house, that thou deliver me from these woes. Go, therefore, I beseech thee, to the haven of Velia, and cast earth upon me for burial; or give me now thy hand, and take me with thee across this river."

Then said the priestess, "O Palinurus, what madness is this? Wilt thou without due burial cross the river, and look upon the awful faces of the Furies? Think not that the Fates can be changed by prayers. Yet hear this, and be comforted. They that slew thee, being sore troubled by many plagues, shall make due expiation to thee, and build a tomb, and make offerings thereon year by year; and the place where they slew thee shall be called after thy name."

Then he took comfort and departed. But when they came near to the river, the Boatman beheld them, and cried, "Stay thou, whoever thou art, that comest armed to this river, and tell me what thou seekest. This is the land of Shadows, of Sleep, and of Night. The living may not be ferried in this boat. An evil day it was when I carried Hercules, and Theseus, and Pirithoüs, though they were children of the gods. For Hercules chained the Watch-dog of hell, and dragged him trembling from his master's seat. And Theseus and his friend sought to carry away the Queen even from the chamber of her husband."

Then the Sibyl made answer: "Be not troubled. We come not hither with evil thoughts. Let the Watch-dog of hell make the pale ghosts afraid; let your Queen abide in her husband's palace; we will not harm them. Æneas of Troy cometh down to hell that he may speak with his father. And if thou takest no account of such piety, yet thou wilt know this token."

And she showed him the bough of gold. And when he saw it he laid aside his anger, rejoicing to behold, now after many years, the marvellous gift. Then he brought near his boat to the bank, and drave out the souls that were therein, and took on board Æneas and the priestess. Much did it groan with the weight, and the water poured apace through the seams thereof. Yet did they come safe across.

Then they saw Cerberus, the Watch-dog, in his cave. And to him the Sibyl gave a cake of honey and poppy-seed, causing sleep. And this he swallowed, opening wide his three ravenous mouths, and straightway stretched himself out asleep across the cave.

After this they heard a great wailing of infants, even the voices of such as are taken away before they have had lot or part in life. And near to these were such as have died by false accusation; yet lack they not justice, for Minos trieth their cause. And yet beyond, they that, being guiltless, have laid hands upon themselves. Fain would they now endure hardships, being yet alive, but may not, for the river keeps them in with his unlovely stream as in a prison. Not far from these are the Mourning Fields, where dwell the souls of those that have died of love, as Procris, whom Cephalus slew in error, and Laodamia, who died of grief for her husband. And among these was Dido, fresh from the wound wherewith she slew herself. And when Æneas saw her darkly through the shadows, even as one who sees, or thinketh that he sees, the new moon lately risen, he wept, and said, "O Dido, it was truth, then, that they told me, saying that thou hadst slain thyself with the sword. Tell me, Was I the cause of thy death? Loath was I, O Queen—I swear it by all that is most holy in heaven or hell—to leave thy land. But the gods, at whose bidding I come hither this day, constrained me; nor did I think that thou wouldst take such sorrow from my departure. But stay; depart not; for never again may I speak to thee but this once only."

So he spake, and would fain have appeased her wrath. But she cast her eyes to the ground, and her heart was hard against him, even as a rock. And she departed into a grove that was hard by, wherein was her first husband, Sichæus, who loved her even as he was loved. After this they came to the land where the heroes dwell. And there they saw Tydeus, who died before Thebes; and Adrastus, and also many men of Troy, as the three sons of Antenor, and Idæus who was the armor-bearer of King Priam, and bare the arms and drave the chariot yet. All these gathered about him, and would fain know wherefore he had come. But when the hosts of Agamemnon saw his shining arms through the darkness, they fled, as in old days they had fled to the ships; and some would have cried aloud, but could not, so thin are the voices of the dead.

Among these he saw Deïphobus, son of Priam. Cruelly mangled was he, for his hands had been cut off, and his ears and his nostrils likewise. Scarce did Æneas know him, and he himself in shame would have hidden his wounds; but the son of Anchises spake to him, saying, "Who hath dealt so foully with thee, great Deïphobus? Men told me that on the last night of Troy thou didst fall dead on a heap of Greeks whom thou hadst slain. Wherefore I built thee a tomb by the sea, and thrice called aloud thy name. But thee I found not, that I might lay thee therein."

Then Deïphobus made answer: "Thou hast left nothing undone, but hast paid me all due honor. But my ill fate and the accursed wickedness of the Spartan woman have destroyed me. How we spent that last night in idle rejoicings thou knowest. And she, while the women of Troy danced before the gods, stood holding a torch on the citadel, as though she were their leader, yet in truth she called therewith the Greeks from Tenedos. But I lay overcome with weariness in my chamber. Then did she, a noble wife, forsooth! take all the arms out of the house, and my trusty sword also from under my head; and after brought thereunto Menelaüs, so hoping to do away her sin against him; and Ulysses also, always ready with evil counsels. What need of more? May the gods do so and more also to them. But tell me why hast thou come hither?"

And it was now past noonday, and the two had spent in talk all the allotted time. Therefore the Sibyl spake: "Night cometh, Æneas, and we waste the day in tears. Lo! here are two roads. This on the right hand leadeth to the palace of Pluto and to the Elysian plains; and that on the left to Tartarus, the abode of the wicked." And Deïphobus answered: "Be not wroth, great priestess; I depart to my own place. Do thou, my friend, go on and prosper."

But as Æneas looked round he saw a great building, and a three-fold wall about it, and round the wall a river of fire. Great gates there were, and a tower of brass, and the fury Tisiphone sat as warder. Also he heard the sound of those that smote upon an anvil, and the clanking of chains. And he stood, and said, "What mean these things that I see and hear?" Then the Sibyl made answer: "The foot of the righteous may not pass that threshold. But when the Queen of hell gave me this office she herself led me through the place and told me all. There sitteth Rhadamanthus the Cretan, and judgeth the dead. And them that be condemned Tisiphone taketh, and the gate which thou seest openeth to receive them. And within is a great pit, and the depth thereof is as the height of heaven. Herein lie the Titans, the sons of Earth, whom Jupiter smote with the thunder; and herein the sons of Aloeus, who strove to thrust the gods from heaven; and Salmoneus, who would have mocked the thunder of Jupiter, riding in his chariot through the cities of Elis, and shaking a torch, and giving himself out to be a god. But the lightning smote him in his pride. Also I saw Tityos, spread over nine acres of ground, and the vulture feeding on his heart. And over some hangs a great stone ready to fall; and some sit at the banquet, but when they would eat, the Fury at their side forbids, and rises and shakes her torch and thunders in their ears. These are they who while they were yet alive hated their brothers, or struck father or mother, or deceived one that trusted to them, or kept their riches for themselves, nor cared for those of their own household (a great multitude are they), or stirred up civil strife. And of these some roll a great stone and cease not, and some are bound to wheels, and some sit forever crying, 'Learn to do righteousness and to fear the gods.'"

And when the priestess had finished these words they hastened on their way. And, after a while, she said, "Lo! here is the palace which the Cyclopés built for Pluto and the Queen of hell. Here must we offer the gift of the bough of gold." And this being accomplished, they came to the dwellings of the righteous. Here are green spaces, with woods about them; and the light of their heaven is fuller and brighter than that which men behold. Another sun they have and other stars. Some of them contend together in wrestling and running; and some dance in measure, singing the while a pleasant song; and Orpheus, clad in a long robe, makes music, touching his harp, now with his fingers and now with an ivory bow. Here did Æneas marvel to see the mighty men of old, such as were Ilus, and Dardanus, builder of Troy. Their spears stood fixed in the earth, and their horses fed about the plain; for they love spear and chariot and horses, even as they loved them upon earth. And others sat and feasted, sitting on the grass in a sweet-smelling grove of bay, whence flows the river which men upon the earth call the Po. Here were they who had died for their country, and holy priests, and poets who had uttered nothing base, and such as had found out witty inventions, or had done great good to men. All these had snow-white garlands on their heads. Then spake the Sibyl to Musæus, who stood in the midst, surpassing them all in stature: "Tell me, happy souls, where shall we find Anchises." And Musæus answered, "We have no certain dwelling-place: but climb this hill, and ye can see the whole plain below, and doubtless him whom ye seek."

Then they beheld Anchises where he sat in a green valley, regarding the spirits of those who should be born in after-time of his race. And when he beheld Æneas coming, he stretched out his hands and cried, "Comest thou, my son? Hast thou won thy way hither to me? Even so I thought that it would be, and lo! my hope hath not failed me."

And Æneas made answer, "Yea, I have come a long way to see thee, even as thy spirit bade me. And now let me embrace thee with my arms."

But when he would have embraced him it was as if he clasped the air.

Then Æneas looked and beheld a river, and a great company of souls thereby, thick as the bees on a calm summer day in a garden of lilies. And when he would know the meaning of the concourse, Anchises said, "These are souls which have yet to live again in a mortal body, and they are constrained to drink of the water of forgetfulness." And Æneas said, "Nay, my father, can any desire to take again upon them the body of death?" Then Anchises made reply: "Listen, my son, and I will tell thee all. There is one soul in heaven and earth and the stars and the shining orb of the moon and the great sun himself; from which soul also cometh the life of man and of beast, and of the birds of the air, and of the fishes of the sea. And this soul is of a divine nature, but the mortal body maketh it slow and dull. Hence come fear and desire, and grief and joy, so that, being as it were shut in a prison, the spirit beholdeth not any more the light that is without. And when the mortal life is ended, yet are not men quit of all the evils of the body, seeing these must needs be put away in many marvellous ways. For some are hung up to the winds, and with some their wickedness is washed out by water, or burnt out with fire. But a ghostly pain we all endure. Then we that are found worthy are sent unto Elysium and the plains of the blest. And when, after many days, the soul is wholly pure, it is called to the river of forgetfulness, that it may drink thereof, and so return to the world that is above."

Then he led Æneas and the Sibyl to a hill whence they could see the whole company, and regard their faces as they came; and he said, "Come, and I will show thee them that shall come after thee. That youth who leans upon a pointless spear is Silvius, thy youngest child, whom Lavinia shall bear to thee in thy old age. He shall reign in Alba, and shall be the father of kings. And many other kings are there who shall build cities great and famous. Lo! there is Romulus, whom Ilia shall bear to Mars. He shall build Rome, whose empire shall reach to the ends of the earth and its glory to the heaven. Seest thou him with the olive crown about his head and the white beard? That is he who shall first give laws to Rome. And next to him is Tullus, the warrior. And there are the Tarquins; and Brutus, who shall set the people free, aye, and shall slay his own sons when they would be false to their country. See also the Decii; and Torquatus, with the cruel axe; and Camillus winning back the standards of Rome. There standeth one who shall subdue Corinth; and there another who shall avenge the blood of Troy upon the race of Achilles. There, too, thou mayest see the Scipios, thunderbolts of war, whom the land of Africa shall fear; and there Regulus, busy in the furrows; and there the Fabii, chiefly him, greatest of the name, who shall save thy country by wise delay. Such, my son, shall be thy children's children. Others with softer touch shall carve the face of man in marble or mould the bronze; some more skilfully shall plead, or map the skies, or tell the rising of the stars. 'Tis thine, man of Rome, to subdue the world. This is thy work, to set the rule of peace over the vanquished, to spare the humble, and to subdue the proud."

Then he spake again: "Regard him who is the first of all the company of conquerors. He is Marcellus; he shall save the state in the day of trouble, and put to flight Carthaginian and Gaul."

Then said Æneas, for he chanced to see by his side a youth clad in shining armor, and very fair to look upon, but sad, and with downcast eyes, "Tell me, father, who is this? How noble is he! What a company is about him! but there is a shadow of darkness round his head."

And Anchises made answer, "O my son, seek not to know the greatest sorrow that shall befall thy children after thee. This youth the Fates shall only show for a brief space to man. Rome would seem too mighty to the gods should he but live! What mourning shall there be for him! What a funeral shalt thou see, O river of Tiber, as thou flowest by the new-made tomb! No youth of the race of Troy shall promise so much as he. Alas! for his righteousness, and truth, and valor unsurpassed! O luckless boy, if thou canst haply break thy evil doom thou shalt be a Marcellus. Give handfuls of lilies. I will scatter the bright flowers and pay the idle honors to my grandson's shade."

Thus did Anchises show his son things to be, and kindled his soul with desire of glory. Also he showed him what wars he must wage, and how he should endure, or, if it might be, avoid the evils to come.

There are two gates of Sleep, of horn the one, by which true dreams go forth; of ivory the other, by which the false. Then did Anchises send forth his son and the Sibyl by the ivory gate. And Æneas returned to the ships, and making sail came to the cape which was afterwards called Caieta.

CHAPTER IV.

WHILE they tarried at Cumæ, Caieta, who was the nurse of Æneas, died and was buried; and they called the cape after her name. And afterwards they set sail, and passed by the island wherein dwelt Circé, who is the daughter of the Sun. Pleasantly doth she sing, sitting at the loom, and burneth torches of sweet-smelling cedar to give her light by night. And round about her dwelling you may hear the growling of lions and wild boars and bears and wolves, which are men whom the goddess with her enchantments hath changed into the shapes of beasts. But Neptune would not that the men of Troy, being fearers of the gods, should suffer such things. Therefore did he send them favorable winds, so that they passed quickly by that land.

Now when it was dawn, the wind being now lulled, they came to a great wood upon the shore, and in the midst of the wood the river Tiber, yellow with much abundance of sand, flowing into the sea. And on the shore and in the wood were many birds. Thither the men of Troy brought their ships safe to land.

Of this country Latinus was king, who was the son of Faunus, who was the son of Picus, who was the son of Saturn. And King Latinus had not a son, but a daughter only, Lavinia by name, who was now of an age to be married. Many chiefs of Latium, and of all Italy, desired to have her to wife; of whom the first was Turnus, a very comely youth, and of a royal house. Now the Queen, the mother of the virgin, loved him, and would fain have married her daughter to him, but the gods hindered the marriage with ill omens and marvels. In the midst of the palace was a great bay-tree, which the King who had builded the house had dedicated to Phœbus. On this there lighted a great swarm of bees, and hung like unto a cluster of grapes from a bough thereof. And the seers, beholding the thing, cried, "There cometh a stranger who shall be husband to Lavinia, and a strange people who shall bear rule in this place." Also when Lavinia lighted the fire upon the altar, standing by her father, a flame leapt therefrom upon her hair, and burned the ornament that was upon her head and the crown of jewels and gold, and spread with smoke and fire over the whole palace. Whereupon the prophets spake, saying, "The virgin indeed shall be famous and great, but there cometh a dreadful war upon her people." And King Latinus, fearing what these things might mean, inquired of the oracle of Faunus, his father, which is by the grove of Albunea. Now the custom is that the priest offereth sacrifice in the grove and lieth down to sleep on the skins of the sheep that he hath slain; and it cometh to pass that he seeth visions in the night and heareth the voice of the gods. So King Latinus, being himself a priest, made a great sacrifice, even of a hundred sheep, and lay down to sleep upon the skins thereof. And when he was laid down, straightway there came a voice from the grove, saying, "Seek not, my son, to marry thy daughter to a chief of this land. There shall come a son-in-law from beyond the sea, who shall exalt our name from the one end of heaven to the other." Nor did the King hide these things, but noised them abroad, and the fame thereof was great in these days when Æneas and his company came to the land of Italy.

Now it so chanced that Æneas and Iülus his son, and

others of the princes, sat down to eat under a tree; and they had platters of dough whereupon to eat their meat. And when they had ended, and were not satisfied, they ate their platters also, not thinking what they did. Then said Iülus, making sport, "What! do we eat even our tables?" And Æneas was right glad to hear this thing, and embraced the boy, and said, "Now know I that we are come to the land which the gods have promised to me and to my people, that they would give us. For my father, Anchises, spake to me, saying, 'My son, when thou shalt come to a land that thou knowest not, and hunger shall constrain thee to eat thy tables, then know that thou hast found thee a home.' Now, therefore, seeing that these things have an accomplishment, let us pour out libations to Jupiter, and make our prayers also to my father, Anchises, and make merry. And in the morning we will search out the country, and see who they be that dwell herein."

Then he bound a garland of leaves about his head, and made his prayers to Mother Earth, and to the gods of the land, of whom indeed he knew not who they were, and to Father Jupiter, and to the other gods also. And when he had ended his prayer, Jupiter thundered thrice from the sky. Then was it noised abroad among the men of Troy that now indeed were they come to the land where they should build them a city; and they eat and drank and made merry.

The next day those who should search out the country went forth. And when it was told Æneas, saying that this river was the Tiber, and that the people who dwelt in the land were the Latins, valiant men of war, he chose out a hundred men who should go, with crowns of olive upon their heads, to the city of the King, having also gifts in their hands, and should pray that there might be peace between the men of Troy and his people. And the men made haste to depart; and in the meanwhile Æneas marked out for himself a camp, and bade that they should make a rampart and a ditch.

Now when they that were sent came nigh to the city, they saw the young men in the plain that was before it, riding upon horses and driving chariots. Others shot with the bow or cast javelins, and some contended in running or boxing. And one rode on horseback and told the king, saying that certain men in strange raiment were come. Then the King commanded that they should be brought into the palace, and sat upon the throne of his fathers, and gave audience to them.

Now the palace stood on the hill that was in the midst of the city, where King Picus had builded it, having woods about it very sacred. Here did the kings first receive the sceptre, that they should bear rule over the people. A senate-house also it was, and a banqueting-house, where the princes sat feasting. Very great was it and magnificent, having a hundred pillars; and in the halls were the statues of ancient kings, carven in cedar, even Italus, and Sabinus the vine-dresser, and Father Saturn, and Janus with the two faces. Also on the wall hung trophies of war, chariots, and battle-axes, and helmets, and the beaks of ships. And sitting on the throne was the image of King Picus, clad in royal apparel, and bearing a shield on his left arm. But the King himself his wife Circé had changed into a bird.

And King Latinus spake, saying, "Tell me, men of Troy, for I know you who you are, what seek ye? For what cause are ye come to the land of Italy? Have ye gone astray in your journey? or have the storms driven you out of the way, as ofttimes befalleth men that sail upon the sea? Ye are welcome. And know that we be of the race of Saturn, who do righteously, not by constraint, but of our own will. From hence also, even from Corythus, which is a city of the Etrurians, went forth Dardanus, and abode in the land of Troy."

Then Ilioneüs made answer, saying, "Great King, we have not gone astray in our journey, nor have storms driven us out of our way. Of set purpose are we come to this land. For we were driven away by ill-fortune from our country, of which things we doubt not, O King, that thou knowest the certainty. For who is there under the whole heaven who knoweth not what a storm of destruction came forth from the land of Greece and overthrew the great city of Troy, Europe and Asia setting themselves in arms against each other? And now are we come to ask for a parcel of land whereon we may dwell; and for air and water, which indeed are common to all men. Nor shall we do dishonor to this realm, nor be unthankful for these benefits. And be sure, O King, that it will not repent thee that thou hast received us. For indeed many nations and lands would fain have joined us to themselves. But the gods laid a command upon us that we should come to this country of Italy. For indeed, as thou sayest, Dardanus came forth from hence, and thither his children, Apollo bidding them, would return. And now, behold, Æneas sends thee these gifts of the things which remain to us of the riches which we had aforetime. This sceptre King Priam held when he did justice among his people; here is a crown also, and garments which the women of Troy have worked with their hands."

Then for awhile King Latinus kept silence, fixing his eyes upon the ground. Deeply did he ponder in his heart upon the marriage of his daughter, and upon the oracles of Faunus his father, whether indeed this stranger that was now come to his land might haply be the son-in-law of whom the prophets had spoken. At the last he spake, saying, "May the gods prosper this matter between you and me. We grant, men of Troy, that which ye ask. Also we regard these your gifts. Know ye that while we reign in this land ye shall not want for riches, even unto the measure of the riches of Troy. And for your King, Æneas, if he desire, as ye say, to join himself with us, let him come and look upon us, face to face. And also take ye back this message to your King. I have a daughter, whom the gods suffer me not to marry to a husband of this land. For they say that there shall come a stranger who shall be my son-in-law, and that from his loins shall come forth those who shall raise our name even unto the stars."

Then the King commanded that they should bring forth horses from the stalls. Now there stood in the stalls three hundred horses, very fleet of foot. And of these they brought forth one hundred, one for each man of Troy; and they were decked with trappings of purple, and champed on bits of gold. And for Æneas himself he sent a chariot, and two horses breathing fire from their nostrils, which were of the breed of the horses of the Sun. So the men of Troy went back riding on horses, and took to Æneas the gifts and the message of peace.

Now Juno beheld how the men of Troy were come to the land of Italy, and were now building them houses to dwell in; and great wrath came into her heart, and she spake to herself, saying, "Of a truth this accursed race hath vanquished me. For the flames of Troy burned them not, neither hath the sea devoured them. And, lo! they are come to the place where they would be, even to the river of Tiber. Yet could Mars destroy the whole nation of the Lapithæ, when he was wroth with them; and Jupiter suffered Diana to prevail against the land of Calydon. Yet had not the Lapithæ or Calydon done so great wickedness as hath this nation of Troy. And I, who am the wife of Jupiter, am vanquished by Æneas! Yet have I means yet remaining to me, for if the gods of heaven will not help me, then will I betake me to the powers of hell. From the kingdom of Latium I may not keep him, and the gods decree that he shall have Lavinia to wife. Yet may I hinder the matter. Surely at a great price shall they buy this alliance; and thy dowry, O virgin, shall be the blood of Italy and of Troy."

Then Juno descended to the lower parts of the earth, and called to her Alecto from the dwellings of her sisters the Furies — Alecto who loveth war and anger and treachery, and all evil deeds. Even Pluto hateth her, aye, and her sisters likewise, so dreadful is she to behold. And Juno spake to her, saying, "Now would I have thee help me, Daughter of Night, that I lose not my proper honor. I will not that Æneas should have the daughter of Latinus to wife, or dwell in the land of Italy. Seeing therefore that thou canst set brother against brother, and bring enmity into houses and kingdoms, that they should fall, break this peace that they have made, and bring to pass some occasion of war."

Then straightway Alecto betook herself to the dwelling of King Latinus. There found she Amata, the Queen, in great trouble and wrath, for she loved not the men of Troy, and would have Turnus for her son-in-law. And the Fury took a snake from her hair, and thrust it into the bosom of the Queen. About her breast it glided unfelt, and breathed poisonous breath into her heart.

And now it became a collar of twisted gold about her neck, and now a crown about her head, binding her hair. At the first indeed, when the poison began to work, and her whole heart was not as yet filled with the fever, she spake gently and after the wont of a mother, weeping much the while over her daughter. "Art thou then ready, my husband, to give thy daughter to this exile of Troy? Hast thou no pity for thyself, or thy daughter, or me? Well know I that with the first north wind he will fly and carry her away over the sea. And what of thy word, and of the faith that thou hast pledged so many times to Turnus thy kinsman? If thou must seek a son-in-law from the land of the stranger, I hold that they all be strangers who obey not thy rule, and that the gods mean not other than this. And Turnus, if thou wilt inquire more deeply into his descent, is of the lineage of Inachus, and cometh in the beginning from the land of Mycenæ."

But when she perceived that her husband heeded not these words, and when also the poison of the serpent had now altogether prevailed over her, she ran through the city like to one that is mad. Nay, she feigned that the frenzy of Bacchus was upon her, and fled into the woods, taking her daughter with her, to the end that she might hinder the marriage. Many other women also, when they heard this thing, went forth, leaving their homes. With bare necks and hair unbound they went, crying aloud the while; and in their hands they held staves of pine, and were clad in the skins of wild beasts. And in the midst of them stood the Queen, holding a great pine torch in her hand, and singing the marriage song of her daughter and Turnus; and her eyes were red as blood.

Next after this the Fury, deeming that she had overthrown the counsels of Latinus, sped to the city of Turnus the Rutulian. Now the name of the city was called Ardea, and Danaë builded it in old time; Ardea is it called to this day, but its glory hath departed. Now Turnus was asleep in his palace, and Alecto took upon her the shape of an old woman, even of Chalybé, who was the priestess of Juno; and she spake, saying, "Turnus, wilt thou suffer all thy toil to be in vain, and thy kingdom to be given to another? King Latinus taketh from thee thy betrothed wife, and chooseth a stranger that he should inherit his kingdom. Juno commanded that I should tell thee this in thy sleep. Rise, therefore, and arm thy people. Consume these strangers and their ships with fire. And if King Latinus yet will not abide by his promise, let him know for himself what Turnus can do in the day of battle."

But Turnus laughed her to scorn. "That the ships of the stranger have come to the Tiber, I know full well. But tell me not these tales. Queen Juno forgetteth me not, therefore I am not afraid; but thou, mother, art old, and wanderest from the truth, and troublest thyself for nought, and art mocked with idle fear. Thy business it is to tend the temples of the gods and their images, but as for war, leave that to men, seeing that it is their care."

Greatly wroth was Alecto to hear such words. And even while he spake the young man shuddered and stared with his eyes, for the Fury hissed before him with a thousand snakes. And when he would have spoken more, she thrust him back, and caught two snakes from her hair, and lashed him therewith, and cried aloud, "Old am I! and wander from the truth! and am mocked with idle fears! Nay, but I come from the dwelling of the Furies, and war and death are in my hand!"

And she cast a torch at the youth, and fixed it smoking with baleful light in his heart. Then, in great fear, he woke, and a cold sweat burst forth upon him, and he cried aloud for his arms, and was exceedingly mad for battle. Also he bade the youth arm themselves, saying that he would thrust the men of Troy out of Italy, aye, and fight, if need were, with the Latins also. And the people hearkened unto him, so fair was he, and of noble birth, and great renown in war.

Then Alecto hied her to the place where Iülus was hunting the beasts of the forest. Now there was a stag, very stately, with exceeding great horns, which Tyrrheus and his children had brought up from a fawn. And Silvia, a fair virgin who was his daughter, was wont to adorn it with garlands, and to comb it, and to wash it with water. By day it would wander in the woods, and at nightfall come back to the house. This stag, then, the dogs of Iülus having scented pursued, and indeed Alecto brought it to pass that this mischief shall befall; and Iülus also, following hard upon his dogs, shot an arrow at it, nor missed (for the Fury would have it so), but pierced it through. Then the wounded beast flew back to the house which it knew, being covered with blood, and filled it with a lamentable voice, as one that crieth for help. And Silvia heard it, and cried to the country folk for aid, who came forthwith, Alecto urging them (for the accursed thing lay hid in the woods). And one had a charred firebrand and another a knotted stick, each such weapon as came to his hand. And Tyrrheus, who chanced to be splitting a tall oak with wedges, led the way, having a great axe in his hand.

Then did Alecto climb upon the roof, and, sounding with hellish voice through a clarion, sent abroad the shepherds' signal. And all the forest trembled at the sound, and Trivia's lake and Nar, with his white sulphurous wave, and the fountains of Velia; and trembling mothers pressed their children to their breasts.

Then ran together all the country folk, and the youth of Troy hasted also to the help of Iülus. And now they fought not with clubs and charred stakes, but with swords and spears in battle array. Then Almo fell, the eldest of the sons of Tyrrheus, stricken in the throat, with many others round him, and among them the old man Galæsus, even as he offered himself to be a mediator between the two. Most righteous of men was he, and richest likewise, for he had five flocks of sheep and five herds of cattle, and tilled the earth with a hundred ploughs.

But Alecto, when she had accomplished these things, hasted to Juno, and spake, saying, "I have done thy bidding; and now, if thou wilt, I will to the neighboring cities, spreading among them rumors of wars." But Juno answered, "It is enough; there hath been the shedding of blood. It were not well that the Father should see thee wandering in the upper air, wherefore depart, and if aught remain to be done, I will see to it."

After this the shepherds hasted back to the city, and bare with them the dead, even the youth Almo and the old man Galæsus, and cried for vengeance to the gods and to the King. And fiercest of all was Turnus, complaining that men of Troy were called to reign over them, and that he himself was banished. And all the multitude was uregnt with the King that he should make war against the strangers; neither did any man regard the commands of the gods. But the King stood firm, even as a great rock in the sea is not moved though the waves roar about it and the seaweed is dashed upon its sides. But when he saw that he could not prevail against these evil counsels, he called the gods to witness, crying, "The storm strikes upon me, and I may not stand against it. O foolish Latins, ye shall pay for this madness with your blood, and thou, Turnus, shalt suffer the worst punishment of all; and when thou shalt turn to the gods they shall not hear thee. But as for me, my rest is at hand; I lose but the honors of my funeral."

It was a custom in Latium, which Alba kept in after time, and mighty Rome yet keepeth to this day, that when she beginneth to make war, be it on the men of Thrace or the men of the East, Arab, or Indian, or Parthian, they open the great gates of the temple (double they are, and made strong with bolts of brass and iron), on the threshold whereof sitteth Janus, the guardian. For the Consul himself, with robe and girdle, so soon as the fathers give their sentence for war, throweth them wide, and the people follow the Consul, and the horns blow a great blast together. Even so they bade King Latinus, after the custom of his country, declare war against the the men of Troy, and open the gates of slaughter; but he would not, flying and hiding himself in darkness. Then did great Juno herself come down and burst asunder the iron-bound gates of war.

Then through the land of Italy men prepared themselves for battle, making bright shield and spear, and sharpening the axe upon the whetstone. And in five cities did they set up anvils to make arms thereon, head-pieces, and shields of wicker, and breast-plates of bronze, and greaves of silver. Nor did men regard any more the reaping-hook nor the plough, making new for battle the swords of their fathers.

Now the greatest of the chiefs were these:—

First, Prince Mezentius, the Tuscan, who regarded not the gods; and with him Lausus his son, than whom was none fairer in the host but Turnus only. A thousand men followed him from Agylla. Worthy was he of a better father.

Next came, with horses that none might surpass, Aventinus, son of Hercules; and on his shield was the emblem of his father, the Hydra with its hundred snakes. Long swords had his men and Sabine spears; and he himself had about his head and shoulders a great lion's skin, with terrible mane and great white teeth.

And from Tibur came two youths of Argos, twin brothers, Catillus and Coras, swift and strong as two Centaurs from the hills. And Cæculus, who builded Præneste, was there, son of Vulcan, and a great company of country folk with him, whereof many bare not shield nor spear, but slings with bullets of lead, and javelins in either hand, and helmets of wolf's skin upon their heads.

After him marched Messapus, tamer of horses, Neptune's son, whom no man might lay low with fire or sword; and the people followed, singing a war-song of their king, like to a great flock of swans, which flies with many cries across the Asian marsh. And next Clausus the Sabine, from whom is sprung the great Claudian house; and Halesus, companion of Agamemnon, and enemy of Troy from of old, with many nations behind him; clubs had they, fastened with thongs of leather, and wicker shields on their left arms, and their swords were shaped as reaping-hooks. After these came Œbalus, son of Telon, with the men of Campania, wearing helmets of cork, and having shields and swords of bronze; also Ufens, of Neresæ, with his robber bands; and Umbro, the Marsian priest, a mighty wizard and charmer of serpents, who could also heal their bite; but the wound of the Trojan spears he could not heal, nor did all his charms and mighty herbs avail him.

With them also came Virbius, son of Hippolytus, from Egeria. For men say that Hippolytus, when the curse of his father had fallen upon him, and he had perished by the madness of his horses, was made alive by the skill of Æsculapius, and that Jupiter, being wroth that a mortal should return from the dead, slew the healer, the son of Phœbus, with his thunderbolt; but that Hippolytus Diana hid in the grove of Africa, that he might spend the rest of his days obscure and without offence. And therefore do they yet hinder horses from coming near to the temple of Diana. Nevertheless the youth Virbius drave horses in his chariot.

But chief among them all was Turnus, who moved in the midst, clad in armor, and overtopping them all by his head. And he had a helmet with three crests, and the Chimæra thereon for a sign; and on his shield was Io, with her horns lifted to heaven, and Argus the herdsman, and Inachus pouring a river from his urn. A great multitude of footmen followed him, Rutulians and Sicanians, and they that dwelt about the Tiber, and about Anxur, and about the green woods of Feronia.

Last of all came Camilla the Volscian, with a great company on horses, clad in armor of bronze. She loved neither distaff nor the basket of Minerva, but rather to fight and to outstrip the winds in running. And a mighty runner was she, for she would run over the harvest-field nor harm the corn, and when she sped across the waves of the sea she wetted not her foot therein. All the youth marvelled to behold her, and the women stood gazing upon her as she went. For a robe of royal purple was about her shoulders, and a snood of gold about her hair; and she carried a Syrian quiver and a pike of myrtle-wood, as the shepherds are wont.

So the chiefs were gathered together, and much people with them, Mezentius, and Ufens, and Messapus being their leaders. They sent an embassy likewise to Diomed (for Diomed had built him a city in Italy, even Arpi), to tell him that Æneas and the men of Troy were setting up a kingdom in these parts, and to bid him take counsel for himself.

But Æneas was much troubled at these things, and cast about in his mind where he should look for help. And while he meditated thereon he slept. And lo! in his dreams the god of the river, even Father Tiber, appeared to him. An old man was he, and clad in a blue linen robe, and having a crown of reeds upon his head. And he spake, saying, "Thou art welcome to this land, to which thou hast brought the gods of Troy. Be not dismayed at wars and rumors of wars, nor cease from thy enterprise. And this shall be a sign unto thee. Thou shalt find upon the shore a white sow with thirty young, white also, about her teats. And it shall come to pass that after thirty years Iülus shall build him the White City. And now I will tell thee how thou shalt have victory in this war. Certain men of Arcadia, following their King, Evander, have built a city in this land, and called its name Pallantium. These wage war continually with the Latins. To them therefore thou must go, making thy way up the stream of the river. Rise therefore, and offer sacrifice to Juno, appeasing her wrath. And to me thou shalt perform thy vows when thou shalt have prevailed. For know that I am Tiber the river, and that of all the rivers on earth none is dearer to the gods."

Then Æneas roused him from sleep, and made his supplications to the Nymphs and the river god, that they would be favorable to him. And when he looked, lo! upon the shore a white sow with thirty young, white also, about her teats. Of these he made a sacrifice to Juno. And after this he commandèd that they should make ready two ships, and so went on his way. And Tiber stayed his stream so that the men might not toil in rowing. Quickly they sped, and many trees were above their heads, and the image thereof in the water beneath. And at noonday they beheld a city with walls, and a citadel, and a few houses round about.

Now it chanced that Evander and his people were holding a sacrifice that day to Hercules before the city. But when they saw through the trees the ships approaching, they were astonished, and rose all from the feast. But Pallas, who was the son of the King, commanded that they should not interrupt the sacrifice, and snatching a spear, he cried from the mound whereon the altar stood: "Strangers, why come ye? what seek ye? Do ye bring peace or war?"

Then Æneas cried from the stern of his ship, holding out the while an olive branch: "We be men of Troy, enemies of the Latins, and we seek King Evander. Say, therefore, to him that Æneas, prince of Troy, is come, seeking alliance with him."

Much did Pallas marvel to hear this name, and said, "Approach thou, whoever thou art, and hold converse with my father;" and he caught him by the hand.

And when Æneas was set before King Evander he spake, saying, "I come to thee, O King, not unwilling or fearful, though indeed thou art a Greek and akin to the sons of Atreus. For between thee and me also there is kindred. For Dardanus, builder of Troy, was the son of Electra, who was the daughter of Atlas. And ye come from Mercurius, who was the son of Cyllene, who was also the daughter of Atlas. Wherefore, I sent not ambassadors to thee, but came myself, fearing nothing. Know thou that the Daunian race, which warreth against thee, pursueth us also; against whom if they prevail, without doubt they shall rule over Italy, from the one sea even to the other. I would, therefore, that we make alliance together."

And as he spake, Evander ceased not to regard him, and, when he had ended, spake, saying, "Welcome, great son of Troy. Gladly do I recognize the voice and face of Anchises. For I remember how Priam came of old time to the kingdom of his sister Hesioné, who was the wife of Telamon; and many princes were with him, but the mightiest of them was Anchises. Much did I love the man, and took him with me to Pheneus. And he gave me when he departed a quiver and arrows of Lycia, and a cloak with threads of gold, and two bridles of gold, which my son Pallas hath to this day. The alliance that thou seekest I grant. To-morrow shalt thou depart, with such help as I can give. But now, since ye be come at such good time, join us in our sacrifice and feast."

So they feasted together on the flesh of oxen and drank wine, and were merry. And when they had made an end of eating and drinking, King Evander spake, saying, "This great feast, my friend, we hold not without good reason, which thou shalt now hear from me. Seest thou this great ruin of rocks? Here in old time was a cave, running very deep into the cliff, wherein Cacus dwelt, a monster but half man, whose father was Vulcan. The ground thereof reeked with blood, and at the mouth were fixed the heads of dead men. Very great of stature was he, and breathed out fire from his mouth. To this land came Hercules, driving before him the oxen of Geryon, whom he had slain. And when he had left these to feed in the valley by the river, Cacus, that he might fill up the measure of his wickedness, stole four bulls and four heifers, the very chiefest of the herd. And that he might conceal the thing, he dragged them by the tails backwards, so that the tracks lead not to the cave. But it chanced that the herd made a great bellowing when Hercules would have driven them away in the morning. And one of the heifers which Cacus had hidden in the cave bellowed also, making answer. Then was Hercules very wroth, and caught up in his hand his great knotted club, and climbed to the top of the hill. Then was Cacus sore afraid, and fled to his cave swift as the wind, fear giving wings to his feet. And when he was come thither, he shut himself therein, letting fall a great stone which he had caused to hang over the mouth thereof by cunning devices that he had learned from his father. And when Hercules was come he sought to find entrance and could not; but at the last he saw one of the rocks that it was very high and leaned to the river. This he pushed from the other side, so that it fell with a great crash into the water. Then did the whole cave of Cacus lie open to view, horrible to behold, as though the earth were to open her mouth and show the regions of the dead. And first Hercules shot at the monster with arrows, and cast boughs and great stones at him; and Cacus vomited forth from his mouth fire and smoke, filling the whole cave. And Hercules endured not to be so baffled, but plunged into the cave, even where the smoke was thickest, and caught him, twining his arms and legs about him, and strangled him, that he died. Of which deed, O my friends, we keep the remembrance year by year. Do ye, therefore, join in our feast, putting first wreaths of poplar about your heads, for the poplar is the tree of Hercules."

So they feasted; and the priests, even the Salii, being in two companies, young and old, sang the great deeds of Hercules: how, being yet an infant, he strangled the snakes that Juno sent to slay him, and overthrew mighty cities, and endured many grievous labors, slaying the Centaurs and the lion of Nemea; and how he went down to hell, and dragged the dog Cerberus therefrom, and many other things likewise.

And at even they went back to the city, and as they went Evander told Æneas many things concerning the country: how of old a savage race dwelt therein, living even as the beasts, whom Saturn, flying from his son Jupiter, first taught, giving them customs and laws; and how other kings also had borne rule over them, and how he himself had come to the land at the bidding of Apollo. Also he showed him the city which he had founded, and the places thereof: very famous were they in aftertime, when mighty Rome was builded, even on the selfsame ground. And when they came to his palace he said, "Hercules entered this dwelling, though indeed it be small and lowly. Think not, then, overmuch of riches, and so make thyself worthy to ascend to heaven, as he also ascended."

Then he led him within the palace, and bade him rest on a couch, whereon was spread the skin of an African bear.

Very early the next morning the old man Evander rose up from his bed, and donned his tunic, and bound his Tuscan sandals on his feet, and girt his Tegean sword to his side, flinging a panther's hide over his left shoulder. Pallas, his son, also went with him. And two hounds, which lay by his chamber, followed him. For he would fain have speech with Æneas, whom, indeed, he found astir, and Achates with him. Then spake Evander: "Great chief of Troy, good will have we, but scanty means; for our folk are few and our bounds narrow. But I will tell thee of a great people and a wealthy, with whom thou mayest make alliance. Nigh to this place is the famous city **Agylla**, which the men of Lydia, settling in this land of Etruria, builded aforetime. Now of this Agylla Mezentius was King, who surpassed all men in wickedness. For he would join a living man to a dead corpse, and so leave him to perish miserably. But after awhile the citizens rebelled, saying that he should not reign over them, and slew his guards and burnt his palace. But on him they laid not hands, for he fled to Prince Turnus. Therefore there is war between Turnus and Agylla. Now in this war thou shalt be leader; for as yet, when they would have gone forth to battle, the soothsayers have hindered them, saying, 'Though your wrath against Mezentius be just, yet must no man of Italy lead this people; but look you for a stranger.' And they would fain have had me for their leader, but I am old and feeble. And my son Pallas also is akin to them, seeing that he was born of a Sabine mother. But thou art in thy prime, and altogether a stranger in race. Wherefore take this office upon thyself. Pallas also shall go with thee, and learn from thee to bear himself as a warrior. Also I will send with thee two hundred chosen horsemen, and Pallas will give thee as many."

And even before he had made an end of speaking, Venus gave them a sign, even thunder in a clear sky; and there was heard a voice as of a Tuscan trumpet, and when they looked to the heavens, lo! there was a flashing of arms.

And Æneas knew the sign and the interpretation thereof, even that he should prosper in that to which he set his hand. Therefore he bade Evander be of good cheer. Then again they did sacrifice, and afterwards Æneas returned to his companions, of whom he chose some, and them the bravest, who should go with him to Agylla, and the rest he bade return to Iülus, to the camp.

But when he was now ready to depart, Evander took him by the hand, saying, "O that Jupiter would give me back the years that are gone, when I slew, under Præneste, King Erulus, to whom at his birth his mother, Feronia, gave three lives. Thrice must he needs be slain, and thrice I slew him. Then had I not been parted from thee, my son, nor had the wicked Mezentius slain so many of my people. And now, may the gods hear my prayer: If it be their pleasure that Pallas should come back, may I live to see it; but if not, may I die even now while I hold thee in my arms, my son, my one and only joy."

And his spirit left the old man, and they carried him into the palace. Then the horsemen rode out from the gates, with Pallas in the midst, adorned with mantle and blazoned arms, fair as the Morning Star, which Venus loves beyond all others in the sky. The women stood watching them from the walls, while they shouted aloud and galloped across the plain. And after a while they came to a grove, near to which the Etruscans and Tarchon, their leader, had pitched their camp.

Now in the meantime Venus had bestirred herself for her son, for while he slept in the palace of Evander she spake to her husband, even Vulcan, saying, "While the Greeks were fighting against Troy, I sought not thy help, for I would not that thou shouldst labor in vain; but now that Æneas is come to Italy by the command of the gods, I ask thee that thou shouldst make arms and armor for my son. This Aurora asked for Memnon; this Thetis for

Achilles, and thou grantedst it to them. And now thou seest how the nations join themselves to destroy him. Wherefore I pray thee to help me." And he hearkened to her voice. Therefore when the morning was come, very early, even as a woman who maketh her living by the distaff riseth and kindleth her fire, and giveth tasks to her maidens, that she may provide for her husband and her children, even so Vulcan rose betimes to his work. Now there is an island, Liparé, nigh unto the shore of Sicily, and there the god had set up his furnace and anvil, and the Cyclopés were at work, forging thunderbolts for Jupiter, whereof one remained half wrought. Three parts of hail had they used, and three of rain-cloud, and three of red fire and the south wind; and now they were adding to it lightning, and noise, and fear, and wrath, with avenging flames. And elsewhere they wrought a chariot for Mars, and a shirt of mail for Minerva, even the Ægis, with golden scales as of a serpent, and in the midst the Gorgon's head, lopped at the nape, with rolling eyes. But the god cried, "Cease ye your toils. Ye must make arms for a hero." Then they all bent them to their toil. Then bronze, and gold, and iron flowed in streams; and some plied the bellows, and others dipped the hissing mass in water, and a third turned the ore in griping pincers.

A helmet they made with nodding crest, that blazed like fire, and a sword, and a cuirass of ruddy bronze, and greaves of gold molten many times, and a spear, and a shield whereon was wrought a marvellous story of things to come. For the god had set forth all the story of Rome. There lay the she-wolf in the cave of Mars, suckling the twin babes that feared her not—and she, bending back her neck, licked them with her tongue; and there the men of Rome carried off the Sabine virgins to be their wives; and hard by the battle raged, and there again the kings made peace together, with offerings and sacrifice. Also there were wrought the chariots that tore asunder Mettus of Alba for his treachery, and Porsenna bidding the Romans take back their King, besieging the city, but the men of Rome stood in arms against him. Angry and threatening stood the King to see how Cocles broke down the bridge, and Cloelia burst her bonds to swim across the river. There Manlius stood to guard the Capitol, and a goose of silver flapped his wings in arcades of gold, and showed the Gauls at hand. And they, under cover of the darkness, were climbing through the thickets even to the ridge of the hill. Their hair was wrought in gold, in gold their raiment; and their cloaks were of divers colors crossed; milk-white their necks and clasped with gold; two spears had each and an oblong shield. Likewise he wrought the dwellings of the dead, of the just and of the unjust. Here Catiline hung from the rock while the Furies threatened him; there Cato gave the people laws. And all about was the sea wrought in gold; but the waves were blue, and white the foam, and therein sported dolphins of silver. But in the midst was wrought a great battle of ships at the cape of Actium. On the one side Augustus led the men of Italy to battle, standing very high on the stern of the ship. From either temple of his head blazed forth a fire. And Agrippa also led on his array with a naval crown about his head. And on the other side stood Antony, having with him barbarous soldiers arrayed in divers fashions, and leading to battle Egypt and Persia and the armies of the East; and lo! behind him — a shameful sight — his Egyptian wife. But in another part the battle raged, and all the sea was in a foam with oars and triple beaks. It seemed as though islands were torn from their places, or mountain clashed against mountain, so great was the shock of the ships. And all about flew javelins with burning tow, and the sea was red with blood. In the midst stood Cleopatra, with a timbrel in her hand, and called her armies to the battle: behind her you might see the snakes by whose bite she should die. And on one side the dog Anubis, with other monstrous shapes of gods, and over against them Neptune, and Venus, and Minerva. And in the midst Mars was seen to rage, embossed in steel; and the Furies hovered above, and Discord stalked with garment rent, while high above Apollo stretched his bow, and Egyptian and Indian and Arab fled before him. And in a third place great Cæsar rode through Rome in triumph, and the city was full of joy, and the matrons were gathered in the temples; and through the street there passed a long array of nations that he had conquered, from the east, and from the west, and from the north, and from the south. Such was the shield which Vulcan wrought.

And Venus, when she saw her son that none was with him, — for he had wandered apart from his companions, — brought the arms and laid them down before him, saying, "See the arms that I promised I would give thee. These my husband, the Fire-god, hath wrought for thee. With these thou needst shun no enemy; no, not Turnus himself." Right glad was he to see them, and fitted them upon him, and swung the shield upon his shoulder, nor knew what mighty fates of his children he bare thereon.

CHAPTER V.

AFTER this Æneas made a covenant with the men of Etruria, of whom one Tarchon was chief. And a great company of these went with him to the war.

But in the meanwhile Turnus had fought against the camp of the Trojans, and had slain many of the people. And when they that remained were now ready to despair, they looked up, and behold! Æneas was there, for he stood upon the stern of his ship and lifted in his left hand a flashing shield. Much did the men of Troy rejoice to see that sight, and shouted amain. And Turnus and his companions marvelled, till they looked behind them, and lo! the sea was covered with ships, and in the midst was Æneas. And it was as if a flame poured forth from his helmet and his shield, bright as is a comet when it shines in the night-time red as blood, or as the Dog Star in the hot summer-tide with baleful light bringing fevers to the race of men.

Yet did not Turnus lose heart, but would occupy the shore, and hinder from landing those that came. Wherefore he cried, "Now have ye that which ye wished for. Lo! the enemy hides not himself behind a wall, but meets us face to face. Remember wife and child and home and the great deeds of your fathers. Let us meet them on the shore ere yet their footing is firm." And he thought within himself who should watch the walls, and who should meet the enemy when he would gain the shore.

But in the meanwhile Æneas landed his men on gangways from the ships. And some leapt on shore, having watched for the ebb of the waves, and some ran along the oars. Tarchon also, the Etrurian, having spied a place where the sea broke not in waves, commanded his men that they should beach the ships. Which indeed they did without harm. Only the ship of Tarchon himself was caught upon a ridge and the men thrown therefrom. Yet these also, after a while, got safe to the shore.

Then did Æneas do great deeds against the enemy. For first he slew Theron, who surpassed all men in stature, smiting through his coat of mail; and Cisseus and Gyas, who wielded clubs after the manner of Hercules. Sons were they of Melampus, who had borne Hercules company in all his labors. Then the sons of Phorcus came against him, seven in number; and they cast at him seven spears, whereof some rebounded from his shield and some grazed his body, but harmed him not. Then cried Æneas to Achates, "Give me spears enough. Spears which have slain the Greeks on the fields of Troy shall not be cast in vain against these Latins." Then of the seven he slew Mæon and Alcanor, for the spear pierced the breast-plate and heart of Mæon, and when Alcanor would have held him up, passed through his arm and yet kept on its way. And many others fell on this side and on that, for they fought with equal fortune. On the very threshold of Italy they fought, and neither would the Italians give place nor yet the men of Troy, for foot was planted close to foot, and man stood fast by man.

In another part of the battle Pallas fought with his Arcadians. And when he saw that they fled, not being wont to fight on foot (for by reason of the ground they had sent away their horses), he cried, "Now, by the name of your King Evander, and by my hope that I may win praise like unto his, I beseech you that ye trust not to your feet.

Ye must make your way through the enemy with your swords. Where the crowd is the thickest follow me. Nor have ye now gods against you. These are but mortal men that ye see." And he rushed into the midst of the enemy. First he smote Lagus with his spear, even as he was lifting a great stone from the earth. In the back he smote him, and, having smitten him, strove to draw forth the spear; and while he strove, Hisbo would have slain him; but Pallas was aware of his coming, and pierced him in the breast with his sword. Next he slew the twin brothers, Larides and Thymber. Very like they were, and it pleased father and mother that they knew not the one from the other; but Pallas made a cruel difference between them, for from Thymber he struck off the head, and from Larides the right hand. And after these he slew Rhœtus, as he fled past him in his chariot. And now, even as a shepherd sets fire to a wood, and the flames are borne along by the wind, so Pallas, and his Arcadians following, raged through the battle. And when Halæsus, the companion of Agamemnon, would have stayed them, Pallas, first praying to Father Tiber, smote him through the breast with a spear, that he died. Then came to the help of the Latins, Lausus, the son of King Mezentius, and slew Abas of Populonia, and others also. Then the battle was equal for a space, for Pallas supported it on the one side and Lausus on the other. Fair were they both to behold and of equal age, and for both it was ordained that they should not return to their native country. Yet they met not in battle, seeing that the doom of each was that he should fall by a greater hand.

And now the nymph Juturna, who was sister to Turnus, bade her brother haste to the help of Lausus. And when he was come, he cried to the Latins, "Give place: I only will deal with Pallas. I only would that his father were here to see." Much did Pallas marvel to behold him and to see the men give place. But, being no whit afraid, he went forth into the space between the hosts, and the blood of the Arcadians ran cold when they saw him go. Then Turnus leapt from his chariot, for he would meet him on foot. And first Pallas prayed, saying, "O Hercules! if thou wast indeed my father's guest, help me to-day!" And Hercules heard him where he sat in heaven, and wept because he could avail nothing. Then said Father Jupiter, "My son, the days of men are numbered; yet may they live forever by noble deeds. This at least can valor do. Did not many sons of the gods fall at Troy? yea, and my own Sarpedon. And for Turnus, too, the day of doom is at hand." And he turned his eyes from the battle. Then Pallas cast his spear with all his might. Through the shield of Turnus it passed, and through the corselet, yea, and grazed the top of his shoulder. Then Turnus balanced his spear awhile, and said, "This, methinks, shall better make its way," and he cast it. Through the shield, through the stout bull's hide, and through the folds of bronze it passed, and through the corselet, and pierced the breast of Pallas from front to back. And Pallas tore from the wound the reeking steel, and the blood gushed out, and the life therewith. Then Turnus stood above the corpse, and said, "Men of Arcadia, tell these my words to Evander: 'Pallas I send him back, even as he deserved that I should send him. I grudge him not due honors of burial. Yet of a truth the friendship of Æneas hath cost him dear.'" Then he put his foot upon the body and dragged therefrom the belt. Great and heavy it was, and Clonius had wrought thereon in gold the deed of the fifty daughters of Danaüs, how they slew their husbands in one night. But even then the time was very near when Turnus would wish that he had left that spoil untouched. And afterwards, with much groaning and weeping, the companions of Pallas laid him upon a shield and bare him back.

And now tidings came to Æneas that it fared ill with his men, and that Pallas was slain. Across the field he sped, and all his heart was full of wrath against Turnus and pity for the old man Evander; and first he took alive eight youths, whom he should slay upon the tomb. Then he cast his spear at Lagus; but Lagus avoided it by craft, and rushed forward, and caught him by the knees, beseeching him by the spirit of his father and the hopes of Iülus that he would spare him, and take a ransom for his life. But Æneas made answer, "Talk not of sparing nor of ransom; for to all courtesy of war there is an end now that Turnus hath slain Pallas." And he caught the man's helmet with his left hand, and, bending back his neck, thrust in the sword up to the hilt. And many other valiant chiefs he slew, as Hæmonides, priest of Phœbus and Diana, and Tarquitus, son of Faunus, and dark Camers, son of Volscens. And now there met him two brethren on one chariot, Lucagus and Liger. And Liger, who indeed drave the horses, cried aloud, "These are not the horses of Diomed, nor this the chariot of Achilles, from which thou mayest escape. Lo! the end of thy battles and thy life is come." But Æneas spake not, but cast his spear, and even as Lucagus made himself ready for battle, it sped through his shield and pierced his thigh. Then he fell dying on the plain. And Æneas cried, mocking him, "Thy horses are not slow to flee, nor frightened by a shadow. Of thine own will thou leavest thy chariot." And he caught the horses by the head. Then Liger stretched out his hands to him in supplication, saying, "I beseech thee, by thy parents, have pity upon me." But Æneas made answer, "Nay, but thou speakest not thus before. Die! and desert not thy brother." And he thrust the sword into his breast. Thus did Æneas deal death through the host, even as he had been the giant Typhœus with the hundred hands. And when Iülus and the men of Troy beheld him they brake forth from the camp.

And now Juno bethought her how she might save Turnus, whom she loved. So she caused that there should pass before his eyes an image as of Æneas, which seemed to defy him to battle. And when Turnus would have fought, lo! the false Æneas fled, and Turnus followed him. Now there chanced to be lying moored to a great rock a certain ship, on which King Asinius had come from Clusium. Into this the false Æneas fled, and Turnus followed hard upon him, but found not the man. And when he looked, Juno had burst the moorings of the ship, and the sea was about him on every side. Then he cried, "What have I done, great Jupiter, that I should suffer such shame? What think the Latins of my flight? Drown me, ye winds and waves, or drive me where no man may see me more." Thrice he would have cast himself into the sea; thrice would he have slain himself with the sword; but Juno forbade, and brought him safe to the city of Daunus, his father.

In the meanwhile King Mezentius joined the battle. Nor could the men of Troy, nor yet the Tuscans, stay him. Many valiant men he slew, as Mimas, whom his mother Theano bare the same night that Hecuba bare Paris to King Priam; and Actor, a Greek, who had left his promised wife, and carried her purple favor in his helmet; and tall Orodes. Orodes, indeed, was flying, but the King deigned not to slay him in his flight, but met him face to face and smote him. Also when Orodes cried, "Whoever thou art, thou goest not long unpunished: a like doom awaits thee; and in this land shalt thou find thy grave," Mezentius laughed, and made answer, "Die thou, but let the King of gods and men see to me."

But after awhile Æneas spied Mezentius as he fought, and made haste to meet him. Nor did the King give place, but cried, "Now may this right hand and the spear which I wield be my gods, and help me." And he cast his spear. It smote the shield of Æneas, but pierced it not. Yet did it not fly in vain, for glancing off it smote Antores in the side — Antores who once had been comrade to Hercules, and afterwards followed Evander. Now he fell, and in his death remembered the city which he loved, even Argos. Then in his turn Æneas cast his spear. Through the bull's-hide shield it passed, wounding the King in the groin, but not to death. And Æneas was right glad to see the blood flow forth, and drew his sword and pressed on ; and Mezentius, much cumbered with the spear and the wound, gave place. But when Lausus, his son, saw this, he groaned aloud and leapt forward, and took the blow upon his sword ; and his companions followed him with a shout, and cast their spears at Æneas, staying him till Mezentius had gotten himself safe away. And Æneas stood awhile under the shower of spears, even as a traveller stands hiding himself from a storm. Then he cried to Lausus, "What seekest thou, madman? Why venturest thou that which thy strength may not endure?" But Lausus heeded him not at all, but still pressed on. Then the heart of Æneas was filled with wrath, and the day was come for Lausus that he should die. For the King smote him with his sword: through shield it passed and tunic woven with gold, and was hidden to the hilt in his body. And Æneas pitied him as he lay dead, bethinking him how he, too, would fain have died for his father, and spake, saying, "What shall Æneas give thee, unhappy boy, for this thy nobleness? Keep thy arms, in which thou hadst such delight, and let thy father care as he will for thy body; and take this comfort in thy death, that thou fallest by the hand of the great Æneas." Then he lifted him from the earth, and bade his companions carry him away.

In the meantime his father tended his wounds, leaning on the trunk of a tree by the Tiber bank. His helmet hung from a branch, and his arms lay upon the ground, while his followers stood around. And ever he asked tidings of Lausus, and sent those who should bid him return. But when they brought back his body on a shield, his father knew it from afar, and threw dust upon his white hair, and fell upon the body, crying, "Had I such desire to live, my son, that I suffered thee to meet in my stead the sword of the enemy? Am I saved by these wounds? Do I live by thy death? And indeed, my son, I did dishonor to thee by my misdeeds. Would that I had given my guilty life for thine! But indeed I die; nevertheless not yet, for I have first somewhat that I must do."

Then he raised himself on his thigh, and commanded that they should bring his horse. His pride it was and comfort, and had borne him conqueror from many fights. Very sad was the beast, and he spake to it, saying, "O Rhœbus, thou and I have lived long enough, if indeed aught on earth be long. To-day thou shalt bring back the head and the arms of Æneas, and so avenge my Lausus; or thou shalt die with me. For a Trojan master thou wilt not, I know, endure."

Then he mounted the horse, and took spears in both his hands, and so hasted to meet Æneas. Thrice he called him by name, and Æneas rejoiced to hear his voice, and cried, "Now may Jupiter and Apollo grant that this be true. Begin the fight." And Mezentius made answer: "Seek not to make afraid. Thou canst do me no harm now that thou hast slain my son. I am come to die, but take thou first this gift; and he cast his spear, and then another, and yet another, as he rode in a great circle about the enemy. But they brake not the boss of gold. And Æneas stood firm, bearing the forest of spears in his shield. But at last issuing forth in anger from behind his shield, he cast his spear and smote the war-horse Rhœbus between his temples. Then the horse reared himself and lashed the air with his feet, and fell with his rider beneath him. And the men of Troy and the Latins sent up a great shout. Then Æneas hasted and drew his sword, and stood above him, crying, "Where is the fierce Mezentius now?" And the King said, when he breathed again, "Why threatenest thou me with death? Slay me; thou wrongest me not. I made no covenant with thee for life, nor did my Lausus when he died for me. Yet grant me this one thing. Thou knowest how my people hateth me. Keep my body, I pray thee, from them, that they do it no wrong. And let my son be buried with me in my grave." And he gave his throat to the sword, and feared not.

So the battle had an end. And the next day, early in the morning, Æneas paid his vows. For he took an oak-tree, and lopped the branches round about, and set it on a mound. And thereon he hung, for a trophy to Mars, the arms of King Mezentius, the crest dripping with blood, and the headless spears, and the corselet pierced in twelve places. Also he fastened on the left hand the shield, and hung about the neck the ivory-hilted sword. And next, the chiefs being gathered about him, he spake, saying, "We have wrought a great deed. Here ye see all that remaineth of Mezentius. Now, therefore, let us make ready to carry the war against the city of Latinus. This therefore will we do with the first light to-morrow. And now let us bury the dead, doing such honor to them as we may, for indeed they have purchased a country for us with their own blood. But first will I send back Pallas to the city of Evander."

Then he went to the tent where the dead body was laid, and old Acœtes kept watch thereby — Acœtes, who had been armor-bearer to Evander, and now had followed his son, but with evil fortune; and the women of Troy, with their hair unbound, mourned about him. But when they saw Æneas they beat their breasts, and sent up a great cry even to heaven. And when the King saw the pillowed head, and the great wound in the breast, he wept, and said, "Ah! why did Fortune grudge me this, that thou shouldst see my kingdom, and go back in triumph to thy father's home? This is not what I promised to Evander when he gave thee to my charge, and warned me that the men of Italy were valiant and fierce. And now haply, old man, thou makest offerings and prayers for him who oweth not service any more to the gods of heaven. Yet, at least, thou wilt see that he beareth an honorable wound. But what a son thou losest, O Italy! and what a friend, thou, Iülus!"

Then he choose a thousand men who should go with the dead and share the father's grief. After this they made a bier of arbutus boughs and oak, and put also over it a canopy of branches, and laid the dead thereon, like unto a flower of violet or hyacinth which a girl hath plucked, which still hath beauty and color, but the earth nourisheth it no more. And Æneas took two robes of purple, which Dido had woven with thread of gold, and with one he wrapped the body and with the other the head. And behind were carried the arms which Pallas had won in fight; and they led the old man Acœtes, smiting on his breast and tearing his cheeks, and throwing himself upon the ground; and the war-horse Æthon walked beside, with the great tears rolling down his cheeks. And also they bare behind him his helmet and shield, for all else Turnus had taken: and then followed the whole company, the men of Troy, the Arcadians, and the Tuscans, with arms reversed. And Æneas said, "The same cares and sorrows of war call me elsewhere. Farewell, my Pallas, for ever!" And he departed to the camp.

And now there came ambassadors from the city, having olive branches about their heads, praying for a truce, that they might bury their dead. Then Æneas made answer, "Ye ask peace for the dead; fain would I give it to the living. I had not come to this land but for the bidding of the Fates. And if your King changeth from me and my friendship to Turnus, I am blameless. Yet methinks Turnus should rather have taken this danger upon himself. And even now, if he be willing to fight with me, man to man, so be it. But now bury ye your dead."

Then they made a truce for twelve days. And the men of Troy and the Latins labored together, hewing wood upon the hills, pine and cedar and mountain ash. And the men of Troy built great piles upon the shore, and burned the dead bodies of their companions thereon, and their arms with them. And the Latins did likewise. Also they that had been chosen to do this thing carried the body of Pallas to his city. And King Evander and the Arcadians made a great mourning for him.

CHAPTER VI.

After these things there was again battle between the Trojans and the Latins; and many were slain on either side, but at the last the men of Troy prevailed. Then Prince Turnus, seeing that the Latins had fled in the battle, and that men looked to him that he should perform that which he had promised, even to meet Æneas face to face, was filled with rage. Even as a lion which a hunter hath wounded breaketh the arrow wherewith he hath been stricken, and rouseth himself to battle, shaking his mane and roaring, so Turnus arose. And first he spake to King Latinus, saying, "Not for me, my father, shall these cowards of Troy go back from that which they have covenanted. I will meet this man face to face, and slay him while ye look on; or, if the gods will that he vanquish me so, he shall rule over you, and have Lavinia to wife."

But King Latinus made answer: "Yet think awhile, my son. Thou hast the kingdom of thy father Daunus; and there are other noble virgins in Latium whom thou mayest have to wife. Wilt thou not then be content? For to give my daughter to any husband of this nation I was forbidden, as thou knowest. Yet did I disobey, being moved by love of thee, my wife also beseeching me with many tears. Thou seest what troubles I and my people, and thou more than all, have suffered from that time. Twice have we fled in the battle, and now the city only is left to us. If I must yield me to these men, let me yield whilst thou art yet alive. For what doth it profit me that thou shouldst die? Nay, but all men would cry shame on me if I gave thee to death!"

Now for a space Turnus spake not for wrath. Then he said, "Be not troubled for me, my father. For I, too, can smite with the spear; and as for this Æneas, his mother will not be at hand to snatch him in a cloud from my sight."

Then Amata cried to him, saying, "Fight not, I beseech thee, with these men of Troy, my son; for surely what thou sufferest I also shall suffer. Nor will I live to see Æneas my son-in-law."

And Lavinia heard the voice of her mother, and wept. As a man stains ivory with crimson, or as roses are seen mixed with lilies, even so the virgin's face burned with crimson. And Turnus, regarding her, loved her exceedingly, and made answer: "Trouble me not with tears or idle words, my mother, for to this battle I must go. And do thou, Idmon the herald, say to the Phrygian king, 'To-morrow, when the sun shall rise, let the people have peace, but we two will fight together. And let him that prevaileth have Lavinia to wife.'"

Then first he went to the stalls of his horses. The wife of the North Wind gave them to Pilumnus. Whiter than snow were they, and swifter than the wind. Then he put the coat of mail about his shoulders, and fitted a helmet on his head, and took the great sword which Vulcan had made for Daunus his father, and had dipped it when it was white-hot in the river of Styx. His spear also he took where it stood against a pillar, saying, "Serve me well, my spear, that has never failed me before, that I may lay low this womanish robber of Phrygia, and soil with dust his curled and perfumed hair."

The next day the men of Italy and the men of Troy

measured out a space for the battle. And in the midst they built an altar of turf. And the two armies sat on the one side and on the other, having fixed their spears in the earth and laid down their shields. Also the women and the old men stood on the towers and roofs of the city, that they might see the fight.

But Queen Juno spake to Juturna, the sister of Turnus, saying, "Seest thou how these two are now about to fight, face to face? And indeed Turnus goeth to his death. As for me, I endure not to look upon this covenant or this battle. But if thou canst do aught for thy brother, lo! the time is at hand." And when the Nymph wept and beat her breast, Juno said, "This is no time for tears. Save thy brother, if thou canst, from death; or cause that they break this covenant."

After this came the kings, that they might make the covenant together. And King Latinus rode in a chariot with four horses, and he had on his head a crown with twelve rays of gold, for he was of the race of the Sun; and Turnus came in a chariot with two white horses, having a javelin in either hand; and Æneas had donned the arms which Vulcan had made, and with him was the young Iülus. And after due offering Æneas sware, calling on all the gods, "If the victory shall fall this day to Turnus, the men of Troy shall depart to the city of Evander, nor trouble this land any more. But if it fall to me, I will not that the Latins should serve the men of Troy. Let the nations be equal one with the other. The gods that I bring we will worship together, but King Latinus shall reign as before. A new city shall the men of Troy build for me, and Lavinia shall call it after her own name."

Then King Latinus sware, calling on the gods that are above and the gods that are below, saying, "This covenant shall stand for ever, whatsoever may befall. As sure as this sceptre which I bear — once it was a tree, but a cunning workman closed it in bronze, to be the glory of Latium's kings — shall never again bear twig or leaf, so surely shall this covenant be kept."

But the thing pleased not the Latins; for before, indeed, they judged that the battle would not be equal between the two; and now were they the more assured, seeing them when they came together, and that Turnus walked with eyes cast to the ground, and was pale and wan. Wherefore there arose a murmuring among the people, which when Juturna perceived, she took upon herself the likeness of Camers, who was a prince and a great warrior among them, and passed through the host, saying, "Are ye not ashamed, men of Italy, that one man should do battle for you all? For count these men: surely they are scarce one against two. And if he be vanquished, what shame for you! As for him, indeed, though he die, yet shall his glory reach to the heavens; but ye shall suffer disgrace, serving these strangers for ever."

And when she saw that the people were moved, she gave also a sign from heaven. For lo! an eagle that drave a crowd of sea-fowl before him, swooped down to the water, and caught a great swan; and even while the Italians looked, the birds that before had fled turned and pursued the eagle, and drave him before them, so that he dropped the swan and fled away. Which thing when the Italians perceived, they shouted, and made them ready for battle. And the augur Tolumnius cried, "This is the token that I have looked for. For this eagle is the stranger and ye are the birds, which before, indeed, have fled, but shall now make him to flee."

And he ran forward and cast his spear, smiting a man

of Arcadia below the belt, upon the groin. One of nine brothers was he, sons of a Tuscan mother, but their father was a Greek; and they, when they saw him slain, caught swords and spears, and ran forward. And straightway the battle was begun. First they brake down the altars, that they might take firebrands therefrom; and King Latinus fled from the place. Then did Messapus drive his horses against King Aulestes of Mantua, who, being fain to fly, stumbled upon the altar and fell headlong on the ground. And Messapus smote him with a spear that was like a weaver's beam, saying, "This, of a truth, is a worthier victim." After this Coryneüs the Arcadian, when Ebysus would have smitten him, snatched a brand from the altar and set fire to the beard of the man, and, before he came to himself, caught him by the hair, and thrusting him to the ground, so slew him. And when Podalirius pursued Alsus the shepherd, and now held his sword over him ready to strike, the other turned, and with a battle-axe cleft the man's head from forehead to chin.

But all the while the righteous Æneas, having his head bare, and holding neither spear nor sword, cried to the people, "What seek ye? what madness is this? The covenant is established, and I only have the right to do battle." But even while he spake an arrow smote him, wounding him. But who let it fly no man knoweth; for who, of a truth, would boast that he had wounded Æneas? And he departed from the battle.

Now when Turnus saw that Æneas had departed from the battle he called for his chariot. And when he had mounted thereon he drave it through the host of the enemy, slaying many valiant heroes, as Sthenelus and Pholus, and the two sons of Imbrasus the Lycian, Glaucus and Lades. Then he saw Eumedes, son of that Dolon who would have spied out the camp of the Greeks, asking as his reward the horses of Achilles (but Diomed slew him). Him Turnus smote with a javelin from afar, and, when he fell, came near and put his foot upon him, and taking his sword drave it into his neck, saying, "Lo! now thou hast the land which thou soughtest. Lie there, and measure out Italy for thyself." Many others he slew, for the army fled before him. Yet did one man, Phegeus by name, stand against him, and would have stayed the chariot, catching the bridles of the horses in his hand. But as he clung to the yoke and was dragged along, Turnus broke his cuirass with his spear, and wounded him. And when the man set his shield before him, and made at Turnus with his sword, the wheels dashed him to the ground and Turnus struck him between the helmet and the breast-plate, and smote off his head.

But in the meanwhile Mnestheus and Achates and Iülus led Æneas to the camp, leaning on his spear. Very wrath was he and strove to draw forth the arrow. And when he could not, he commanded that they should open the wound with the knife, and so send him back to the battle. Iapis also, the physician, ministered to him. Now this Iapis was dearer than all other men to Apollo, and when the god would have given him all his arts, even prophecy and music and archery, he chose rather to know the virtues of herbs and the art of healing, that so he might prolong the life of his father, who was even ready to die. This Iapis, then, having his garments girt about him in healer's fashion, would have drawn forth the arrow with the pincers but could not. And while he strove, the battle came nearer, and the sky was hidden by clouds of dust, and javelins fell thick into the camp. But when Venus saw how grievously her son was troubled, she brought from

Ida, which is a mountain of Crete, the herb dittany. A hairy stalk it hath and a purple flower. The wild goats know it well if so be that they have been wounded by arrows. This, then, Venus, having hidden her face, brought and dipped into the water, and sprinkled there with ambrosia and sweet-smelling panacea.

And Iapis, unawares, applied the water that had been healed; and low! the pain was stayed and the blood was staunched, and the arrow came forth, though no man drew it, and Æneas's strength came back to him as before. Then said Iapis, "Art of mine hath not healed thee, my son. The gods call thee to thy work." Then did Æneas arm himself again, and when he had kissed Iülus and bidden him farewell, he went forth to the battle. And all the chiefs went with him, and the men of Troy took courage and drave back to the Latins. Then befell a great slaughter, for Gyas slew Ufens who was the leader of the Æquians; also Tolumnius, the great augur, was slain, who had first broken the covenant, slaying a man with his spear. But Æneas deigned not to turn his hand against any man, seeking only for Turnus, that he might fight with him. But when the nymph Juturna perceived this she was sore afraid. Therefore she came near to the chariot of her brother, and thrust out Metiscus, his charioteer, where he held the reins, and herself stood in his room, having made herself like to him in shape and voice. Then as a swallow flies through the halls and arcades of some rich man's house, seeking food for its young, so Juturna drave the chariot of her brother hither and thither. And ever Æneas followed behind, and called to him that he should stay; but whenever he espied the man, and would have overtaken him by running, then again did Juturna turn the horses about and flee. And as he sped Messapus cast a spear at him. But

Æneas saw it coming, and put his shield over him, resting on his knee. Yet did the spear smite him on the helmet-top and shear off the crest. Then indeed was his wrath kindled, and he rushed into the army of the enemy, slaying many as he went.

Then there was a great slaughter made on this side and on that. But after a while Venus put it into the heart of Æneas that he should lead his army against the city. Therefore he called together the chiefs, and, standing in the midst of them on a mound, spake, saying, "Hearken now to my words, and delay not to fulfil them, for of a truth Jupiter is on our side. I am purposed this day to lay this city of Latinus even with the ground, if they still refuse to obey. For why should I wait for Turnus till it please him to meet me in battle?"

Then did the whole array make for the walls of the city. And some carried firebrands, and some scaling-ladders, and some slew the warders at the gates, and cast javelins at them who stood on the walls. And then there arose a great strife in the city, for some would have opened the gates that the men of Troy might enter, and others made haste to defend the walls. Hither and thither did they run with much tumult, even as bees in a hive in a rock which a shepherd hath filled with smoke, having first shut all the doors thereof.

Then also did other ill fortune befall the Latins, for when Queen Amata saw from the roof of the palace that the enemy were come near to the walls, and saw not anywhere the army of the Latins, she supposed Turnus to have fallen in the battle. Whereupon, crying out that she was the cause of all these woes, she made a noose of the purple garment wherewith she was clad, and hanged herself from a beam of the roof. Then did lamentation go through the city, for the women wailed and tore their hair, and King Latinus rent his clothes and threw dust upon his head.

But the cry that went up from the city came to the ears of Turnus where he fought in the furthest part of the plain. And he caught the reins and said, "What meaneth this sound of trouble and wailing that I hear?" And the false Metiscus, who was in truth his sister, made answer, "Let us fight, O Turnus, here where the gods give us victory. There are enough to defend the city." But Turnus spake, saying, "Nay, my sister, for who thou art I have known even from the beginning, it must not be so. Why camest thou down from heaven? Was it to see thy brother die? And now what shall I do? Have I not seen Murranus die and Ufens the Æquian? And shall I suffer this city to be destroyed? Shall this land see Turnus flee before his enemies? Be ye kind to me, O gods of the dead, seeing that the gods of heaven hate me. I come down to you a righteous spirit, and not unworthy of my fathers."

And even as he spake came Saces, riding on a horse that was covered with foam, and on his face was the wound of an arrow. And he cried, "O Turnus, our last hopes are in thee. For Æneas is about to destroy the city, and the firebrands are cast upon the roofs. And King Latinus is sore tried with doubt, and the Queen hath laid hands upon herself and is dead. And now only Messapus and Atinas maintain the battle, and the fight grows fierce around them, while thou drivest thy chariot about these empty fields."

Then for a while Turnus stood speechless, and shame and grief and madness were in his soul; and he looked to the city, and lo! the fire went up even to the top of the tower which he himself had builded upon the walls to be a defence against the enemy. And when he saw it, he cried, "It is enough, my sister; I go whither the gods call me. I will meet with Æneas face to face, and endure my doom."

And as he spake he leapt down from his chariot, and ran across the plain till he came near to the city, even where the blood was deepest upon the earth and the arrows were thickest in the air. And he beckoned with the hand and called to the Italians, saying, "Stay now your arrows. I am come to fight this battle for you all." And when they heard it they left a space in the midst. Æneas also, when he heard the name of Turnus, left attacking the city, and came to meet him, mighty as Athos, or Eryx, or Father Apenninus, that raiseth his snowy head to the heavens. And the men of Troy and the Latins and King Latinus marvelled to see them meet, so mighty they were.

First they cast their spears at each other, and then ran together, and their shields struck one against the other with a crash that went up to the sky. And Jupiter held the balance in heaven, weighing their doom. Then Turnus, rising to the stroke, smote fiercly with his sword. And the men of Troy and the Latins cried out when they saw him strike. But the treacherous sword brake in the blow. And when he saw the empty hilt in his hand he turned to flee. They say that when he mounted his chariot that day to enter the battle, not heeding the matter in his haste, he left his father's sword behind him, and took the sword of Metiscus, which, indeed, served him well while the men of Troy fled before him, but brake, even as ice breaks, when it came to the shield which Vulcan had made. Thereupon Turnus fled, and Æneas, though the wound which the arrow had made hindered him, pursued.

Even as a hound follows a stag that is penned within some narrow space, for the beast flees hither and thither, and the staunch Umbrian hound follows close upon him, and almost holds him, and snaps his teeth, yet bites him not, so did Æneas follow hard on Turnus. And still Turnus cried out that some one should give him his sword, and Æneas threatened that he would destroy the city if any should help him. Five times about the space they ran; not for some prize they strove, but for the life of Turnus. Now there stood in the plain the stump of a wild olive-tree. The tree was sacred to Faunus, but the men of Troy had cut it, and the stump only was left. Herein the spear of Æneas was fixed, and now he would have drawn it forth that he might slay Turnus therewith, seeing that he could not overtake him by running. Which when Turnus perceived, he cried to Faunus, saying, "O Faunus, if I have kept holy for thee that which the men of Troy have profaned, hold fast this spear." And the god heard him; nor could Æneas draw it forth. But while he strove, Juturna, taking again the form of Metiscus, ran and gave to Turnus his sword. And Venus, perceiving it, wrenched forth the spear from the stump. So the two stood again face to face.

Then spake Jupiter to Juno, where she sat in a cloud watching the battle, "How long wilt thou fight against fate? What purpose hast thou now in thy heart? Was it well that Juturna — for what could she avail without thy help? — should give back to Turnus his sword? Thou hast driven the men of Troy over land and sea, and kindled a dreadful war, and mingled the song of marriage with mourning. Further thou mayest not go."

And Juno humbly made answer, "This is thy will, great Father; else had I not sat here, but stood in the battle smiting the men of Troy. And indeed I spake to Juturna that she should help her brother; but aught else I know not. And now I yield. Yet grant me this. Suffer not that the Latins should be called after the name of Troy, nor change their speech nor their garb. Let Rome rule the world, but let Troy perish forever."

Then spake with a smile the Maker of all things, "Truly thou art a daughter of Saturn, so fierce is the wrath of thy soul! And now what thou prayest I give. The Italians shall not change name, nor speech, nor garb. The men of Troy shall mingle with them, and I will give them a new worship, and call them all Latins. Nor shall any race pay thee more honor than they."

Then Jupiter sent a Fury from the pit. And she took the form of a bird, even of an owl that sitteth by night on the roof of a desolate house, and flew before the face of Turnus and flapped her wings against his shield. Then was Turnus stricken with great fear, so that his hair stood up and his tongue clave to the roof of his mouth. And when Juturna knew the sound of the false bird what it was, she cried aloud for fear, and left her brother and fled, hiding herself in the river of Tiber.

But Æneas came on, shaking his spear that was like unto a tree, and said, "Why delayest thou, O Turnus? Why drawest thou back? Fly now if thou canst through the air, or hide thyself in the earth." And Turnus made answer, "I fear not thy threats, but the gods and Jupiter, that are against me this day." And as he spake he saw a great stone which lay hard by, the landmark of a field. Scarce could twelve chosen men, such as men are now, lift it on their shoulders. This he caught from the earth and cast it at his enemy, running forward as he cast. But he knew not, so troubled was he in his soul, that he ran or that he cast, for his knees tottered beneath him and his blood grew cold with fear. And the stone fell short, nor reached the mark. Even as in a dream, when dull sleep is on the eyes of a man, he would fain run but cannot, for his strength faileth him, neither cometh there any voice when he would speak; so it fared with Turnus. For he looked to the Latins and to the city, and saw the dreadful spear approach, nor knew how he might fly, neither how he might fight, and could not spy anywhere his chariot or his sister. And all the while Æneas shook his spear and waited that his aim should be sure. And at last he threw it with all his might. Even as a whirlwind it flew, and brake through the seven folds of the shield and pierced the thigh. And Turnus dropped with his knee bent to the ground. And all the Latins groaned aloud to see him fall. Then he entreated Æneas, saying, "I have deserved my fate. Take thou that which thou hast won. Yet per chance thou mayest have pity on the old man, my father, even Daunus, for such an one was thy father Anchises, and give me back to my own people, if it be but my body that thou givest. Yet hast thou conquered, and the Latins have seen me beg my life of thee, and Lavinia is thine. Therefore, I pray thee, stay now thy wrath."

Then for awhile Æneas stood doubting; aye, and might have spared the man, when lo! he spied upon his shoulders the belt of Pallas, whom he had slain. And his wrath was greatly kindled, and he cried with a dreadful voice, "Shalt thou who art clothed with the spoils of my friends escape me? 'Tis Pallas slays thee with this wound, and takes vengeance on thy accursed blood." And as he spake he drave the steel into his breast. And with a groan the wrathful spirit passed into darkness.

www.ingramcontent.com/pod-product-compliance
Lightning Source LLC
Chambersburg PA
CBHW032354230426
43672CB00007B/698